STEPHEN POTTER

The Sense of Humour

PENGUIN BOOKS

Penguin Books Ltd, Harmondsworth, Middlesex, England
Penguin Books Pty Ltd, Ringwood, Victoria, Australia

—

First published by Max Reinhardt 1954
Published in Penguin Books 1964

—

Copyright © Stephen Potter, 1954

—

Made and printed in Great Britain
by C. Nicholls & Company Ltd
Set in Monotype Times

Stephen Potter was born in 1900 and educated at Westminster School and Merton College, Oxford, where he read English. In 1926 he became a lecturer in English at London University, and in 1938 he joined the staff of the B.B.C. as a writer-producer. There he became Editor of the literary features and poetry, and in 1943 Chairman of the Literary Committee. His principal programmes were the 'How' series (with Joyce Grenfell) and Professional Portraits, and he was originator and editor of the New Judgement series. He has been dramatic critic of the *New Statesman*, book critic of the *News Chronicle*, and editor of the *Leader Magazine*. His other books include *D. H. Lawrence* (1930), *The Nonesuch Coleridge* (1934), *Minnow among Tritons: Letters of Mrs S. T. Coleridge* (1934), *Potter on America* (1956), *Steps to Immaturity* (1959). Also available in Penguins are *Gamesmanship*, *Lifemanship*, *One-Upmanship*, and *Supermanship*. Stephen Potter lives in London.

U Ron

1965

In grateful memory of
MY FATHER

ACKNOWLEDGEMENT

This book would not have been possible without the helpful cooperation of the authors, publishers, and executors concerned with the more recent quotations. My sincere thanks are due to them. Detailed acknowledgements will be found at the end of the book.

Contents

CONTENTS

CONTENTS

11

CONTENTS

CONTENTS

EDITOR'S NOTE. In the body of the text, titles printed within
brackets are the editor's, not the author's

PART I
THE THEME

THE LINCOLN IMP

Hidden among the angelic faces of the sacred
images carved above the columns of Lincoln Cathe-
dral is this figure of a kindly but impertinent devil
or imp – symbol perhaps of the intrusion of humour into even the serious moments of English life

The day of English Humour is declining. I am not suggesting that *Punch* is less what it was than tradition demands, nor that at the other end, the acid end, of the scale (towards which *Punch* incidentally has begun to shift after eighty years of alkali), our Barren Leaves and Vile Bodies are pulverized less efficiently by the novelists of 1953 than they were by the Waughs and Huxleys of a quarter of a century ago. It is simply that times have changed. A sub-era in the evolution of Englishness, in which humour has been regarded as an essential part of the Good, as a graceful and necessary congruity of social life, as something to be taken for granted as right, is beginning to pass away.

For many occasions the humorous approach is still the safest diagnostic proof of the Englishness in our blood. 'How are you?' There, at the bar, is my solid friend G., the ornithologist. 'Jolly D,' he says. 'Well played,' I say. No smile, of course: it is something less than being facetious, even. This exhausted parody of prep-school slang is one of four traditional methods of starting a conversation. We shake jokes, as it were, instead of shaking hands, to show that there is no hostility. It is as automatic as the cough reflex for clearing the throat. True, the 'humour' need not necessarily be so worn out and automatic as this. On the other hand it may be worse, taking the shape of the comic story – 'stop me if you've heard it,' (for it is part of the tribal custom never to 'stop me', but to listen helplessly and wait for the point, get the feel and inflexion of the place where the laugh should come, in the story, and then laugh in unison with the teller).

It is true that most of these preliminary parries, these chewings of a worn-out old cud, are a symptom of a decadent

19

tendency to live-off-the-land in the world of humour, without putting anything back. And it is true that most people who deliberately make humorous remarks have no humour in the special English sense which this essay tries to define. An hour from my home by car on the road from London there is a pub which I visit partly for a drink and partly to refresh myself with the character of the landlord. He is, I think, an exceptionally shy man and feels more than most of us the never-admitted horror of meeting strangers – a characteristic which is surprisingly common in his profession. He is without humour, yet he too makes use of humour to bridge the gap. Every now and then he utters some of the accepted comic phrases of our age, quite isolated, quite without reference. 'Mind my bike,' he will say. Then a little later: 'Time I gave it the old one-two.' Gave what he does not say. Nobody smiles or comments, but he will himself laugh. This does not embarrass him – only the absence of the funny saying embarrasses him. Another customer comes in. With reference to nothing: 'Yes,' says the landlord laughingly, as if he and I had been having a rattling good conversation. Then, 'Don't forget the diver,' perhaps is the next phrase which happens to come to the surface. Between times the pause is always uneasy. But the general implication is that common ground has been found, if not a safe conduct into the stranger's territory.

But whether we chew over other people's humour or create it ourselves, our most usual reflex is to detach ourselves by smiling. It might be called the English Reflex. It is part of the framework of our social life. Cockney wit, for instance, shows it particularly clearly. Writing in the nineteenth century, on the habits of the English, French writers like Taine make the strange mistake, as it seems to us, of talking of the 'grim savagery and gloom' of Cockney humour – a classic misapprehension of a tone of voice which on the contrary is a making ordinary of the grim, taking the sting out of it, to make bearable life in the back streets of the Whitechapel of mid nineteenth century London. It flourishes in such unsquashable characters as Sam Weller, constantly cheering everybody up by making tragedy ludicrous. . . . 'It's over and can't be helped . . .and that's one consolation, as they always say in Turkey, ven they cuts the wrong man's head off.' Half modern Cockneyisms, equally, are used to take the edge off reality: rhyming slang, shortened as it usually is to the first word of the phrase only, keeps the reality at double remove. Far nearer than rhyming slang to essential English Humour is the slang of the Services – euphemisms like 'fishes' eyes' for tapioca pudding or the phrase next below it in Eric Partridge's *Dictionary* – 'the fishing fleet' for the women who frequent the Ladies' Lounge at the Union Club, Malta; or 'The Flap' for the great retreat which ended at Alamein.

More specifically Cockney is the extension of this kind of humour to rub in the awkwardness of the slightly embarrassing situation. The bus driver, made to brake rather hard when the woman in the Baby Austin unexpectedly swerves, pretends to faint over the steering wheel. Or a bus conductor I remember. It was in the days when a leather thong had to be pulled to stop the bus. Boldly and breezily, and to show my familiarity with the workings of the thing, I pulled it myself. But too hard – embarrassingly it came off in my hand. The conductor never seemed so much to glance at me over his shoulder, as he began to move down inside to take tickets. 'Look at Hercules' was all he said; but it gave universal satisfaction.

Is this English Reflex really peculiar to the English? We are certainly not the only country to fall back on a technique when dealing with first contacts. It is usual to contrast French wit with British humour. The French have their more supple armour of chain mail; an armoury of *finesse* and poise, an ancient fabric of manners which can be almost hostile in its correctness. Even the irresponsibility and gaiety

21

which seems to deny this, has a slight taste of ritual. The contrast between the North and South German approach is just as strong. Whether 'Heil Hitler' is the phrase or not, the salute to a northern national hero is implied. The Southern Teuton, the Austrian, on the other hand, seems to suggest by humorous implication that he is a sceptic on such matters. 'We are artists together,' he seems to say, 'humouring the junior and philistine races.' The American (U.S.) óften makes his approach in solemnity. Voice and manner seem to say 'We believe, you and I, in the great ordinary things. There is nothing whimsical or eccentric about you and me. We are solid citizens, right? Now we can talk.' Some sound British types use the same method; but for the majority of the English, humour is still the way.

FUNNINESS BY THEORY

It has not always been so. I have my own theory of a date, of a certain piece of writing which could be called the beginning of English Humour. But let us compare notes, for a moment, with the authorities.

Hazlitt on the English Comic Writers is the classic; Leigh Hunt is effectively diffuse on the subject of Wit and Humour: but in their day the word was ambiguous and vague, the culture of the English sense of humour had not begun. On the other hand, there are plenty of modern books on the theory and anatomy of humour: and so far from being inappropriately solid and learned as one might expect from the academic treatment of such a quick-silver subject, they are judicious and entertaining. To take the best since 1900: first comes Bergson's celebrated *Le Rire*, full of audacious theorizing, and entertainingly 'explaining' laughter as a shout of 'Beware!' to the rest of the community. 'I am laughing at that man' (who put his foot in a coalhole, who is wearing the wrong clothes, who does not know it is the host he is talking to when he is abusing the wine) 'because of his failure to adjust.' Next came Freud's *Wit and the Unconscious*. He approves of Bergson, and is naturally sympathetic to Bergson's theory of the reference back, through laughter, to the memory of childhood amusements with toys, and toy soldiers. Yet Freud is not truly writing about humour, nor about the kind of wit which is native here. The wit involved is *Simplicissimus* – puns, and primitive jokes, occasionally rather cruel and coarse, sometimes innocent and feeble. Though the wonderful imaginative wisdom of Freud appears here as in all his work, and though he himself was a man of delightful humour, humour is never the theme of his book.

More recently, there have been two small English books and a big treatise, the size and weight of a large firebrick, by a great French student of English.

The first of the two English books is by J. B. Priestley – the *English Humorists*: date 1929. Outwardly the book is unpromising. It belongs to the 'English Heritage' series; there is an introduction by Stanley Baldwin which dwells on the pleasures of gardens scented by Gillyflowers, and the savour of new-baked bread. But on inspection even this introduction is perfectly pleasant, and the book itself maintains a refreshingly high level of positive criticism. How good everybody is, Mr Priestley says in effect; and the enthusiasm is infectious. Mr Priestley can appreciate equally the humour of Ben Jonson and *Tristram Shandy*, of Charles Lamb and Heath Robinson. But Priestley then was one of J. C. Squire's men, and the Squirarchy really did have a warmth and enjoyment about their criticism which we seem to have lost. And when Priestley concludes, as he does, that English humour is a product of the close observation of character, it seems a natural, not a manufactured, conclusion.

Sir Harold Nicolson, in a limited edition so privately printed unfortunately as to be almost invisible, has also written on the *English Sense of Humour*, measuring up its characteristics

23

with those of Englishness in general. It touches on the all-important question of the When – *when* this sense of humour was accepted and became part of our life.* Then comes the big definitive-style work (Vol. II 1950) of the Professor of English at the Sorbonne, Louis Cazamian, who sifts the whole of English Literature, from the beginnings to Shakespeare, for first examples and early signs. Some literary research workers sink beneath the weight of their materials – buried in their enthusiasm. The historian of wit, scraping his way through the sandy centuries before English humour was created, is inclined, in the desert, to see green spots of humour where it doesn't exist. 'There is more than one touch of slyest humour in' – the Anglo-Saxon Chronicle? In Beowulf? When the real humour comes: 'Touchstone is a thing of pure joy for ever,' he says, losing proportion. Not pure joy. But on the whole M. Cazamian keeps his head. He disinters interesting early examples; he carefully picks out the change of attitude which turned laughing *at* into laughing *with*; and he tries to plot the history, with the help of the staff of the O.E.D., of the meaning of the difficult word Humour, which wobbles indecisively between three meanings before the modern sense is established.

THE IRRELEVANCE OF LAUGHTER

What is this 'English humour' which as soon as it is persuaded on to the slide under the microscope swims out of focus? Particularly misleading, all the humour authorities agree, is the connexion between humour and laughter. There are in fact very few situations to which laughter is not appropriate. We laugh when the sea touches our navel, the first June bathe. But we only laugh in company. Under the the age of six we cry – and cry the harder the bigger the crowd. Do we laugh when we play and frown when we work?

*I am deeply indebted both to this book and to Mr Priestley's.

In England, particularly, this is often reversed. It is only children who are irresponsible and ill-educated enough to make a game of games. We laugh at something because it is familiar and something else because it is unfamiliar. We laugh at misfortunes if they do not incur danger, though what constitutes 'danger' varies enormously between nations and centuries. The day before yesterday, in ethnological time, we laughed to see a lunatic on the end of a chain, or a bear tied to a post and bitten to death by dogs. We just about permit ourselves now, in our unworthier moments, to smile behind our pipe at somebody looking seasick, if we ourselves are immune. We laugh because other people are laughing uncontrollably; but controlled or calculated laughter, on the other hand, can drive our own smiles underground for hours. We laugh if and because we are supposed not to laugh. Sometimes, if we are middle-aged, we like to try to slide into the irrepressible laughter of young people, thinking perhaps they will say 'He's only a boy' whereas in fact they are thinking, at this youthful and therefore most solemn period of their lives, 'he's only elderly'. We laugh at the clothes and customs of savages, as savages laugh at the clothes and customs of ourselves, and we claim to be superior to savages by 'being able to laugh at our own idiosyncrasies'; though this is itself a highly complex kind of laughter connected with the kind of self-dispraise which Dr Johnson said is often self-praise.

Then there is the laugh which fills up a blank in the conversation, often associated with a thoughtful 'Yes, isn't it amazing?' The laugh of the older man talking to a girl, which can suggest: 'You are charming, but I am charming too.' The laugh to attract attention, similar to that attention-attracting cough, that large confident chest-clearing, kept for a *pianissimo* passage, by the man who feels out of his depth at a concert. The laugh, similar, which we hear in the hall from the new arrival not sure of himself, who wishes to appear sure of himself, and it makes us sure we are not sure of him. The laugh of the lone man at the theatre, who wishes to show that he understands the play or understands the foreign language which is being spoken, or gets the point of the joke quickest, or has seen the play. The laugh of creative pleasure uttered by someone who has managed to say something precise and descriptive in a conversation, whether witty or not. The laugh of relief from physical danger, or from the reprieve of the worse danger of separation. We laugh at funny hats.

Finally, we laugh at sex jokes. We do not laugh at sex jokes if they are not funny unless other people are present. It is possible to roar with laughter at a very minute impropriety if it is delivered from the stage to an auditorium the size of the Palladium. We laugh even at bad sex jokes if we are young and virginal, to show we are not young and virginal; the elderly man's 'Have you heard this one?' is equally, perhaps, to show that he has not yet returned to virginity but partly it is to show that everything is all right, I am all right, and I know the password. We also smile at people laughing at sex jokes, and the analytical-minded may enjoy a hidden smile, half clinical, half affectionate, when he sees Miss Joan Hunter Dunn, at the Café de Cannes in Compton Street, her strong brown tennis-playing upper arms shaking with laughter at cabaret songs which home in Green Loamings she would scarcely understand. It also makes us feel nostalgic for that most pertinent lyric by Herbert Farjeon, about the cabaret singer at the piano who sings every evening in a nice white tie, nice dirty songs to go with the nice clean food:

> To the bees and the breeze and the trees, no doubt,
> A kitchenmaid heart responds,
> But when men who are really men go out
> With blondes who are really blondes,
> You give 'em smut,

> You give 'em dirt,
> In a nice white tie
> And a nice white shirt,
> And they'll clap you loud,
> They'll clap you long,
> Till you give 'em a dirtier
> Dirty song.

How can it be possible to tie all these different kinds of laughs to one cause? The motives for laughter, in fact, could not be more diverse and contradictory; but it is difficult to resist the old game of trying to tag them all on to one human characteristic. Theories ... Bergson is still the favourite, with his laughter which calls out 'Beware', his smile which is a Darwinianly correct expostulation at any deviation from human adaptability. Bergson's diagnosis is certainly gayer than the somewhat schoolmastery laughter of the Freudians, who can take the Christmas out of smiles, even, by putting them all down to the sadistic impulse. Hobbes and Spencer, after philosophical speculation, have held that laughter is a way of saying 'I'm the king of the castle', is a 'feeling of sudden glory', a rush of self-esteem. It is a question of taste. If my life depended on it and I had to find a link between the happy yell of the schoolboy released from the schoolroom and that buried quiver of satisfaction, that smile curling round the most deeply buried ventricle of the heart, of the Dean when he observes that his Bishop, referring to what he calls Isaiah in the pulpit, is in fact quoting Micah – if I was forced to explain the pleasure of both parties in one word, I would say 'release'. The Dean, inwardly, has put on his gym shoes and is running like fury to pull Isobel Jones's pigtail.

Are these definitions of laughter relevant to the theme of humour? And if so, is it because humour is itself a sub-department of the comic? Or is it not truer to say that the humorous attitude runs parallel to the laughing attitude, looking at laughter from next-door, as it were, examining it? The grin of laughter – the poker face of humour. Surely laughter and humour are opposed. Or at nearest humour is buried laughter – 'laughter with a sad brow', as Falstaff says.

Maybe 'release of inhibition' is the key which unlocks both kinds of laughter, extravert and introvert: certainly humour has something to do with 'getting outside ourselves' ... 'seeing things in a new light' ... 'turning over the soil at the roots'. It is difficult to define because it is something which is always growing and changing. Perhaps its history is its meaning.

THE GREAT ORIGINATOR

One of the rewards of the Lit. man – of the academic student of English Literature – is the appreciation of the first bursts; and there never was such a first burst as happened to English in the fourteenth century. Humour came suddenly to our literature without warning. Old English epics and Middle English romances give no sign. They were solemn and severe at a time when, across the Channel, wit and *finesse* were already developing. Malory's version of *Morte d'Arthur* misses the satirical point of its French original. It is as richly pleasant, as comfortably stabilizing as a homecoming to feel ourselves only a few steps away from these medieval ancestors. The remains of their churches and carvings and laws and castles and place names often give us this feeling: their writings hardly ever.

The change came in the fourteenth century with one man. No Eng. Lit. disciple will ever believe that there is a greater innovator in any art than Chaucer in his. There is the language he chose, the dialect of that language, the making rhythm out of that language, the attitude to his writing and his audience and the sense of communication between them, the eye turned intently to the contemporary reality of life instead of the repeated fantasy of allegory and personification, the originality which reversed medieval practice, the recognition of the sacred importance of detail, the recognition that character is not an abstraction from, but a fusion into, small unpredictable traits none of which have very much to do with any seven deadly sins or moribund virtues – no need to add humour to these attributes which together make up Humour itself.

Because Chaucer did not show his full power till late in life, it is possible to see when, in his evolution, these different newnesses appeared. Chaucer was perfectly at ease with the feathery Gallic spirit of the *Roman de la Rose*. At the other end of his writing life, the *Prologue* shows Chaucer's newness, and therefore Chaucer's humour, concentrated. Perhaps the best examples of it before the *Canterbury Tales* are in *Troilus and Criseyde*; but for a good clear landmark in this history, I would like to choose Chaucer's treatment of the Theme of the Henpecked Husband.

While humour was being evolved by Chaucer, a rough kind of comedy was already in existence elsewhere. The religious Miracle Plays of Chaucer's century and before were evolving the first stock comic characters, which were soon fitting as naturally into religious plays as the impolite carvings of the miserere seats and the gargoyles into the dreamy curves and mystical perpendiculars of our cathedrals. One of the favourite plays – 'turns' would perhaps be the word – in the Miracle cycle is from the Towneley sequence, the *Play of Noah*. A tradition which seems always to have been ancient is that Noah drank. Another, that he was nagged by his wife. In the Towneley version there is this kind of dialogue, as Noah and his wife quarrel:

Hold thy tongue, ramskyt, or I shall make thee be still ...
Have at thee, Gill!

29

But the wife has the last word when Noah at last gets her into the ark: 'Better take a cloth to your shoes, or they won't last!' Noah's wife is not the only comic character in these series. If the theme has to be religious by order and custom, it is not surprising that to a generation indulging in its first literary high spirits Genesis should appear to be potentially the funniest book in the world. But the henpecked husband seems to have been the favourite theme of them all.

Now the point is that in one of his most famous stories, the Canterbury Tale told by the Nun's Priest, Chaucer takes this honoured farcical theme of the family quarrel. Chanticleer the cock is the husband, and the hen who pecks him is Perthelote.

How does Chaucer do it? First, by describing, with tenderness, not the hatred but the love between this husband and wife. Chanticleer's comb, embattled like a castle wall, is redder than the fine coral. His bill 'black and shiny like jet – like azure were his legs and toes. His nails were whiter than the lily flower, his colour like burnished gold'.

Then Perthelote. Of all the seven hens to do his pleasure 'his sisters and his paramours, Perthelote had the most prettily coloured throat, she was the most courteous and debonair'. And the two were devoted to each other: 'Truly she hath the heart of Chanticleer locked in every limb. He loved her so that well it was with him.'

Instead of settling down to a stock laugh for a stock joke, we feel on the contrary full of sympathy and interest. When the quarrel comes, it is all the more effective, just because it is so gentle. Chanticleer has had a dream, of a fox. Is it a warning dream? He quotes at length a wealth of authorities for believing that it is; and Perthelote listens patiently. Her comment, when it comes, is more like solicitude than reproof. 'I understand,' she says in effect, 'but ... are not dreams the result of eating ... perhaps too much? ... If you would take a little laxative? ... a few worms?' Chanticleer does not immediately collapse; he scarcely realizes that the ground has gone from his feet. He talks on: but he has lost the argument for ever. What a technique! It is best described by Dryden, when he warns against the use of the bludgeon, in Satire: more effective, he says, is the scimitar, so sharp that, capable of severing the head from the neck with one blow, it can leave the head still standing in position.

Is this the first example of English humour? There is evidence that the Nun's Priest's Tale was written before the *Prologue*. There are, I know, odd exceptional examples of true English humour even before Chaucer's century.* But none of them begin to show so clearly the essentials of highly developed humour – the gentleness, the seeing both sides of the argument at once, and that something which I once heard Professor Walter Raleigh describe as the 'china blue eye' of Chaucer. The Nun's Priest's Tale seems to have this rather wide open, pale blue and innocent eye; which I suppose is another way of saying that Chaucer never laughs at his own jokes. In fact the reader must be ever on the alert to make sure that Chaucer is not smiling at *him*, for taking some grave-seeming passage too seriously.

After Chaucer came the desert, for whatever the merits of the Scottish Chaucerians, English followers were certainly not Chaucerian in their humour. Young Lit. students can never agree whether Gower or Langland is the least funny writer in history. There are now many admirers of John Heywood, the tutor of Henry VIII, and his truly original mind and wit: but the influence of the spirit of Chaucer was blocked for at least three hundred years. Till then, humour had to be recreated.

*Far the best pre-Chaucerian humorist is agreed to be the author of the dialogue *The Owl and the Nightingale*, date about 1180 The Owl stands for the Old Poetry and the old way of life; the Nightingale for the New.

HUMOUR IN THREE DIMENSIONS: SHAKESPEARE

Even when we come to Shakespeare, there is a certain prejudice to be broken down. The absolute freshness and originality of Shakespeare's humour is tarnished for many of us by a veil of schoolroom experience. By Eileen Philpot being Toby Belch when they did *Twelfth Night* for the Prize-giving. By learning up those terrible puns of the funny men, the Gobbos and the Llewellyns, which depended on a glance at the introduction, p.xvi, before you could see the point. *Enter the clowns* – and we crouched more earnestly still over the footnotes. True, we were quite soon old enough to laugh really heartily at these parts – but this seemed to depend on the luck of there being, for us in the late twenties, at any rate, two great Shakespeare comedians, Hay Petrie and Miles Malleson, to make them funny. In other words, if we laughed, it was always at Petrie as Aguecheek, Miles Malleson as young Gobbo; Miles Malleson as Snout, turning his head so completely towards Bottom, fastening his attention on him with such overwhelming abandonment to the hypnotic powers of Bottom's genius. Or remember, later still, Laurence Olivier as Justice Shallow reflecting on his past, and the satisfaction with which he repeats the information, well known to him already of course, that some of those early contemporaries of his are dead, as he reiterates the question:

> 'And is old Double dead?'
> 'Dead.'

'Dead,' he echoes, with all the secret and self-congratulatory satisfaction which, as Bernard Shaw once said, so completely, as one gets older, replaces grief at the death of friends. In the theatre, we say 'what acting'. It is only afterwards that we realize we should have said 'what Shakespeare'; for it is the completeness of Shakespeare's understanding and humour which makes possible so many different interpretations.

Within the history of Shakespeare's drama – from *Henry VI* at one end to *The Tempest* at the other – are comprehended the beginnings, growth and maturity of English drama. Shakespeare, living whole cycles of development in his own literary evolution, included English humour among them. In the earliest plays are portraits of characters marked down for satire by considerations which were considered fashionable or politic. Shakespeare's first humour is more subtle than his first gravities: it seems as if it is through humour that he first emerges, that the first sharp Shakespearean distinctiveness shows. Shakespeare shows his first trace of Shakespeare, as it were, in the prose speeches, the Jack Cade speeches, of *Henry VI*, Part 2. Jack Cade – a rebel against a Tudor ancestor and therefore opposed to all that is right – apprehends Lord Say and accuses him of causing education:

> Thou hast most traitorously corrupted the youth of the realm in erecting a grammar-school . . . it will be proved to thy face that thou hast men about thee that usually talk of a noun and a verb, and such abominable words as no Christian ear can endure to hear.

Nouns and verbs, word consciousness, word tricks, word battles and word parodies much concerned Shakespeare in this trial and error period. Soon after he began his first humorous character sketches, he was enjoying himself with tongue twisters and verbal knockabout. It is the habit of youthful writers to utter at least one great 'yah' to schooldays and grammar days. *Love's Labour's Lost*, with its schoolmasters and euphuists, is the setting of this word revelry.

ARMADO: Fetch hither the swain: he must carry me a letter.

MOTH: A message well sympathized; a horse to be ambassador for an ass.

ARMADO: Ha, ha! what sayest thou?

MOTH: Marry, sir, you must send the ass upon the horse, for
he is very slow-gaited. But I go.

ARMADO: The way is but short: away!

MOTH: As swift as lead, sir.

ARMADO: Thy meaning, pretty ingenious?
Is not lead a metal heavy, dull, and slow?

MOTH: Minime, honest master; or rather, master, no.

ARMADO: I say lead is slow.

MOTH: You are too swift, sir, to say so:
Is that lead slow which is fired from a gun?

ARMADO: Sweet smoke of rhetoric!
He reputes me a cannon, and the bullet,
that's he; –
I shoot thee at the swain.

MOTH: Thump, then, and I flee.

As humour it seems to us now excruciating. It is useless for
modern producers to burst themselves with invention of
business to make such scenes 'go'. Contemporary-to-the-
minute reference and inflexion are the essence of much dialogue. We must think in terms of *Much Binding* or *Itma*.
Tommy Handley's dialogue depended just as much on puns
and word idiocies, and catch-phrases, and seemed to us
delightful. But remember, that kind of Shakespeare dialogue
should be delivered at Handley-speed, not at scholar-speed.

A third development came with the comic types based on
observation. Here, too, a certain amount of period-swallow-
ing and note-nibbling is necessary, but experience will soon
show how close these thin but precisely studied characters
are to their modern equivalents. There is a bad tradition in
our own theatre of overplaying these parts. The first time I
saw Dogberry acted with a little observation, a little subtlety
– it was in a Gielgud production of *Much Ado* – I came awake
to the character and began to watch and enjoy. 'But policemen *are* like that *now*,' I thought, 'especially the one who
examined my car licence in Dorset last March.' The humour
of these characters increases in us: for just as Shakespeare's

34

profound or tragic words become true for us one after another as we live longer, so do his quick perceptions and sketches seem nearer to life, and therefore nearer to humour, as our experience widens.

There is a fourth kind of Shakespearean humour, however, which surpasses all these, and is surely first conceived by Shakespeare. It is Shakespeare's creation of the man with a sense of what is humorous. More precisely, the man who is capable of perceiving the character-humour of a situation – of perceiving the human traits of others that is, and consequently also the human traits in himself. It is known that there can be seen developing in the sequence of the 'great' plays of Shakespeare, and beginning even before these, in *Richard III*, but seen first most certainly, though slightly, in the person of Faulconbridge in *King John*, a 'Shakespeare protagonist' – a character in which not only some of Shakespeare's own tastes, but his powers of psychological insight are manifest as well. I wonder if my experience is often shared – the shock of first discovering this Shakespearish person in one particular scene, the second scene of *Henry IV* Part 1, where the conspirators are arguing against each other while they count their chickens before they are hatched? Here Hotspur is this Shakespeare protagonist, understanding the characters of the others, and (being the Hotspur part of Shakespeare) impatient with them. Shakespeare, and particularly Hotspur-Shakespeare, is irritated above all by superstition.

'Do you realize who I am?' says Glendower in effect. 'I can call spirits from the vasty deep.'

HOTSPUR: Why, so can I and so can any man,
But do they come when you do call to them?

I remember so many years ago – when this gave me the first, free *contemporary* laugh from Shakespeare; and this Hotspur humour plays against the humourlessness of Glendower

Worcester and Northumberland through the play. Shakespeare seems to delight in this situation, and his sympathy is never with the humourless man, whether it is Claudius being taunted by Hamlet, or the 'good' Gloucester by the 'bad' Edmund.

THE GREAT AGE

In none of its manifold styles does seventeenth century literature seem to turn naturally to humour. It is true the century begins with Ben Jonson. Ben Jonson is responsible for the Comedy of Humours; yet as every Cert. A schoolboy knows, 'humour' meant something totally different in Jonson's day. Talk of Humour, then, was a way of describing a prevailing characteristic and tying it to a theory of the humours, explaining bad temper or serenity, for instance, by reference to a predominance of certain qualities in the blood which combined to make a sanguine, choleric, melancholy or phlegmatic 'complexion'. The meaning of every one of these words has now changed, and the theory is dead; although it would be a little difficult to explain to an Elizabethan *precisely* how it differs from our contemporary theory of the influence on character of the secretions of the pituitary or the adrenals.

Whatever the theory, in practice 'comedy of humours' meant comedy of set types in plain black and white. The laughter in Ben Jonson is high spirits given permanence by a gloriously athletic command of language. To read aloud a good speech in *Volpone* is like exercises before breakfast; and just about as far from the spirit of the English Sense of Humour.

Of the other literary directions of the seventeenth century, none of them are peculiar for humour, although there are exceptions. Neither Webster nor Milton, Cowley nor the raw farces of Dryden, to name a few of the fixed points in the bewilderment of contrasts in this century, could have existed quite as they were after the Age of Humour had been invented. The Jacobean tragedies, for instance, have scarcely a sign of that deliciously light touch considered so necessary in serious plays in Shaftesbury Avenue, 1954. On the other hand they usually find a more adequate line, at the high moment of tragedy, than 'O, my dear, if only I had understood.' Seventeenth-century humour does exist, of course, even in the middle period of fighting satire and hard feeling. What there is round the corner, so to speak – in the caustic verse asides in the lesser poems of Herrick, in Dryden's prose, in the half-self-amused self-parody of Pepys, in the bland detail of Overbury. But the Age of Humour was still to come.

If we had to pin it down to a tone of voice, or a page, we should not be far out if we looked into the 1709 *Tatler*. We shouldn't be far away to say that the Age of Humour was born early in the eighteenth century, out of the warmth of Steele, married to the urbanity of Addison. Swift is not of the true line: his satire is too passionately identified with purpose. *Moll Flanders* and the other less wonderful works of Defoe seem too direct from life to have the at-one-removeness necessary for humour. We have to wait for the works of Fielding before we are conscious of a novelist-author smiling in the background. In mid century, Dr Johnson made his own unique addition to the character of humour – the power of taking the offensive without meaning, or giving, offence. Boswell, hopping along anxiously in Johnson's wake, seldom realized how often the Master was smiling at him. When Johnson is disapproving over a Shakespeare stage direction, when he writes in a grave footnote to the 'Enter a Third Friar' of *Romeo and Juliet* the comment 'I do not perceive the purpose of this Friar', Boswell would no doubt have called this a 'very severe judgment'.

Who, besides Johnson, are the eighteenth-century geniuses of humour? The effect of Gibbon's amusement, like Johnson's, is increased by the solemnity of his sentence structure. At the other extreme, the wide-open-ness of Smollett – ('Smollett's robust gusto' was the phrase by which, following a special system of memorizing, I learnt to distinguish him in order to get through Matriculation English, from other novelists) – all belong to a chapter on The Comic rather than one on The Humorous.

Sterne is the obvious choice. His break through the rules of syntax and even of printing was a wonderful private joke for his own time, perhaps: but the humane humour of his characterizing make him officially the First of the great humorists of the eighteenth century.

For myself, however, the choice is Boswell. The character of Boswell's humour is not easy to describe. The modern worship of this trait was too embryonic then to affect his attitude – fortunately so, because part of our pleasure in his humour is due to the unconsciousness with which he purveys it. Yet for the purposes of my own working definition of descriptive humour, Boswell is the man. If humour is really the recording of small but insignificant human traits, Boswell is the man. He did not know about humour, but he did know about character. It was even correct literary fashion to be observant about character, as Richardson and Rousseau and the sentimental movement were observant of it. But what may have started in Boswell as a respectably fashionable activity emerged as a great artistic enterprise.

I always think of one particular passage in the *Journal* of the Hebrides tour as an epitome of Boswellism. After a good deal of engineering, Boswell, with Johnson, has 'made' the Duke of Argyll's. What luck – and what delight! They are his guests at dinner. Boswell is excited and, no doubt, convivial. But the artist, as always, retains his detachment. He observes:

A gentleman in company after dinner, was desired by the duke to go to another room for a specimen of curious marble, which his grace wished to show us. He brought a wrong piece, upon which the duke sent him back again. He could not refuse; but, to avoid any appearance of servility, he whistled as he walked out of the room, to show his independency.

That kind of observation is to me the perfection of humour and the art of recording. Because of Boswell, that slight disjointed whistle through the teeth, heard by all the company yet listened to by only one of them, will go on thinly sounding for ten thousand years. Needless to say, Boswell does not record it because it is 'funny'. 'On mentioning this afterwards to Dr Johnson,' writes Boswell, 'he said, it was a nice trait of character.'

Boswell would certainly not have thought of himself as humorous in the modern sense. Indeed he disapproved of fooling in himself and other people, as he disapproved of and misunderstood the fooling of Goldsmith.* Yet it is through the warmth and subtlety of Goldsmith, rather than through Boswell, that the path leads to the first completely conscious humorist, the first real English Sense of Humour man, Charles Lamb. The delicate and separate flame of Charles Lamb is indistinct now in the hard light of a thousand Lamb imitators. Yet to what extent the idea of humorousness is tinged by his influence is obvious when we reflect that even now traits of Lamb which are not themselves necessarily humorous at all, such as a more or less pleasingly sentimental attitude to children, or a perfectly serious treatment of a trivial subject, or puns, are regarded as a kind of necessary accompaniment of humour. What could sound more modern than this typical Lamb turn of thought?

This very night I am going to leave off tobacco: surely there must be some other world in which this unconquerable purpose

*See page 81

shall be realized. The soul hath not her generous aspirings implanted in her in vain.

Critical interest in the subject of wit and humour begin to be given special place in the writings of Hazlitt and Leigh Hunt: but still the modern conception of the English Sense of Humour had not been born; nor, except in almost chance uses (beginning as far back as Dryden) had the word 'humour' taken on its modern meaning. No doubt it was Dickens who helped to establish and fix it, by being the greatest comic writer of our history. Though his was not the deepest kind of humour, involving as it did two parts of laughing at to one of laughing with, Dickens attacks the more external and fixed traits of human character with such power that superficiality itself becomes a virtue.

Yet Dickens does stand outside his characters, approving or disapproving; the characters can all be divided therefore into what is Good and Bad according to a man who had never in himself achieved inner certainty. Why, then, is he so undoubtedly a genius of humour – what was it new that he added? Perhaps it has something to do with this very word 'external' – 'superficial'. My own best pleasure comes from all the surface habits revealed by Dickens – of clothes and speech and gesture and expression. As soon as we open a page of Dickens we begin to see. It is personality through appearance: even the characters who only appear for a moment are raised out of the flat by their physical shape. The man at the Podsnap party who suddenly leans forward and says 'Esker' to the Frenchman is always before our eyes as 'the young gentleman with the lumpy forehead'. That is why Dickens has been so successful as material for broadcasting. Writing for broadcasting needs above all to be picture making, so that the glazed outward eye of the listener, staring at the art wood of his radio set, can be given something to feed on. That is why, however fond we may be of them out of loyalty to our childhood, the Dickens illustrations are a handicap. His illustrators, like us, were stimulated to see, but they saw in terms of a limited yet powerful taste, rather over-ripe and clinging taste, of the eighteen forties, when gnome-like men, or weightless young women (with feet just showing below their skirts 'like tea-leaves', as Max Beerbohm says), when tiny crippled people or rough

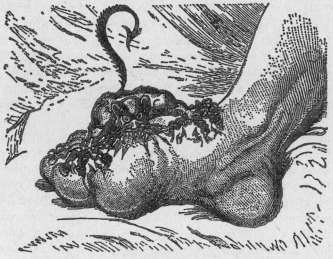

THE GOUT

Dickens re-created English humour out of the harsh fantasy of caricaturists like Gillray. This drawing of 1799 is a relatively mild example of the violence of this period.

fine handsome people, or dark branded people, with manacled brows, were set in gloomy forests illuminated by lightning, or pale glaring meres, or stricken granges, or Gothic High Streets, or ancient slums, or claustrophobious doll's house interiors. So that between Dickens and his descriptions this front-drop picture is lowered. Without the illustrations, Dickens becomes more vivid. More important, his humanity stands out with greater clearness.

Dickens and the prestige of his comedy set the scene for

the last phase of this evolution – the age of the English Sense of Humour, and its entrance as something good and necessary. The word 'humour' was soon to acquire its modern meaning – the sense of *something begetting a quietly analytical amusement – the ready ability to feel that amusement*.

'Humour' is first associated with a way of writing by Sir William Temple. Then, suddenly, we find Addison, who confesses he finds the word difficult, saying that 'humour should not be ill natured' or that 'True Humour generally looks serious' – quite in the modern sense. The new meaning was not finally fixed till half-way through the nineteenth century. And the attitude? When did the English Sense of Humour become established as something vaguely like good sportsmanship, a quality which seemed all at once to be something we had always possessed, always must possess, wouldn't be quite right if we didn't possess, would hate to see absent from our sons-in-law or our policemen or novelists or Prime Ministers? Sir Harold Nicolson points out that Gladstone was not the first Prime Minister who lacked a sense of humour; but he was the first one of whom this was said. When did we acquire the *sense* of the sense of humour? One specific innovation should make it easier to place the dates.

The innovation was *Punch*. *Punch*, founded in 1841, covers our period and to some extent determines it. *Punch*-the-reflection-of-the-English-character and *Punch*-the-social-history-of-our-times is not more important than *Punch* as an influence. We are influenced by our own reflection. We look at *Punch* in our more defenceless and therefore more impressionable moments. We look at the hairdresser's; we looked when we were very young.

The young get most of their education in asides, out of school hours. I knew every page of my father's ten-volume edition of *Punch* selections – *Mr Punch at the Theatre . . . By the Seaside*. When I read about Germany, the picture, and the only picture, which came to my mind was a cartoon of the Kaiser playing with toy battleships on the end of a string. 'Wealth' – and I saw a du Maurier drawing of Sir Gorgius Midas. 'Drunkenness' – there was the John Leach drawing of the man lying in the gutter who had 'dined well but not too wisely', the caption said. 'Peace' or 'Britain' meant thick-waisted females in baggy Grecian skirts, symbolic, difficult affairs to be skipped over quickly. 'Art' was another du Maurier drawing of an aesthetic person in a quilted waistcoat, something not to be approved of. Members of Parliament, equally, were a lot of funny gentlemen with their feet up, with funny collars, and huge heads. The caricatures and the pictures *were* life, it seemed, as I turned to them from the shadowy world of real people.

Later on, in my teens, *Punch* was at its English-sense-of-humour peak, all light touches and mild smile. In its beginnings, it could scarcely have been more different. *Punch* arose in the hungry forties filled with a strong sense of social injustice, as reformatory in its satire as Dickens, and as independent. The gentler, more gentlemanly and on the whole more subtle *Punch* came twenty years later with the double change of editor and proprietor, with the advent of Mark Lemon and John Agnew; and a relic of a stronger and more savage humour disappeared. Great 'sense-of-humour' subjects began to turn up – the curate, the Scotsman in London, the Cockney in the country, the fashionable stupid and the stupidly unfashionable, the foolish mothers and the wise children, particularly nice children asking their mothers awkward questions. For Hogarth's drunkard standing over his coffin in Gin Lane was substituted the mildly bibulous Scotsman on the spree, amusingly finding himself 'unco' fu''.

The change in the nature of comic drawing was even greater. Instead of the delicate coarseness of Rowlandson, or the spotty ugliness of some of the comic figures in the Dickens illustrations, the drawings were pleasant, right for the family, and at the best, showing a humour of observation, of gesture, clothes and character more truly humorous than any of the letterpress part of *Punch*. Occasionally its pages were touched by genius – by a Charles Keene, or a Mr Pooter. By 1900 *Punch* was taking on its modern shape. In spite of the figure of Punch himself, facetious finger on hearty nose, in spite of innumerable representations, by Bernard Partridge, of a John Bull obviously incapable of any amusement more subtle than a beefy laugh, the light touch had arrived. English sense of humour was established.

My own generation was almost drowned in it. Our childhood books were humorous, filled with humorously funny animals. My father had been told his stories from *The Parent's Assistant*. I of course learnt to read out of Benjamin Bunny. The inhabitants of my vast story-book zoo were never tragic or touching. They followed Lewis Carroll, not Hans Andersen: anthropomorphism is itself a big sub-department of English humour (pedimorphism, to be more exact. The animals take on a child shape). There are certainly worse places to grow up in than a world in which the eyes were supposed to twinkle and the mouths determined to have deep corners. The mid-nineteenth-century clergymen tended to be grim over nothing. Our own parsons were jolly about nothing, which was certainly an improvement, even though it seemed equally far away from religion. There was a general cheering up among the poets. Georgian poetry was pleasantly smiling in an outdoor sort of way. 'One would think,' – I remember Philip Guedalla first creating the hard-worked epigram, in the days when E. V. Lucas's *Open Road* was the great selling anthology – 'One would think that poetry was a form of deep breathing. Even Mr Chesterton seems to be suffering from a hearty degeneration of the fat.' E. V. in his *Punch* articles had the right, slight, light tone of the period. Sturge Moore unsympathetically dismissed Belloc and

Chesterton as 'two buttocks of one bum', which in the case of Chesterton and perhaps Belloc as well did fairly suggest the degeneration from their youthful mastery of wit into heartiness. Our historians, like Strachey, by exchanging for the telescope the microscope, picked out the amusing detail instead of showing us the majestic panorama. Even our philosophers, especially our don philosophers, smiled frequently in well-written little introductions; and the economists themselves stopped referring to pieces of stuff by the severe title of 'goods', and talked with a sort of wild aboriginal gaiety of 'Mr Smith going into a shop and buying a twelve and fourpenny bicycle tyre from Mr Robinson'. And of course the novelists, or rather our Four Uncles, as Rebecca West once called them, Bennett and Wells, Shaw and Galsworthy, had all written great comic works except Galsworthy, in whom the absence of humour, it was generally agreed, was a pity.

S.B. AND G.B.S.

Of course there was an historical reason for this Age of Humour. It was a reaction against the unmeaning seriousness of the Queen Victoria age; against the solemn furniture and the hypocritical goodness of the Podsnaps and the Veneerings. Something like a 'great breath of Falstaffian laughter' was needed to blow it all away.

Something like G. K. Chesterton? Chesterton had some similarities to a Falstaff, except that he was more a spiritual, and much less a sensual zealot. But the fact is that the physique of Falstaff is by no means what it was as a comedy 'line'. In fact, so far from laughing at a man simply because he is very fat, we are inclined to polite commiseration, and think 'hypertensive ... or hypothyroid ... in a couple of years he'll either have blown up or blown down ... if he hasn't melted away with diabetic sugar ... and think of the arthritis in those over-weighted knee joints. No wonder he says he wants "levers to pull himself up". Poor fellow, let us look away'. Symptoms are not, nowadays, on the list of things we can laugh at.

So it is not surprising that of our two really powerful Falstaffs of 1900, our two boldest sweepers away of conventional morality, one was a bachelor recluse, the other a Puritan ascetic.

It is necessary to have been born with at least one toenail in the Victorian era to enjoy something of the pleasure of incredulous relief which was blessedly given by the humour of Samuel Butler and Bernard Shaw. The effect of Shaw was once compared to an early morning call, 7.30 am, on a fine morning. In comes the maid, brisk and crisp, with a nice cup of tea, and draws the curtains. It is a fine day. We don't want to get up, but how nice it is when we do. We open the window wide, and all those gloomy dreams and night thoughts are blown away. All those Victorian worse-than-deaths, unnecessary fears, and moral scars, and not-mentioning-things-because-we-take-them-I-hope-for-granted were blown out of the window.

When these two great writers are studied as classics they will be approached, I have no doubt, through the opening chapters of Butler's *Erewhon*. As the explorer approaches the boundaries of the unknown country he is alone. His guide has deserted him. Lost in the mist at the crest of the pass, he hears the sound of music – more terrifying because it is beautiful. Suddenly giant figures are above him and then the man brave enough to go on sees that the figures are sham; the music is the wind playing through their backless heads. A rift in the clouds and he sees the fresh and sunny fields of a new country.

It was Butler who in this splendid metaphor suggested that the morality effigies of the Victorians, if they could be taken unawares and turned back to front, would seem merely absurd. All these things we were supposed to look solemn about – it's all right, we needn't. O heavenly release. 'I sat for two hours before the statue of Laocoon in the Uffizzi,' Theobald Pontifex records in his diary. 'I wonder how often he looked at his watch to see if the two hours was up,' says Butler.

In spite of the poetry of *Erewhon*, and in spite of an infectiously optimistic philosophy of progress and the human will, Butler, so far as his ideas and beliefs were concerned, never succeeded even in his two greatest works, the *Notebooks* and *The Way of all Flesh*, in opposing anything more fruitful than a No to the great Victorian Negative. Even his philosophy was a No to Darwin. But Butler was certainly positive in his humour – in his description of Theobald and Christina Pontifex; in the humour of the characterization of his own character, if one may so put it. In the richness of the flavour of his own particular No-ness, Butler was unique.

Talking it over, we agreed that Blake was no good because he learnt Italian at sixty in order to study Dante, and we knew Dante was no good because he was so fond of Virgil, and Virgil was no good because Tennyson ran him, and as for Tennyson – well, Tennyson goes without saying.

There was always something much more positive about Shaw. Great occasions at Court meant the Court Theatre in those days; and then later, for my generation, Everyman meant the Everyman, Hampstead. How well I can remember, after my weekly dash to see the latest G.B.S. revival, standing on the platform of Hampstead Underground and feeling as if the keenest mountain air was blowing through my brains: as if every old bit of furniture in my head had been taken out, dusted, and put back again in a new, tidy, and sensible order.

For us then, of course, much of the laughter was release-of-inhibition laughter. But once the chains have been broken, can the emancipator hope to retain his audience? This is a test of genius which Shaw does not always pass. In *The Doctor's Dilemma*, a rich play of the second rank, the doctors are 'scandalized' (favourite word of Shaw's stage directions) when Dubedat, the artist, makes them believe that he and his adored Jennifer are married only in the eyes of God, not in the legal or church-door sense. 'Why not?' says Dubedat:

Lots of people do it: just as good people as you. Why don't you learn to think, instead of bleating and baahing like a lot of sheep when you come up against anything you're not accustomed to ... I can just play with people like you. I only asked you had you seen Jennifer's marriage lines; and you concluded straight away that she hadn't got any. You don't know a lady when you see one ... Now I'm only an immoral artist; but if you'd told me that Jennifer wasn't married, I'd have had the gentlemanly feeling and artistic instinct to say that she carried her marriage certificate in her face and in her character.

How does such a passage stand the test of time? It is good Shaw, certainly; the last line lifts it: but the fact that the doctors were scandalized loses its impact unless the audience, and perhaps even Shaw himself, in some unconscious but ineradicable way, is secretly scandalized as well. In 1906 this may well have been. But in the audience of 1953 it is Shaw we smile at – Shaw suggesting that four experienced doctors, of all people, could be shocked by the absence of legitimacy; and we are inclined to regard Dubedat's not-being-actually-married boast as a bit of tiresome nineteen-ten-ishness. The fact is that Shaw's scorn of false convention created a crowd of superior little Shavians and People who Couldn't be Shocked. And it was these very people who turned up their noses at the man who had done their emancipating for them.

What is there left? What place does Shaw take in this account of English humour? There is nothing specifically English, certainly, about the satire of outworn institutions.

Early, rubber-stamp criticism of Shaw compared him to Aristophanes and Molière. The outstandingly un-English Swift was mentioned and so, therefore, was *saeva indignatio*. All this, it is true, had some kind of appositeness to *Widowers' Houses* and the rest of 'Plays Unpleasant'. The overlying tone of voice and the rigid form of Shaw's earliest work belonged to Ibsen. Shaw the delightfully shocking, the outrageously sensible, came later. And this later Shaw, whatever his birth and his dogmatic denial of citizenship, was the most Anglian thing which ever existed, mixed up as he was with such overwhelming Englishnesses as the Fabian Society and the West End Theatre, a strong touch of Jaeger puritanism, the lively but hopelessly unprofound and mechanistic religion of the Prefaces (a true Englishman's version of mysticism if ever there was one) and a strong natural suspicion of artists as artists.

Shaw is the chief pope and apostle of English humour. Yet there are times, it must be said, when Shaw exhibits its worst defects – when he shows a kind of nervous revulsion from the undiluted seriousness of the tragic moment. As if to prove his equality with Shakespeare, for instance, Shaw introduces humour and humorous character at his highest moments to reinforce the tragic effect. But Shaw's humour has too much of a life and purpose of its own to be used in this merely complementary fashion. Go back to the *Doctor's Dilemma*. At the crescendo moments of the death of Dubedat, judiciously and imaginatively contrived, Shaw introduces a comic journalist. In the theatre this just gets by. But Shaw means his plays to be read as well, and in the text he spoils the effect by overdoing it when he adds a long stage direction:

Walpole returns with the Newspaper Man, a cheerful, affable young man who is disabled for ordinary business pursuits by a congenital erroneousness which renders him incapable of describing accurately anything he hears. As the only employment in which these defects do not matter is journalism (etc., etc.) . . .

49

Moderately funny in itself, the intrusion of this ridiculous Guy Fawkes casts a chill of doubt over the tragic climax of the play, and puts Shaw as an artist under suspicion.

A still more serious defect of English humour is exemplified in this Third Act. Dubedat is the artist without conscience. Outside his art he is without morality. To those like Max Beerbohm who watched the first performance of this play in 1906, a new edition of a certain novel by Henry James was a recent memory. Dubedat was Mr Shaw's Roderick Hudson, they thought : but less impressive because, so far as his activities outside the world of art and Jennifer are concerned, Dubedat is not so much amoral as an inexpert borrower of fivers, an unsuccessful cardsharper on a third rate provincial racecourse. The fact is that Shaw enjoys himself over Dubedat's taste for fiddling and caricatures it for laughs ; and the master of English humour shows its weaknesses as well as its strength when on this occasion, as on many others, he has allowed humour to master him. In such plays, when Shaw does want to strike the note of deepest seriousness, the sound is sometimes tinny, the solemn music even sentimental.

To appreciate Shaw's humour at its best it is necessary to throw away the most often repeated criticism of Shaw which is also the shallowest – that his characters are not so much characters as the mouthpiece of his views, or of the opposite of his views. The answer is of course that sometimes they are and sometimes they aren't. When they are not as in the character of 'B.B.' (the vaguely disarming doctor of the *Dilemma*, who tries to resolve a galloping T.B. by bedside manner) the humorous observation of detail is perfect, and highly English, in its humour, according to our definition.

In the half-dozen great plays, we see a different kind of humour altogether. In these, humour comes near to compassion. Drama is conflict, moving, effective and memorable according to the depths of the involvement of the opposing sides. By that definition, Shaw's *Candida*, as drama, reduces nearly all the best in our modern box-office drama to the level of tinkling teacups. The struggle between those two mighty opposites, Morell the idealist and Marchbanks the poet, is imbued by a sort of heavenly gaiety; but this in no way impairs the everlasting seriousness of it. *Eugene, you are making a fool of yourself.* 'Do you think I don't know all that? Do you think that things people make fools of themselves about are any less real and true than the things they behave sensibly about?' And so on, for the whole battle. No doubt in some sense both characters 'are' Shaw, but they are his soulpieces, not his mouthpieces, reflecting the division in his own nature. The play is full of humour – but in the case even of the comedy types, like Prossy the love-crossed, the humour is tinged with sympathy and comprehension.

DECLINE

To me Shaw is the climax of the age of English Humour. For it soon becomes apparent that it was an 'Age', to which limits were set – one in fact which was shortly to decline.

Shaw's advice to young dramatists was always 'First, never copy me'. But there were squadrons of imitators of his tone of thought emancipating away after the last link had been broken. Then there were other regiments who set out to be 'debunkers', to use the word invented for the historical approach of Lytton Strachey. This word is more fittingly applied to Shaw, who took the nonsense out of the nonsensical part of the nineteenth century: but Strachey, by a simple process of concentrating on the ordinary human and therefore the humorous traits in the notable figures of the past, to the exclusion of those characteristics which made them outstanding, might be described more justly as a de-great-er.

Shaw might have been said with his great wagging beard

to have huffed and dusted out the cobwebs to make way for the clear light of day. The Aldous Huxleys dusted out the daylight to make room for nothing at all. Huxley once wrote amusingly about the intent, the annotating, the not quite open, stare of what he called the 'psycho-analytic look'. I remember that after reading the latest early Huxley novel, my own youthful and normally quite cheerful face would feel stiff with the attempt to twist it into the blasted and grimly sophisticated smile of a Huxley look.

Perhaps more truly typical as products of this age of the English Sense of Humour are the half-dozen writers who made of it a grace and an adornment. One type of the English humorous man, in the modern sense, will always be, for me, Professor Walter Raleigh. His was not at all the kind of humorousness which was a barrier to serious writing. His neglected book on Shakespeare, though it particularly reveals the humour-human-ness of Shakespeare, is warmly serious as well. But it was Raleigh's sense of humour which made him the perfect academic literary man, the ideal creator, at Oxford, of the new School. It made him keep his head in the then comparatively uncharted jungle of the Eng. Lit. subject; it helped him to make us remember that besides criticizing the English classics, it was possible, it was even more important, to like them. It helped him to keep at bay the encroaching forests of the Book On. It gave him the power to prevent critical inquiry from wandering too far down the opposite but equally irrelevant paths of Scandinavian psychologizing and the Teutonic footnote. It was Raleigh who brought criticism back to the sanity of Dr Johnson.

But it was in his letters and his talk and his person – his face – that Raleigh exuded humour. The wide-eyed curiosity of his glance; the slight twitch of the mouth. It was Raleigh's way of reading the Foreign Gentleman passage from *Our Mutual Friend* or the description of the Pardoner in

Chaucer's *Prologue* – Raleigh constantly endeavouring, by pulling down the corners of his mouth as he read, not to spoil the effect of the funniness by laughing himself – which first made me able to appreciate the genius of those pieces.

Another great Man of Humour was Max Beerbohm. Unlike Raleigh, one thinks of Beerbohm as representing not the sympathy of humour, but its impartiality. 'I am a *philosophic* sympathetic person,' is what he seems to say. 'I never can be angry with anyone,' he actually does say, 'never having been able to cure myself of the power to see other people's points of view.' So mild – so reasonable. Yet if I had written a vulgar and unworthy play, I know which, of Bernard Shaw and Max Beerbohm, I should most fear to see in the audience of first-night critics. Max used humour as a salve, as an unguent to soften the hardness of judgements which never temporized.

One other name I would add to this list of men who have exemplified the different virtues of the great Age of Humour: Sir Harold Nicolson. Humour seems in him to be connected in some way with the rule of good manners and the good manners with the etiquette of the art of writing. Even if his subject is foreign policy in the Near East, and it often has been, the humanization of humour lightly spread over the surface makes what he writes easy and pleasurable to read. Is this gift in this writer sometimes a limitation? When Nicolson deals with the mysteries of the human spirit – when, that is, he comes to write those biographies of the poets who fascinate him, 'he is forced,' says Edmund Wilson, 'in a reflex action to detach himself socially from their company by a quiet but well-placed accent of amusement, disapproval, disdain'. This is a perfect description of defensive humour which takes refuge in the axiom: *It is impossible to laugh at the man who is laughing at.* But I do not feel it is a true description of Nicolson. At first the reader thinks, perhaps, 'another Lytton – no doubt his subjects are in for a thorough

Stracheyfication'. True this is what happens to the mortal human side of the poets and statesmen he describes; but to balance this there is, for example, a sense of the submerged and thwarted genius of Tennyson, or of the essential disinterestedness of Curzon, which Strachey would never have been able to give us.

But this array of the protagonists of the Age of Humour does not alter the fact that while some of them were still only beginning, the period itself was already in decay. Humour had taken a long road from the days when hunchbacks, persecuted Jews, madmen, and a cat stuck in a bottle to be stoned to death were considered fit subjects for laughter. It had evolved from the self-congratulation and even sadism of laughing at, to the sympathy and even compassion of laughing with. In fact there were signs, now, that it was toppling over the other side into sweetness and 'niceness'. The atmosphere of Ian Hay and A. A. Milne, in the very early twenties, was of this nice-nice kind; even if, perhaps because they seemed so deliciously funny to us then, it is difficult to pin these able writers to a fault by quotation. The *Oxford Book of English Verse*, the most successful anthology of our time, is a curiously typical product of this age. English poetry is a mighty and animal force, beating against the bars of logic and the rules of expression. But in Quiller-Couch's selection it is as calm, as suitable, and sometimes even as cosy as a Sunday on the river, with rather the same kind of nature on view – a monument to the pleasantness, sometimes fatally inappropriate, which the Age of Humour produced. Taking *Punch* as our touchstone once more, it is obvious that by 1918 humour was becoming mechanized. Indeed this unique journal was entering on an unworthy phase. Cockney wit was degraded into the oh-so-funny Cockney-accent joke. In its natural desire, for the sake of the more solid advertising, to feed the prejudices of the lower half of the upper middle-class or income group B2, a collection of socially conscious jokes at the expense of income groups B3 to D4, and an endless series of drawings of Jewish gentlemen who had taken up hunting, reached a new low level in snobbery. The nice people, in the elegant drawings of Shepperson, the right people, were being eternally puzzled by the not so very awkward questions of their equally nice and right children. And it must have been in 1920 that the first of three thousand jokes at the expense of 'modern painting' was first aimed against a target which, every reader capable of appreciating the Scottish glen backgrounds to the whisky bottles in the advertisement pages of the paper must agree, was really worth attacking.

This is not to say that humour, even in *Punch*, never flourished, as an attitude to life, in the twenties. There was a

BORED LITTLE GIRL: 'AREN'T YOU NEARLY
CLEAN NOW, MUMMY?'

The innumerable children who made their sweet remarks in the pages of *Punch* of the early twenties were almost invariably upper-class.

magnificent absence of reverence for the wrong things shown by the Sitwells at one level, by Coward and the tart, smart revues of the twenties at another. Penetrating if minute social satire was seen in *Punch*, not from the letterpress, which except for Alan Herbert and E.V. had decayed into unspeakable nicification ('On the lawn this morning approached, in echelon, our two ants, Edwin and Angelina'). It came from those virtuosos of line, first W. K. Haselden, the effortless; then the Man who Breathed on the Glass at the British Museum and all those other immortal tragedies of H. M. Bateman, then Kenneth Bird – 'Fougasse' the deft, the decorative, who can put a small volume of social comment into a drawing of one very small man in one very large First Eleven scarf. Like Garrick, who was said to be able to act even with his coat-tails, so can Fougasse, in his drawing, animate and humanize a pocket handkerchief. Fougasse, one of our most warmly humorous satirists, would himself choose Laidlaw as the greatest of the *Punch* contributors. In 'Pont', as Laidlaw signed himself, the perfection is in the satire of the social traits of the class of *Punch*-readers themselves. He seems to observe closely – yet so too did such careful contemporaries as F. H. Townshend and George Belcher. But Pont, like a wildly talented but mad child, seems to single out one detail of a head, draw the detail and almost leave out the rest of the face. It is hard not to throw about words like 'genius' and 'masterpiece' and 'significant line' in the Pont discussions which have gone on ever since his tragically early death.

REACTION

Agreeable lightheartedness began to be less acceptable before and during the war years. The most brilliant humorist of this period, Osbert Lancaster, is a satirist. The rest of our humorous artists had or should have had the 'awfully jolly' nonsense frozen out of them by the cold and ever formidable

Drawings by Pont: he was the first to break the sweet little children convention, which was finally swept away by Giles and Ronald Searle.

stare of the *New Yorker*, whose anti-sentimental tradition some of them have attempted, with more or less success, to imitate. The purely English genius of Giles yet reflects this reaction in the carefully drawn grimness of his backgrounds, and in his very funny substitution, for nice-nice little boys in his child drawings, of nasty-nasty spotty little blobs. The change in attitude particularly suits the essential seriousness of Ronald Searle. For the daydream or wish-fulfilment country-house background of the old high-class *Punch* joke, he substitutes the nightmare of St Trinian's. Very recently, under a new editor, the character of *Punch* has begun to turn once more towards its own origins and is going back to a sharper less kindly satire, which aims at the roots without any longer being Radical. By the current generation of poets and philosophers humour has been put back in its place, where it belongs; and there is a feeling that this is salutary and a change for the better. 'He has such a sense of humour' is a phrase heard now much less often; taken for granted as a term of praise, it is decidedly suspect.

We have worked our English humorousness a little too long. Wit is like some kinds of poetry in this respect, that unless it comes as naturally 'as leaves to the tree', it will not give pleasure. Robert Nichols saw the dangers in the twenties – 'Conquer humour,' he said, 'or humour will conquer you.' Even the restrained smiles of Bloomsbury were able to warp the reputation and success of a writer like D. H. Lawrence whose writing needed the kind of acceptance for itself which Humour could never allow.

But English humour has conferred many blessings. It has given many of our writers who are below the first rank a modesty and proportion which makes 'the Sense' – the good sense – 'of Humour' the best general title for this book. It has done more. Coleridge notes as the first excellence of Sterne the 'bringing forward into distinct consciousness those minutiae of thought and feeling which appear trifles, have an importance only for the moment, and yet almost every man feels in one way or another'. This will do, surely, for the definition I have been looking for through this essay. Coleridge, revealing as always the heights, shows that at its best humour can be near to poetry. Even if it is not one of the Graces, humour can at least be called a saving grace. It is not unworthy to want to be in the company of those who show that saying what we mean is not helped by a pompous tone of voice – who can demonstrate, even, that the highest gaiety and the highest sincerity can be one and the same thing. It is not a mean ambition to wish to touch the hem of Mozart's garment.

PART II

THE THEME ILLUSTRATED

The selections which follow are intended for enjoyment and have been chosen because they still, or have newly, given me pleasure. If I had chosen from the works which seemed funniest in my whole life, half would not seem funny now. I do not choose The Adventures of Professor Radium in *Puck* (the only coloured comic in 1910), or P. G. Wodehouse's school stories, in the *Captain*, about Psmith, or *When Knights Were Bold*, or the serial in the *Boy's Own Paper* called 'From the Slums to the Quarter-Deck, the Story of a Lad of Grit', or *The Safety Match* by Ian Hay. It is as sadly painful for me not to laugh at these now, as it was unbearably pleasure-painful laughing at them then. Beatrix Potter, early Dickens and early Wells still seem almost as funny now, but the goodness of Mr Polly and Mr Jingle my readers will know and take for granted.

In a secondary way, I have chosen in order to illustrate my theme of the English sense of humour. The extracts are not arranged in time order: the history I have already tried to sketch. For contrast and to give the elements of the theme a re-shuffle, I have enjoyed trying to place the sections so as to suggest the steps which extend between the humourless, at one extreme, and humour at its most intelligent and perceptive at the other.

Looking at this selection as it goes to press, I regret omissions. One boundary to an unmanageably vast field I have allowed myself. The spoken word – plays, speeches and conversations – is little quoted, and I allow myself the excuse that it is often dependent on inflection and presentation. But I wish now I had included question time in the House, Mr Churchill up. I wish I had included quotations from that wonderfully funny play *Present Laughter*, or the 'very flat, Norfolk' passage from an earlier comedy by the same author, or Mr Coward's cabaret song 'I wonder what's happened to . . .', or Mrs Worthington. I wish I had had time to comb the seventeenth century antiquarians. I would have included early Evelyn Waugh had I not been earlier an early Huxley man. The full pleasures of the laughter of shocked and incredulous recognition only come once in our lives.

CHAPTER 1

The Raw Material

It may seem illogical to include examples of the Unintentionally Funny in an anthology of the humorous. Must there not exist somewhere some kind of argument to the effect that humour and the humourless are opposite characteristics of the same middle? Perhaps it is true that a certain unselfconsciousness or self-forgetfulness provides the necessary raw material for the humorists to work on.

'UNCONSCIOUS HUMOUR'

'Of course,' (I can hear the phrase sounding in my head) 'my favourite humour is unconscious humour.' It is a remark to think, not speak, because it is full of traps. The phrase itself, which Samuel Butler claimed to have invented, seems a silly way of describing the unconsciously humour-*less*. And when we come to list our favourite pieces of 'unconscious humour', are we always completely sure that we are not ourselves the unconscious victims of a leg pull, or that an unpleasing touch of the su-superior in us has blinded our eyes to something fresh and sincere, not less genuine because it is simple?

Or course, if the simplicity is unfresh, as on certain celebrated occasions it is in Wordsworth, for instance, I do think that we can laugh with a clear conscience. Wordsworth describing for instance, the Old Huntsman, Simon Lee, fallen on evil times:

> And he is lean and he is sick,
> His little body's half awry,
> His ankles they are swollen and thick;
> His legs are thin and dry.

> When he was young he little knew
> Of husbandry or tillage,
> And now he's forced to work, though weak,
> – The weakest of the village.

I suppose it is conceivable that a modern reader might think that Wordsworth was writing a light poem: if so, the funniness would be in Wordsworth being light. There was no doubt however about the serious intent of the candidates for the prize which the Government offered, after the victory, for a poem about Blenheim. But English poetry was at a low ebb, and many examples of the unconsciously funny were received:

> Think of three hundred gentlemen at least
> And each man mounted on his capering beast:
> Into the Danube they were flung in shoals.

Dryden, only four years dead, must have turned in his grave – though Dryden himself was capable of writing a funny couplet without meaning to. I always like his verse preface to a translation of the *Metamorphoses* done by a noble patron:

> Now will sweet Ovid's ghost be pleased to hear
> His fame augmented by an English peer ...

Dryden was perfectly serious in this kind of flattery. Equally it is the seriousness of my car Instruction Book (meant to give elementary instruction to the layman) which makes me laugh. One paragraph I particularly enjoy:

> If adjustment of the opening is required, turn engine until contact arm heel is on the point of a cam, slacken off Screw 'A' (nearest the contact breaker points) and turn Screw 'B' (between Screw 'A' and contact arm pivot) until the required gap of ·018 ins. is obtained. Then tighten up Screw 'A'. A small quantity of Vaseline occasionally applied to the lobes of the cam will keep the wear at this point at a minimum.

·018 ins. indeed. But perhaps this is not a fair example. Perhaps the funniness lies in myself, who am so unusually lay that reading this I give up after the first five words. One must beware, also, of too superior a laugh at those wonderful old games-books of the nineties – the Isthmian Book of Croquet for instance, with its directions for etiquette and its reminiscences of great figures of the croquet world ('Everyone will remember the occasion when Colonel Streeter said "There's nothing for it but to go for it" and hooped diagonally across the lawn'). But how much stranger the more passionate and diagrammatic seriousness of our golf manuals will seem in a hundred years' time.

It might be equally dangerous to include as 'unconscious' this extract from the highly conscious Mr Culbertson introducing his sixth new bridge book in five years or so, a space so brief that it takes all Mr Culbertson's wit to show that the new book is as indispensable as the others:*

This *Official Book of Contract Bridge* is the first book of its type I have written. It is a text-book on contract bridge. I have always wanted to write a bridge text-book, and no doubt it is strange that I have achieved this ambition only after fifteen years of bridge writing. My *Blue Book* – in some respects my most successful book – left some questions unanswered. My *Summary* and *Self-Teacher* appeal to specialized groups of bridge players. My *Gold Book*, paradoxically, answers *too many* questions. This *Official Book* is designed to have a more universal appeal.

A very recent republication seems to me an example of the kind of unconscious humour which it is stupid to laugh at. This is a new edition of the *Poetic Gems* of William McGonagall, Poet and Tragedian. These, no doubt, are in a sense Bad Poems, Class One in unconscious humour. McGonagall grew up in the factory-children thirties and the hungry forties. His father was a hand-loom weaver, too poor to keep his son at school; but William developed a passion for reading Shakespeare and reciting it. The boys in the factory subscribed: William was seen as Macbeth in

*No reflection on the greatest of Bridge expositors.

Mr Giles' theatre in the Lindsay Street Quarry, Dundee. 'When I exclaimed "Command, they make a halt upon the heath," ' he writes happily, 'the applause was simply deafening, and was continued throughout the entire evening ...' It was thirty years later that he discovered he was a poet. A voice cried 'Write, write' – and he wrote. His themes are always high – the Tay Bridge Disaster, or Majuba: his verse is always low:

> Alas! noble Prince Leopold, he is dead!
> Who often has his lustre shed:
> Especially by singing for the benefit of Esher School, –
> Which proves he was a wise prince, and no conceited fool.

Poetry, to McGonagall, meant the almost unbelievable miracle of the magic of the line cut – so roughly by him – to a shape. But do we laugh at it? Chesterton says somewhere of Mr Pickwick that because he was simple, because he was taken in by life, he in some way entered deeply into it. The humbleness of McGonagall made small things great. 'The whole world knows of my visit to the Queen,' he says. When he tells the story, it is to say that he was turned away by the porter at the gates of Balmoral, but that the man was not unkind. Indeed, he bought a copy of the McGonagall poems, price twopence. Great events were moving in the poet's world. Unconscious humour blends with unconscious sadness: a perhaps unconscious envy is the prevailing emotion, in the minds of ourselves his readers.

On the whole, however, most of the material which can most fairly be placed in this section seems to be in verse. These next two pieces may be described as self-parody, the first of nineteenth century sentimentalism and the weaker characteristics of the *Oxford Book of English Verse*; the second emphasizes the peculiar talents of a once popular poetess, whose literary skill and apparent sincerity can still leave the reader shaken. Both poems are pleasant to recite.

FREDERICK LOCKER-LAMPSON
At Her Window

Beating Heart! we come again
    Where my Love reposes:
This is Mabel's window-pane;
    These are Mabel's roses.

Let this friendly pebble plead
    At her flowery grating;
If she hear me will she heed?
    Mabel, I am waiting.

Mabel will be deck'd anon,
    Zoned in bride's apparel;
Happy zone! O hark to yon
    Passion-shaken carol!

Sing thy song, thou tranced thrush,
    Pipe thy best, thy clearest; –
Hush, her lattice moves, O hush –
    Dearest Mabel! – dearest ...

Oxford Book of English Verse

ELLA WHEELER WILCOX
Answered

Good-bye – yes, I am going.
    Sudden? Well, you are right.
But a startling truth came home to me
    With sudden force last night.
What is it? shall I tell you? –
    Nay, that is why I go.
I am running away from the battlefield,
    Turning my back on the foe.
Riddles? You think me cruel!
    Have you not been most kind?
Why, when you question me like that,
    What answer can I find?

You fear you failed to amuse me,
  Your husband's friend and guest,
Whom he bade you entertain and please –
  Well, you have done your best.

Then why, you ask, am I going!
  A friend of mine abroad,
Whose theories I have been acting upon
  Has proven himself a fraud.
You have heard me quote from Plato
  A thousand times, no doubt;
Well, I have discovered he did not know
  What he was talking about.
You think I am speaking strangely?
  You cannot understand?
Well, let me look down into your eyes,
  And let me take your hand.
I am running away from danger –
  I am flying before I fall;
I am going because with heart and soul
  I love you – that is all.

There, now, you are white with anger.
  I knew it would be so.
You should not question a man too close
  When he tells you he must go.

                                        Poems of Passion

Here the technique is better than the content. For an example of the reverse I suggest the beginning of *Cymbeline*. If this is not self-parody, it is typical of Shakespeare's impatience, in his last plays, with the more mechanical side of construction: and to blazes, particularly, with disguising the exposition.

Act I. sc. i. *Britain. The garden of* CYMBELINE'S *palace. Enter two* GENTLEMEN
FIRST GENTLEMAN: You do not meet a man but frowns: our
  bloods

No more obey the heavens than our courtiers
Still seem as does the king.

SECOND GENTLEMAN: But what's the matter?

FIRST GENTLEMAN: His daughter, and the heir of's kingdom,
    whom
He purposed to his wife's sole son – a widow
That late he married – hath referr'd herself
Unto a poor but worthy gentleman: she's wedded;
Her husband banisht; she imprison'd: all
Is outward sorrow; though, I think, the king
Be toucht at very heart.

SECOND GENTLEMAN: None but the king? . . .

FIRST GENTLEMAN: I cannot delve him to the root: his father
Was call'd Sicilius, who did join his honour
Against the Romans with Cassibelan,
But had his titles by Tenantius, whom
He served with glory and admired success, –
So gain'd the sur-addition Leonatus:
And had, besides this gentleman in question,
Two other sons, who, in the ward o' the time,
Died with their swords in hand; for which their father,
Then old and fond of issue, took such sorrow,
That he quit being; and his gentle lady,
Big of this gentleman our theme, deceased
As he was born. The king he takes the babe
To his protection; calls him Posthumus Leonatus;
Breeds him, and makes him of his bed-chamber;
Puts him to all the learnings that his time
Could make him the receiver of; which he took
As we do air, fast as 'twas minister'd;
And in 's spring became a harvest; lived in court –
Which rare it is to do – most praised, most loved;
A sample to the youngest; to the more mature
A glass that feated them; and to the graver
A child that guided dotards: to his mistress,
For whom he now is banisht, – her own price
Proclaims how she esteem'd him and his virtue:
By her election may be truly read

What kind of man he is.

SECOND GENTLEMAN: I honour him
Even out of your report. But, pray you, tell me,
Is she sole child to the king?

FIRST GENTLEMAN: His only child.
He had two sons,– if this be worth your hearing.
Mark it,– the eldest of them at three years old,
I' the swathing-clothes the other, from their nursery
Were stoln; and to this hour no guess in knowledge
Which way they went.

SECOND GENTLEMAN: How long is this ago?

FIRST GENTLEMAN: Some twenty years.

SECOND GENTLEMAN: That a king's children should be so con-
vey'd!
So slackly guarded! and the search so slow,
That could not trace them!

FIRST GENTLEMAN: Howsoe'er 'tis strange,
Or that the negligence may well be laught at,
Yet it is true, sir.

SECOND GENTLEMAN: I do well believe you.

FIRST GENTLEMAN: We must forbear: here comes the gentleman,
The queen, and princess. *Exeunt.*

TAKING IT SERIOUSLY

Most countries believe that most other countries take
their games too seriously. A visitor from Mars might con-
ceivably hold that the tone of the best-known croquet
instruction book of the nineties is open to this criticism.
Here are some extracts:

The Isthmian Book of Croquet

THE RULES

It was originally permitted to any ball to 'peg out' another which
had become a rover. By general agreement this became modified,

so that only a rover could peg out a rover. An attempt was made at the 1870 Conference to disallow any pegging out of a rover by the adversary. This attempt fortunately did not succeed.

(LAWN-TENNIS: A TEMPORARY CRAZE)

The whirligig of time brings in his revenges. The game which ousted croquet has itself fallen upon evil days, and recent experience points to the probability of Croquet coming to enjoy a measure of what was formerly her own. Lawn tennis, though an excellent game in every respect, is, nevertheless, one in which middle-aged people, especially ladies, cannot engage with satisfaction to themselves, and its rapidly waning popularity is due largely to this fact ... Captain Drummond, on his lawn at Petworth, continued to play as if nothing had happened and even held private tournaments with conspicuous success. His daughter, Miss Maud Drummond, one of the most brilliant, and quite the most successful lady player of the day, must have learnt all her croquet during this period.

MR WILLIS

To excel at croquet in Mr Willis's style you must be – a Mr Willis.

THE ETHICS

Croquet is, and always has been, a game of the classes. It is, in the nature of things, very unlikely ever to become a pastime of the masses. At first sight one is tempted to conclude that, in these circumstances, any considerations on the subject of this chapter would be superfluous.

*

Serious games of skill call forth particular qualities, which in their turn, demand a certain atmosphere for their proper exhibition, so that what may be unobjectionable at a dinner-table or in a ball-room, may become the acme of bad taste, when a game of skill is being played in public ...

There is more freedom out of doors; we may smoke, we may even lounge – gracefully, if we can – on the lawns and banks.

First and foremost, then, let us have silence on the ground when an important match is afoot. To demand the same degree of silence which is essential in the whist room were unreasonable, but such a degree of silence as indicates that the chief matter of interest is the game which is being played, may justly be expected.

If this were always done there would be less cause for complaint than now, unhappily, exists, on account of onlookers walking across the ground, engaging the players in conversation, making audible remarks about style, tactics, and other subjects of topical interest.

(THE PLAYER OWES THE SPECTATOR A COURTESY TOO)

It is sometimes a little difficult to remember this, as for instance, when a person stalks up to you when you are attempting a difficult stroke, and demands in strident tones how the game stands, or what your other ball is for.

DIET

Moreover, during the week of play, do not indulge your own or anyone else's fads as to the best diet and the best beverage 'to play croquet on'. Eat and drink what you have been accustomed to eat and drink, in the quantities usual with you – neither much more nor appreciably less. If it is to be either, let it be more rather than less. Your functions are active and require feeding. The faster an engine travels, the more fuel does it consume; deprive it of fuel, and its force diminishes.

This is true for all of us, it is especially so for the man who is troubled with nerves. His excitement frequently deprives him of his appetite, and he concludes that he does not want food; so for luncheon he dallies with a biscuit and a brandy and soda – or two. Such a man is foredoomed to ignominious failure.

1899

Last I include an example from my collection of perhaps not entirely necessary footnotes to Shakespeare. This one is attached to the first line, Act I, Scene i, of *Henry IV*, Part 2 (Arden edition).

TEXT

LORD BARDOLPH: Who keeps the gate here, ho!

FOOTNOTE

1. *Who* ... here, ho!] 'Who' is here, I think, the indefinite ('He who'), and not the interrogative pronoun, as is implied, for instance, by the punctuation, 'Who keeps the gate here? ho!' (*Oxford Shakespeare*), and 'Who keeps the gate here, ho?' (*Cambridge Shakespeare*). 'Who keeps the gate' is a periphrasis (= 'Porter') of a kind usual in calling to servants or others, in attendance but out of sight. Cf. 2 *Henry VI*.I.iv.82: 'York ...Who's within there, ho! *Enter a Serving-man*.' (*Oxford Shakespeare*); *Henry VIII*, V.ii.2, 3: '*Cran*. ... Ho! Who waits there! ('there?' *Oxford Shakespeare*). *Enter Keeper*.' Massinger, *The Roman Actor*, III. ii: '*Iphis*. ... I must ... knock ...Within there, ho! something divine come forth. ... (*Enter* Latinus *as a Porter*)'; Jonson, *Every Man in his Humour*, IV. viii; R. Steele, *The Funeral* (1701), II. iii: '*Fardingale*. No – who waits there – pray bring my lute out of the next room. *Enter* Servant, *with a Lute*.' In *Henry VIII*. V. iii. 4, the 'Keeper at the door' is doubtful whether Norfolk's question, 'Who waits there?' is or is not the conventional call to the Doorkeeper, *viz*. 'Who waits there!': '*Nor*. Who waits there? *Keeper at the door*. Without, my noble lords? *Gar*. Yes. *Keep*. My lord archbishop: And has done half-an-hour, to know your pleasures.' Cf. also Beaumont and Fletcher, *Maid's Tragedy*, V. iii: '*Lys*. ... Summon him, Lord Cleon. *Cleon*. Ho, from the walls there!'; and *Jack Straw* (Hazlitt's *Dodsley*, V. 396): 'Neighbours, you that keep the gates.'

THE PERFECTION OF PERIOD

Consciousness of Date is a characteristic and a special pleasure of the present; and if no stronger qualities emerge, this age may become known as the Period period in the history of taste. Any work which fits its date too precisely, too parochially, is a possible source of humour.

For period late Medieval, we might examine the poet Langland demonstrating the greediness of Greed or the virtuousness of Virtues at the rate of ten thousand lines. For Elizabethan drama, Blood period, we might include a grisly stage direction from *Titus Andronicus*. Alternatively, another aspect of this decade can be caught by a quotation from the First Quarto of *Hamlet*. For surely at no other time would either author or law be so indifferent as to allow such a botching – e.g. as here of Hamlet's 'To be or not to be' soliloquy – in a first printing of the text of a great work of art. This is what bad memory and bad shorthand produced between them, in this pirated version made perhaps at the first performance, of the famous speech:

> To be, or not to be, I there's the point,
> To Die, to sleepe, is that all? I all:
> No, to sleepe, to dreame, I mary there it goes,
> For in that dreame of death, when wee awake,
> And borne before an everlasting Judge,
> From whence no passenger ever return'd,
> The undiscovered country, at whose sight
> The happy smile, and the accursed damn'd.
> But for this, the joyfull hope of this,
> Whol'd beare the scornes and flattery of the world,
> Scorned by the right rich, the rich cursed of the poore?

1603

The rest of these few examples (of 'period' in the more accepted sense) I include as material for humour. It may be pointed out that Pepys was giving opinions which he never thought would see the light of day, and that Horace Walpole's novel was a conscious exercise in the Gothic. But, as we can tell from Walpole's preface, it never occurred to him that the results were funny. 'My rule,' he said, 'was nature.'

RESTORATION
SAMUEL PEPYS
(*at the Theatre*)

1661

The Beggars' Bush (B. and F.). The first time that ever I saw women come upon the stage. *The Scornful Lady* (B. and F.) (2 visits). *The Bondman* (Massinger), an excellent play ... Betterton (3 visits). *The Queen's Maske*, or *Love's Mistress* (T. Heywood) (3 visits). *The Silent Woman* (B. Jonson) ... which pleased me. *Harry the Fourth* (Shakespeare) ... a good play. *Bartholomew Fair* (B. Jonson) ... but too much prophane and abusive (4 visits). *The Jovial Crew* (R. Brome) ... as merry and the most innocent play that ever I saw (3 visits). *Hamlet* (Shakespeare) (2 visits). *Love and Honour* (Sir W. Davenant) ... a very good play (three visits on consecutive nights!).

1662

At the Opera saw *Romeo and Juliet* (Shakespeare) the first time it was ever acted, a play the worst that ever I heard in my life. *Midsummer Night's Dream* (Shakespeare), which I had never seen before, nor shall ever again, for it is the most insipid, ridiculous play that ever I saw in my life.

1663

Twelfth Night (Shakespeare), a silly play, and not related at all to the name or day. *Adventure of Five Hours* (transl. from Calderon by S. Tuke), the best for the variety and the most excellent continuance of the plot to the very end, that ever I saw, or think ever shall, and all possible, not only to be done in the time, but in most other respects very admittable, and without one word of ribaldry; and the house, but its frequent plaudits did show their sufficient approbation.

Diary

DR JOHNSON

A Dissertation on the Art of Flying

... I have been long of opinion, that instead of the tardy conveyance of ships and chariots, man might use the swifter migration of wings; that the fields of air are open to knowledge, and that only ignorance and idleness need crawl upon the ground.'

This hint kindled the prince's desire of passing the mountains: having seen what the mechanist had already performed, he was willing to fancy that he could do more; yet resolved to inquire further, before he suffered hope to afflict him by disappointment, 'I am afraid,' said he to the artist, 'that your imagination prevails over your skill, and that you now tell me rather what you wish, than what you know. Every animal has his element assigned him; the birds have the air, and man and beasts the earth.' 'So,' replied the mechanist, 'fishes have the water, in which yet beasts can swim by nature, and men by art. He that can swim needs not despair to fly; to swim is to fly in a grosser fluid, and to fly is to swim in a subtler. We are only to proportion our power of resistance to the different density of matter through which we are to pass. You will be necessarily upborn by the air, if you can renew any impulse upon it faster than the air can recede from the pressure.'

'But the exercise of swimming,' said the prince, 'is very laborious; the strongest limbs are soon wearied: I am afraid the act of flying will be yet more violent; and wings will be of no great use, unless we can fly further than we can swim.'

'The labour of rising from the ground,' said the artist, 'will be great, as we see it in the heavier domestic fowls; but as we mount higher, the earth's attraction, and the body's gravity, will be gradually diminished, till we shall arrive at a region where the man will float in the air without any tendency to fall: no care will then be necessary but to move forwards, which the gentlest impulse will effect. You, sir, whose curiosity is so extensive, will easily conceive with what pleasure a philosopher, furnished with wings, and hovering in the sky, would see the earth, and all its inhabitants, rolling beneath him, and presenting to him successively, by its diurnal motion, all the countries within the same parallel. How it must amuse the pendent spectator to see the moving scene of land and ocean, cities and deserts! To survey with equal security the marts of trade, and the fields of battle; mountains infested by barbarians, and fruitful regions gladdened by plenty and lulled by peace! . . .'

1759   *Rasselas*

HORACE WALPOLE

(*The Frustration of Manfred*)

'Heavens!' cried Isabella, waking from her delusion, 'what do I hear? You, my lord! You! my father-in-law, the father of Conrad! the husband of the virtuous and tender Hippolita!'

'I tell you,' said Manfred imperiously, 'Hippolita is no longer my wife; I divorce her from this hour. Too long has she cursed me by her unfruitfulness. My fate depends on having sons, and this night I trust will give a new date of my hopes.'

At those words he seized the cold hand of Isabella, who was half dead with fright and horror. She shrieked and started from him. Manfred rose to pursue her, when the moon, which was now up and gleamed in at the opposite casement, presented to his sight the plumes of the fatal helmet, which rose to the height of the windows, waving backwards and forwards in a tempestuous manner, and accompanied with a hollow and rustling sound. Isabella, who gathered courage from her situation, and who dreaded nothing so much as Manfred's pursuit of his declaration, cried:

'Look, my lord! see, Heaven itself declares against your impious intentions!'

'Heaven nor hell shall impede my designs,' said Manfred, advancing again to seize the princess. At that instant the portrait of his grandfather, which hung over the bench where they had been sitting, uttered a deep sigh, and heaved its breast. Isabella, whose back was turned to the picture, saw not the motion, nor whence the sound came but started, and said:

'Hark, my Lord! What sound was that?' and at the same time

made towards the door. Manfred, distracted between the flight of Isabella, who had now reached the stairs, and yet unable to keep his eyes from the picture, which began to move, had, however, advanced some steps after her, still looking backwards on the portrait, when he saw it quit its panel, and descend on the floor with a grave and melancholy air.

'Do I dream?' cried Manfred, returning; 'or are the devils themselves in league against me? Speak, infernal spectre! or, if thou art my grandsire, why dost thou, too, conspire against thy wretched descendant, who too dearly pays for –' Ere he could finish the sentence, the vision sighed again, and made a sign to Manfred to follow him.

'Lead on!' cried Manfred: 'I will follow thee to the gulf of perdition.' The spectre marched sedately, but dejected, to the end of the gallery, and turned into a chamber on the right hand. Manfred accompanied him at a little distance, full of anxiety and horror, but resolved. As he would have entered the chamber, the door was clapped to with violence by an invisible hand. The prince, collecting courage from this delay, would have forcibly burst open the door with his foot, but found that it resisted his utmost efforts.

'Since hell will not satisfy my curiosity,' said Manfred, 'I will use the human means in my power for preserving my race; Isabella shall not escape me.'

(Theodore Revealed)

The youth, who felt his indignation rise, and who was touched with the sorrow which he saw he had infused into all the spectators, as well as into the friar, suppressed his emotions, and putting off his doublet, and unbuttoning his collar, knelt down to his prayers. As he stooped, his shirt slipped down below his shoulder, and discovered the mark of a bloody arrow.

'Gracious Heaven!' cried the holy man, starting, 'what do I see? It is my child, my Theodore!'

The passions that ensued must be conceived; they cannot be painted. The tears of the assistants were suspended by wonder, rather than stopped by joy. They seemed to inquire into the eyes of their lord what they ought to feel. Surprise, doubt, tenderness, respect, succeeded each other in the countenance of the youth. He received with modest submission the effusion of the old man's tears and embraces; yet, afraid of giving a loose to hope, and suspecting, from what had passed, the inflexibility of Manfred's temper, he cast a glance towards the prince, as if to say, Canst thou be unmoved at such a scene as this?

Manfred's heart was capable of being touched. He forgot his anger in his astonishment; yet his pride forbade his owning himself affected. He even doubted whether this discovery was not a contrivance of the friar to save the youth. 'What may this mean?' said he; 'how can he be thy son? Is it consistent with thy profession or reputed sanctity to avow a peasant's offspring for the fruit of thy irregular amours?'

'Oh God!' said the holy man, 'dost thou question his being mine? Could I feel the anguish I do, if I were not his father? Spare him, good prince! spare him! and revile me as thou pleasest.'

'Spare him! spare him!' cried the attendants, 'for this good man's sake.'

'Peace!' said Manfred, sternly; 'I must know, ere I am disposed to pardon. A saint's bastard may be no saint himself.'

'Injurious lord!' said Theodore; 'add not insult to cruelty. If I am this venerable man's son, though no prince, as thou art, know, the blood that flows in my veins –'

'Yes,' said the friar, interrupting him, 'his blood is noble; nor is he that abject thing, my lord, you speak him. He is my lawful son; and Sicily can boast of a few houses more ancient than that of Falconara – but alas! my lord, what is blood? what is nobility? We are all reptiles, miserable, sinful creatures. It is piety alone that can distinguish us from the dust whence we sprung, and whither we must return.'

'Truce to your sermon,' said Manfred. ...

1764   *Castle of Otranto*

NINETEENTH CENTURY

Finally, two brief examples from the two halves of the nineteenth century. The first is an example of the *Keepsake* school: the second belongs to the *Cynara* class (the man of the world who hides his true feelings under a mask).*

HAYNES BAYLY
from *She Wore a Wreath of Roses*

A wreath of orange-blossoms,
When next we met, she wore.
The expression of her features
Was more thoughtful than before.

CHARLES MACKAY
Only a Passing Thought

'Twas only a passing thought, my love,
Only a passing thought,
That came o'er my mind like a ray of the sun
In the ripples of waters caught;
And it seemed to me, and I say to thee,
That sorrow and shame and sin
Might disappear from our happy sphere,
If we knew but how to begin;
If we knew but how to profit
By wisdom dearly bought:
'Twas only a passing thought, my love,
Only a passing thought.

E. S. Turner, in *The Shocking History of Advertising*, from which the illustration on page 81 is taken, writes:

Modernized baths, furnaces, stoves and water-closets also began pressing on to the market. In the latter years of the century there was a campaign to install a Turkish bath in every middle-class home. Many of the pictures of these advertisements suggested scenes of penance. In one cabinet a naked male is about to sit gingerly on a skeleton stool under which burns what appears to be an equally naked lamp. From another emerges the head of a woman bearing an expression such as

*These and many more admirable nineteenth-century examples can be found in *The Stuffed Owl*, D. B. Wyndham Lewis and Charles Lee.

1900: Science and the
New Health

THE LADY WITH THE LAMP

might be found on an elderly governess who has had the mis-
fortune to be buried up to her neck by Touaregs. As time went
on the bathers' expressions became less strained and most of
them were depicted reading books.

CHARACTER ON THE SLEEVE

If unconscious self-revelation is the deepest of all the
reservoirs of humour, it also provides us with the subtlest
variations between smiling at and smiling with – when
indeed a smile is involved at all. We should not enjoy Dr
Johnson's criticisms of a rival Shakespeare editor, nor
Blake's of the head of all the Royal Academicians, if we did
not know already something of their character and genius.
The all-too-human Coleridge-the-family-man is only comic
in the godlike context of Coleridge the genius.

DR JOHNSON
on *Warburton on Shakespeare*

I Henry IV, ii. 3 Who falling in the *flaws* of her own youth,
 Hath *blister'd* her report:

WARBURTON: Who doth not see that the integrity of the metaphor requires we should read FLAMES *of her own youth.*

JOHNSON: Who does not see that upon such principles there is no end of correction.

I Henry IV, iii. Methinks, my moiety, north from Burton here
In quantity equals not one of yours.

WARBURTON: *Hotspur* is here just such a divider as the *Irishman* who made *three* halves: Therefore, for the honour of *Shakespeare*, I will suppose, with the *Oxford Editor*, that he wrote *portion*.

JOHNSON: I will not suppose it.

1765

The next extract I place in this section because Boswell is here partly revealing his half-jealous dislike of one of Dr Johnson's favourites.

JAMES BOSWELL

on Goldsmith

During this argument, Goldsmith sat in restless agitation, from a wish to get in and *shine*. Finding himself excluded, he had taken his hat to go away, but remained for some time with it in his hand, like a gamester, who, at the close of a long night lingers for a little while to see if he can have a favourable opening to finish with success. Once when he was beginning to speak, he found himself over-powered by the loud voice of Johnson, who was at the opposite end of the table, and did not perceive Goldsmith's attempt. Thus disappointed of his wish to obtain the attention of the company, Goldsmith in a passion threw down his hat, looking angrily at Johnson, and exclaimed in a bitter tone, 'Take it'. When Toplady was going to speak, Johnson uttered some sound which led Goldsmith to think that he was beginning again, and taking the words from Toplady. Upon which, he seized this opportunity of venting his *own* envy and spleen, under the pretext of supporting another person: 'Sir,' said he to Johnson, 'the gentleman has heard you patiently for an hour; pray allow us now to hear him.'

JOHNSON (sternly): '*Sir, I was not interrupting the gentleman. I was only giving him a signal of my attention. Sir, you are impertinent.*' Goldsmith made no reply but continued in the company for some time.

1790   *The Life*

WILLIAM BLAKE

Annotations to Sir Joshua Reynolds's Discourses

'...I found myself in the midst of works executed upon principles with which I was unacquainted: I felt my ignorance, and stood abashed.'

A Liar! he never was Abashed in his Life and never felt his Ignorance.

'It is the florid style, which strikes at once, and captivates the eye for a time, ...'

A Lie! The Florid Style, such as the Venetian and the Flemish, Never Struck Me at Once nor At-All.

The Style that Strikes the Eye is the True Style, But A Fool's Eye is Not to be a Criterion.

'He (Mr Mudge, Prebendary of Exeter) was a learned and venerable old man: and as I thought, very much conversant in the Platonick Philosophy ...'

Slang!

'He had been originally a dissenting minister.'

Villainy!

c.1808   *The Nonesuch Blake*

S. T. COLERIDGE

(*on a walking tour, writing to his Wife, an expectant mother*)

Nov. 22, 1802

... 2. Permit me, my dear Sara, without offence to you, as Heaven knows! it is without any feeling of pride in myself, to say, that in six acquirements, and in the quantity and quality of natural endowments whether of feeling, or of intellect, you are the inferior. Therefore it would be preposterous to expect that I should see with your eyes, and dismiss my friends from *my* heart; but it is not preposterous in me, on the contrary I have a *right* to expect and demand that you should to a certain degree love and act kindly to those whom I deem worthy of my Love. If you read this letter with half the tenderness with which it is written, it will do you and both of us *good* ... (erasure) You know Sally Pally! I must have a joke or it would not be me!

Crescelly,   Thursday morning, 7 o'clock. Dec. 16, 1802.

MY DEAR LOVE, – I write with trembling – at what time or in what state my letter may find you, how can I tell? Small need is there for saying, how anxious I am, how full of terrors and prayers! I trust in God, that this letter which I write with a palpitating heart, you will read with a chearful one – the new baby at your breast – O may God Almighty preserve you!

We leave this place in less than an hour. Our route lies thro' St Clears, Carmarthen, Llandilo, Llandovery, Trecastle, Brecon, Hay, Hereford, Worcester, Birmingham, Litchfield, Abbots Bromly, Uttoxeter, Ashborn, Newbury, Buxton, Stockport, Manchester, Bolton, Preston, Garstang, Lancaster, Burton, Kendal, Ambleside, Keswick – 346 miles. From Keswick I must go with T. Wedgwood to Mr Clarkson's, and so on to Luff's. I calculate that we shall not much exceed forty miles a day: and that we shall be at Ambleside, Thursday Evening, December 23rd – Mrs Wilson will be so good as to have a fire kept in Peach's Parlour, and likewise in Peach's bedroom and great care taken that the bed and bedding shall be thoroughly warmed and aired. I should think it would be advisable to order immediately a pair of bed blankets from Miss Crosthwaite's. My dearest Love! T.W. will not stay above a day or two in Keswick – and for God's sake do not let (him) be any weight or bustle on your mind – let him be entirely Mr Jackson's visitor, and let a girl from the town come up for the time he stays – and Mrs W. will probably accommodate you with a fowl or two – But above all, Mr Jackson will be so good as immediately to write a line to be left for me at the Post Office, Kendal, informing me how you are – *and of all I am to know.* Any letters you may have written to Gunville will be sent back again to Keswick.

Mrs Wilson will be so good as to procure a pound or so of the best salt potted butter which Mr T. Wedgwood likes.

Again and again, my dear Love

God bless you

S. T. Coleridge

(*Advice to a Son: Coleridge to Hartley*)

April 3, 1807.

Among the lesser faults I beg you to endeavour to remember not to stand between the half-opened door, either while you are speaking, or spoken to. But come *in* or go out, and always speak and listen with the door shut. Likewise, not to speak so loud, or abruptly, and never to interrupt your elders while they are speaking, and not to talk at all during meals. I pray you, keep this letter, and read it over every two or three days.

(*Thanks for a loan: Coleridge to Byron*)

Calne, Wiltshire, Thursday   (Postmark February 17, 1816).

MY LORD, – I have to acknowledge the receipt of your Letter with the 100 £ enclosed. What can I say? Till a Friend and House-mate addressed me at my bedside, with – 'You have had a letter franked by Lord Byron? Is it from *him?*' I had, as it were for-gotten that I was myself the object of your kindness – so com-pletely lost was I in thinking of the thing itself and the manner in which it was done.

Whether, my Lord! it shall be a Loan or not, depends on cir-cumstances not in my power tho' in my hope and expectation. Thank God! this is of the least importance – the debt and the *pleasure* of Love and Gratitude stand unaffected by anything accidental.   *The Nonesuch Coleridge*

A Literary Friendship:
HUGH WALPOLE *and* ARNOLD BENNETT
October 1923

My dearest Arnold,

You'll have a meal with me, won't you, before I go up to

Scotland? I hardly dare to suggest it as I see that you are attending every conceivable function from a dinner to an American band to a luncheon to Mrs Randolph Hearst! I watch and wonder ... I sent you *J. and H.** because you liked some of the first one. But of course don't bother with it.

Your loving

Hugh

My sweet Hughie,

Thank you. Dinner suits me far the best. I'll come on Wednesday 24th, if I may. You might confirm this. I haven't received *J. and H.* yet; but am looking forward to it. You won't like my *Riceyman Steps*, but you shall damn well have it.

Not a luncheon *to* Mrs Hearst, but a luncheon *by* Mrs Hearst. The 'to' was newspaper work. My lad, I sat on her right, Hutchinson on her left, and G.K.C. far down the table level with W. L. George! Quelle vie! (P.S. She was very nice.)

Also, not a dinner *to* an American band. A dinner given by my friends the bosses of the Savoy Hotel, at which the international (*not* American) band played for us, never having played for anybody before since time was. You must get these things right.

Ever thine

A.B.

My dear Arnold,

For our dinner next week whom else would you wish? Would you like to bring someone? We won't be more than four anyway, shall we?

And why do you tell conversational strangers I don't work? I work as hard as you do anyway! – and that's damned hard. Do sometimes bless my crimson head in my absence. All the world thinks you consider me the dung by the roadside. If you do tell me so.

Affectionately,

Hugh

My sweet Hughie,

Thanks. I don't care a damn who is or isn't there on Wednesday so long as you're there. Don't listen to tattle about yourself.

*Jeremy and Hamlet.

Most of it is necessarily untrue and all of it is reported with a malicious intent. If I took notice of a quarter of the things which you are reported to have said about me my appetite would be impaired. But I don't. I have said nothing to other people about you beyond what I have said to you, and shall probably say again.

Thine ever

A.B.

My dearest Arnold,

You are truly a pet. I never doubted your inside loyalty to me for a moment, but for years past people have seemed to wish to separate me from you more than from anyone else alive. Why I can't conceive. And apparently they've tried the same game the other end. However I love you, and although I chatter like a magpie out of sheer excitement, no one could doubt but that I *do* love you. So that's that.

However I'd like to talk to you about novel-writing one day. It's time I did again. Not especially yours or mine but in general I think you're wrong on several points. And if you read *J. and H*. admit that the last two episodes are true.

I'm asking E.V. on Wednesday night – 8.15 Garrick – no one else. Will you be bringing a copy of *Riceyman Steps* with you?

Your loving

Hugh

My dearest Arnold,

I've been a long while writing about *Riceyman* because I took four days motoring up here and very heavenly days they were.

The book is absorbing – your best to me since *The Pretty Lady*. You have had such fine reviews (I was delighted to see, although James Douglas always makes me sick) that I won't emphasize the virtues. Of the detail you are a master. Elsie is A.1. and her young man is still better. Two criticisms. I think in the miser you have drawn two men and you haven't combined them. 1. The miser. 2. A kindly mild little R[iceyman] S[teps] bookseller. Now I am sure that the miser vice is so devastating to its victim that it makes him *bloody*. Your little man is never bloody. In truth he would have squeezed Elsie's throat and wrung his wife's neck. He would have been horrible, terrible, thirstily cruel (*not* Grandet but of Grandet's family).

Secondly (and this is so charmingly quid pro quo that I adore to write it) I think you have written rather carelessly. Your passion for emphatic adjectives knows no check (I saw that Squire said it did. I don't care a twopenny cuss for Squire). Open where I will I find 'blazing', 'extravagant', 'fatal combination', 'thundered', 'stupid', 'misguided', 'heedless', all on p. 166. Or again at random – 'thunderingly', 'rarest', 'deceitful', 'blazing', 'celestial', 'wonderful', 'potent'. To give small things big adjectives has been long your habit, but surely here you overdo it.

I can say this the more confidently in that you at once murmur 'Poor old Hughie' and with that affectionate contemptuous patronage that is your gift to me you will pass on unperturbed.

And I wouldn't have you perturbed. I love you dearly. You are one of the finest artists of our time and this is a damned good book.

I have bought a cottage in the Lakes.

Your loving
Hugh

My dear Hughie,

I thank thee. No. You are probably wrong and Jack Squire probably right. He does know *something* about style; you know nothing; or at any rate you write as if you know nothing. I see you believe rather in Edith Wharton, and assert that at her worst she has never descended as low as Wells and me in certain books. Innocence, you ought to see a doctor; the case is urgent. The excellent Edith is nobody at all, and she has deceived you. She never *began* to write. And what I have charged you with is not violent writing but slipshod writing. Have you ever *known* a miser, personally and well? I have, and I am in a position to tell you that you are quite wrong. In fact your idea is stagey, pseudo-romantic and beautiful absurd. My miser is a real miser.

Why the Lakes, my misguided friend? You will get wet through, and it is the hell of a way from London. Your touching sentimentality has led you to the Lakes. You wanted to get 'into contact with Nature,' didn't you? I bet you did, and of course the Lakes are the spiritual home of Nature. Never mind, my dear Hughie, I am entirely yours, A.B.

Darling Arnold,

What an insulting letter! But you've got nearly twenty years more cocksureness in your bundle than I have, so I'll say I know that I am sentimental, romantic and slipshod – that's *my* 'pattern in the carpet'. And you're shrewd, mathematical, and know far more about a certain section of real life than I do of any. But yours *is* only a section, and even though I'm Mrs Henry Wood (with whom I have many affinities) that's ME. I never said or thought that Wharton approached you as an artist, nor do I think she amounts to much, but she *has* kept her level better than you. As to 'going back to Nature', haven't I lived in the depths of Cornwall all my life? I went to the Lakes eight years running during my youth, so it's no new thing to me. And it *don't* rain all the time, and it's only seven hours from Keswick to London.

Meanwhile I'm in the happy position of differing from most of your opinions and caring for you more and more. Is *that* sentimental? Surely not, because I have excellent sound honest-to-God reasons for my affection. I'm not such a fool as you think, nor is my style so bad as you say, and I believe that when I'm between fifty and sixty I shall produce a slipshod sentimental novel that will have real people in a world of its own. Let me be myself, damn you ...

Your loving

Hugh

Rupert Hart-Davis. *Hugh Walpole*

The Rouse trial presents us with many classic examples of self-revelation in the witness-box. The 'Blazing Car Mystery' murder executed by Rouse was sound in plan but weak in execution. The unknown hitchhiker, found dead in the burnt-out wreck of Rouse's car, might easily have been taken for Rouse himself. But Rouse was neurotically incapable of telling the truth, and under cross-examination by Norman Birkett he self-revealed this fact not so much by contradictions as by a constant repetition of phrases like 'as a matter of fact' or 'well, to be frank'.

At the end of the trial, as comic relief to the tragedy, the defence produced a last-minute expert 'of great experience' who said, among other things, that nuts on petrol pipes could, if greatly heated, unscrew themselves. No need to suspect foul play, as suggested by the prosecution.

But next morning – the last day of the trial – Norman Birkett planned his examinations of this witness. He decided, particularly, on his first question.

NORMAN BIRKETT

(Cross-examines the Witness for the Defence)

ARTHUR ISAACS, *examined by* MR FINNEMORE: I am managing director of the Bramber Engineering Company Limited, of Cricklewood, London, manufacturers and specialists in the heat treatment of metals. I am an engineer and fire assessor, and I have acted for insurance companies in numerous cases for more than eighteen years. I have had a very vast experience of assessing damage in connexion with fires to motor cars. I had nothing, however, to do with this case until two days ago, when I read a report of some of the proceedings, and I thought I had certain information and experience which I ought to bring before the Court. As regards the loose nut on this joint, the idea of the manufacturers in making that, as we term it, a male nipple, all in one piece with the pipe, is for cheapness. It would not be used on an expensive car. A better method is to have the brass nipple either brazed or sweated on to the pipe. I heard the point made that, one being brass and the other copper, when they were tightened up, the softer metal would compress and make a better union. I agree with that. That happens the first time, and it also happens the second time, but not with such effect. The effect gets less and less as it goes on, because the metal is becoming compressed.

With regard to the findings of that nut a whole turn loose after the fire, what do you say? – I say it is invariably found at all fires that have been very intense that these nuts are loose. As a matter of fact, I go so far as to say that in the last twenty-five cases that I have done, where the fire has been intense, these nuts have always been loose. By that I mean in consequence of the action of the fire; it might have been absolutely spanner-tight before the fire, or slightly loose, but over a long experience I have practically always found that as long as the fire has been round this particular nut you get that effect. As a matter of fact, I was inquiring into a case at the time that I read about the one with which we are dealing; I left London on Tuesday morning only to go to a fire case.

*

Cross-examined by MR NORMAN BIRKETT: What is the co-efficient of the expansion of brass? I am afraid I cannot answer that question off-hand.

If you do not know, say so. What do I mean by the term? – You want to know what is the expansion of the metal under heat?

I asked you what is the co-efficient of the expansion of brass? Do you know what it means? – Put that way, probably I do not.

You are an engineer? – I dare say I am. I am not a doctor, nor a crime investigator, nor an amateur detective. I am an engineer.

What is the co-efficient of the expansion of brass? You do not know? – No, not put that way. My company deals with the heat treating of metals. We make commercial laminated springs, car laminated springs, forgings, and all types of parts. We employ 70 people. I do not have any degrees. I have had training as a fire assessor.

Where? – Well, all over the place – in South Africa and in this country.

Let us take South Africa. When was that? – Prior to the war. Subsequent to the war my experience was in this country. It was not with my present firm; it was with insurance companies. I started through an insurance company employing me. I had to assess the damage of the fire and try to locate the cause of it. I still do that. I do it as part of the firm's work. The firm are not fire assessors.

Do you mean that the insurance company go to a limited company engaged in spring manufacturing for fire assessing? – Long before I got to that firm I was assessing ...

...When you say that you have had a 'very vast experience', does it amount to 15 to 20 cars in 1930, and the number of roadside fires you cannot name? – I say that the majority of those fires I have attended are roadside fires.

Did you ever find a loose union joint as the cause of the fire? – No, I could not say that I have.

Would the insurance company you advised pay if you had found it? – They have done, in every case.

When did you find a case? – Of a loose union?

Yes? – In every case.

Tell me the last? – Tuesday.

Have you a report? – Yes, but I do not have it with me. It was Tuesday of this week.

I am asking if you have a case where there was a loose union joint as the cause of fire? – I have no definite proof of such a thing ...

...You come here, I understand, voluntarily. You arrive on Wednesday, and on Friday you tell the jury that a nut will be loosened by heat, and you cannot tell them how much? – I cannot tell you that. I will put it in this way, that the expansion and the looseness of the nut can also depend upon the thread of the male in this case. This is a coarse thread, and then you have a fine thread. (Shown the nut and referred to the thread and cone.) The cone is put into the hole? – That is right.

The nut remains upon the thread? – That is right.

The heat would expand the thread? – Yes, both threads.

And the nuts? – Yes.

When the heat subsides they will contract? – Yes.

And the position would be as they were before? – Oh, no.

They are both expanding? – Oh, not exactly. It does not come back to its natural place.

Do you say that one does and one does not? – I say that they do not get back.

Why? – For the simple reason that I have found it so.

You are an engineer, assisting the jury as an expert witness. Do you tell this jury, as an engineer, that if you put metal, as I have described, nut and tube, one will expand and one will contract? – One will contract more than the other.

Which? – The nut.

Why? – Because one is inside and the other is outside, allowing more room.

If that means anything at all, it means it ought to be tighter and not looser? – No, not necessarily at all.

I am not talking about what is necessary. Is it not the inevitable conclusion from the answer you gave that it would be tighter after the fire than looser? – No.

1931   *Notable British Trials Series*

BARONESS ORCZY
(*The Birth of the Scarlet Pimpernel*)

... I remember Arnold Bennett saying once to me: 'A book will live by the characters that people its story, characters that make the story real; it will never live by the story alone, however well-constructed or interesting it may be.' And he added in his dry, sarcastic way: 'Do not be afraid about the future of your *Scarlet Pimpernel*. It will live because of its character long after far finer books have gone the way of oblivion.' He did not mean this either ironically or carpingly.

We went on talking about Dickens' immortality as against Thackeray, in many ways by far the finer writer of the two, certainly the more literary: however contemptuously modern youth may refer to Dickens (whom for the most part they have never read), there is no getting away from the fact that Mr Micawber, Mr Mantalini, Pecksniff, Squeers, and all the rest, are as alive today as they were when enthusiastic readers fought for the privilege of being the first to read the instalments of *Pickwick Papers* or *The Old Curiosity Shop* as they appeared week by week in *Household Words*.

Does Esmond or Barry Lindon, fine as they are, ever mean the same to millions of thoughtful readers as does Mr Pickwick or Mr Pecksniff and so many others? And even in the case of that greatest writer of all time, does not one's mind dwell on *Hamlet* and *Othello*, *Lady Macbeth* and *King Lear* rather than on the story of *Two Gentlemen of Verona* or *Love's Labour's Lost*? But this, perhaps, is beside the point. The conversation with Arnold

Bennett occurred long after my book had overstepped its umpteenth edition. For the moment I was intent on the personality which would make my story live.

Strangely enough that personality of the Scarlet Pimpernel came to me in a very curious way. I first saw him standing before me – don't gasp, please – on the platform of an underground station, The Temple. I had been to see someone on the *Daily Express*, *à propos* of some minor work, and was waiting for my Inner Circle train for Kensington. Now, of all the dull, prosy places in the world, can you beat an Underground Railway Station? It was foggy too, and smelly and cold. But I give you my word that as I was sitting there, I saw – yes, I saw – Sir Percy Blakeney just as you know him now.

I saw him in his exquisite clothes, his slender hands holding up his spy-glass : I heard his lazy drawling speech, his quaint laugh. I can't tell you in detail everything I saw and heard – it was a mental vision, of course, and lasted but a few seconds – but it was the whole life-story of the Scarlet Pimpernel that was there and then revealed to me. The rest of the day has remained a blur in my mind, but my thoughts were clear enough for me to tell my beloved husband about the wonder that had occurred : the birth of the Scarlet Pimpernel.

1947   *Links in the Chain of Life*

MASS OBSERVATION
(*Me and My Brother and My Cousin*)

The first thing I did wrong was on a Sunday evening. I was about 12 years old then, there were three of us my brother my cousin and me. We started to fool around behind an old warehouse and we found that one of the windows was partly open and gets in and sees typewriters big books and samples of toffy choclates biscits sweets corned beef sauce 'eat' until we was really full up when we started to search in the other rooms and we find cases full of watches, so we takes one each and searches in the other draws and find a box of stamps and a small box of money, so that was all we wanted for the time being so we gets out the same way as we got in, and we makes our way for the cafe and we spends five shillings of our money by 9 o'clock and then its time to go home so we counts the money we have got left and divide it between us and we have twelve and threepence each.

I hides the money on the side of the path as I go up to the house and dad asks the usual question and sends us to bed and we put heads underneath the bedclothes and switches on the torches and looks at the watches until we falls off to sleep, and we spends the money quietly, and Thursday the three of us disides to break into the pop stores so we goes out soon after tea and quietly takes a sheet of tin off the side and goes in and switches on our torches and we see cases and cases of pop so we drinks as much as we can and then we sees tins of crisps so we gets stuck into them and goes into the office and ransacle the draws and we finds two bundles of candles and a bag of crisps through a door and we disides to take some cases of pop and tins of crisps so my brother goes homes and gets the big four wheal troly and we puts about six cases of pop and three tins of crisps and we takes them under the old castle ruins and lights the candles and we hides the cases and tins until tomorrow night.

We goes Friday and saterday night to have a blow out, and on the Sunday we disides to go unto the warhouse again so we goes in and we made a good haul and hid the stuff the same place as the pop and crisps and as we goes past the wearhouse we sees a light in there so I tells them to keep away it might be the police, and my cousin went over to look in the room a PC Woods puts his hand on his shoulder and says what do you know about it and he tells him and Matthew and me dashes off and waits about five minits and my cousin comes running up saying that we have got to go down to the Wearhouse and he says that if we go down he will let us off so we goes down for my cousins sake and the copper asks us to go to his house to clear things up so we goes to his house and he asks us our names and addresses, so I says to him I wont tell you, so my cousin tells him his address and he locks the door and goes of to find his father.

While he is gone we opens the window and dashes of to our hideout under the castle, and we hides there for a week and our food and stuff runs out so we disides to break into the grocers and on our way we sees dad coming up the road and we try to make a bunk but dad soon catches us and he takes us home and sends my other brother to fetch the copper.

We find something to eat by the time he came and he asks us the questions in the house, and tells dad that we have got to attend court on Friday and when he had gone dad got me in the corner and belted hell out of me, and the same happened to my brother, and when we asked my cousin what happened to him and he says he did not get a hideing, because he was only led into it so we gave him a hideing.

On Friday we goes to court in front of D— and he sentences me and my brother to twelve months probation and a fine of ten shillings each, and my cousin gets six months probation when he ought to get three years aprove school.

1949   *Report on Juvenile Delinquency*

CHAPTER 2

Humour of Release

FROM THE BONDS OF WORDS AND SYNTAX

First, the most primitive humour. Under this heading could be included any joke which says 'yah' to authority, from the mildest pun or the tea-cup Spoonerism (the authority of the Word), to the most ruthlessly violent sex story.

But because this humour is ancient, it does not follow that it cannot in treatment be sophisticated, The Handley-Kavanagh pun dialogue of Itma depends on timing and inflection so subtle that only the microphone is capable of doing it justice. The highest refinement of the pun seems to me to have been achieved by that genius of the cross-word clue, the intricate Torquemada (the second example in this section).

The carefree punctuation and grammatical euphorics of Laurence Sterne can, I think, only be properly appreciated if placed in the context of the writing of his age (a page of *Rasselas*, for instance), when exact syntax and the freezing of language was at its height.

Another way of breaking the bonds of the written language is by restoring to it the colloquialism of ordinary speech. Through the theatre? But not very often does even 'first-class light comedy dialogue' show us our speaking mannerisms as they are. Much of the delicious effect of a Herbert Farjeon revue sketch depends on his observation of our talking habits.

TOMMY AND JACK

BOTH: We'll tell you our names, and we'll tell them quite blandly.

TOM: I'm Handley,

JACK: I'm Hylton.

JACK: I'm Hylton.

TOM: I'm Handley.

JACK: Now I'm a big cheese.

TOM: A regular Stilton.

JACK: I'm Hylton.

TOM: I'm Handley.

TOM: Tom Handley.

JACK: Jack Hylton.

BOTH: These are the names that our fame has been built on.

TOM: You ought to see Hylton when he's got his kilt on.

JACK: Tommy can't wear one – his legs are too bandly.

BOTH: Yours very sincerely, Hylton and Handley.

Itma

(DOOR OPENS)

VOICE: Do you know what you can do with a carrot?

TOMMY: Yes.

(DOOR CLOSES)

SO-SO: Ah, Mr Hangnail, you sent for me: again you have an attack of the anni domini – yes?

TOM: No; only a touch of the titti-folols – a kind of concert party on the chest. I want a thorough overhaul, Dr So-So.

SO-SO: First, I test your blood. You're anaemic.

TOM: No, you're thinking of Jack Train. He's a mimic.

SO-SO: I think you glup your food.

TOM: Glup my food? You mean gulp my food?

SO-SO: Yes – glup your food.

TOM: Listen – G-U-L-P – Glup.

SO-SO: You mean – gulp – now I feel your plus.

> Tĕd Kavanagh. *Tommy Handley*

TORQUEMADA
Crossword Clues

Pure, yet no spinster (Lily).

What the cook said to the pancake (P.T.O.).

A light woman: if excessively so, Torquemada puts her on the rack (Baggage).

Heggs! (Exasperated).

Evading the issue (Birth Control).

S.O.S. (Naughtinesses).

What the sailor sits on without results (Hatch).

Makes father late (Parricide).

A little more than kith and less than kind (Taunt).

Limit of human understanding (Toenail).

Land of waving palms (Whitechapel).

Mr Robinson's common name (Heath)

Poetical six balls (O'er).

Solomon's sluggards must have been (Sycophants).

'Drink and the devil' (Impale).

How many can get this bird? (Toucan).

The explorer said it to a goose in pussy's mouth (Cabot).

You can't drink out of these (Hours).

Her motto might well be, 'Let joy be unconfined' (Marie Stopes).

Melba breaks into a walk (Amble).

Both you and I surrender to money in the end (Yields).

The Ring and the Book (not Browning) and One Clear Call for Me (Telephone).

Side issue (Eve).

Edible at the feast, audible after it (Tripe).

The first three letters would not cover the whole (Figure).

Invocation to a Manx cat for work (Opus).

By Massenet out of Scotland Yard (Cid).

Hobson's Choice (Ge-or-ge).

Unpunctual yawn (Behindhand).

Napoleon died in 1066 (Howler).

Puts the parson in his place (Induction).

H.I.J.K.L.M.N.O. (Water – H_2O).

Is Euclid pondering over this in Elysium? (Eternal triangle).

Apotheosis of the palindrome (Deified).

Sarah at evensong (Psalm).

Decrepit horses turned into the wood (Screws).

Male theologian in a car in Somerset (Cheddar).

Sinister solver of the unemployment problem (Satan).

A simple clue (Herb).

Capacity for saying the last word (Amenability).

What is it goes ninety-nine plonk? This, with a wooden leg (Centipede).

Estate suggestive of vulgar incitement to matricide (Domain).

Might sport with Amaryllis in the shed (Rake).

The orphan has neither this – a widely-accepted view (Panorama).

A roughly handled footballer may be in need of one (N.J. – New Jersey).

The piper's twins (Tom-tom).

Device for the alleviation of childbearing (Pram).

LAURENCE STERNE
(*The Male Midwife, Dr Slop, is Urgently Wanted*)

Imagine to yourself a little squat, uncourtly figure of a Dr Slop, of about four feet and a half perpendicular height with a breadth of back, and a sesquipedality of belly, which might have done honour to a serjeant in the horse-guards.

Such were the outlines of Dr Slop's figure, which – if you have read Hogarth's analysis of beauty, and if you have not, I wish you would; – you must know, may as certainly be caricatured, and conveyed to the mind by three strokes as three hundred.

Imagine such a one, – for such, I say, were the outlines of Dr Slop's figure, coming slowly along, foot by foot, waddling thro' the dirt upon the vertebrae of a little diminutive pony, of a pretty colour – but of strength, – alack! – scarce able to have made an amble of it, under such a fardel, had the roads been in an ambling condition. – They were not. – Imagine to yourself, Obadiah mounted upon a strong monster of a coach-horse, pricked into a full gallop, and making all practical speed the adverse way.

Pray, Sir, let me interest you a moment in this description.

Had Dr Slop beheld Obadiah a mile off, posting in a narrow lane directly towards him, at that monstrous rate, – splashing and plunging like a devil thro' thick and thin, as he approached would not such a phenomenon, with such a vortex of mud and water moving along with it, round its axis, – have been a subject of juster apprehension to Dr Slop in his situation, than the worst of Whiston's comets? – To say nothing of the Nucleus; that is, of Obadiah and the coach-horse. In my idea, the vortex alone of 'em was enough to have involved and carried, if not the doctor, at least the doctor's pony, quite away with it. What then do you think must the terror and hydrophobia of Dr Slop have been, when you read (which you are just going to do) that he was advancing thus warily along towards Shandy Hall, and had approached to within sixty yards of it, and within five yards of a sudden turn, made by an acute angle of the garden-wall, – and in the dirtiest part of a dirty lane, – when Obadiah and his coach-horse turned the corner, rapid, furious, – pop, – full upon him! – Nothing, I think, in nature, can be supposed more terrible than such a rencounter, – so imprompt! so ill prepared to stand the shock of it as Dr Slop was.

What could Dr Slop do? – he crossed himself + – Pugh! – but the doctor, Sir, was a Papist. – No matter; he had better have kept hold of the pummel. – He had so; – nay, as it happened, he had better have done nothing at all; for in crossing himself he let go his whip, – and in attempting to save his whip betwixt his knee and his saddle's skirt, as it slipped, he lost his stirrup, – and in losing which he lost his seat; – and in the multitude of all these losses (which, by the bye, shews what little advantage there is in crossing) the unfortunate doctor lost his presence of mind. So that without waiting for Obadiah's onset, he left his pony to its destiny, tumbling off it diagonally, something in the style and manner of a pack of wool, and without any other consequence from the fall, save that of being left (as it would have been) with the broadest part of him sunk about twelve inches deep in the mire.

1759   *Tristram Shandy*

HERBERT FARJEON
Contract Bridge

Tabs part. Four players at card table: TWO MEN, TWO WOMEN. *The last cards are being dealt as lights go up. The players examine their hands. When they talk, they do not look at each other, but concentrate entirely on their cards.*

FIRST MAN (*humming softly as he sorts*: Pom-pom-pom-pom, pom-pom-pom, pom-pom-pom-pom, pom-pom-pom, pom-pom-pom-pom – – –

SECOND MAN (*whistling through his teeth*): Ss, ss-ss-ss-ss, ss-ss – ss, ss-ss-ss, ss-ss – ss, ss-ss-ss-ss –

FIRST LADY: Bub-bub-bub-bub, bub-bub-bub-bub, bub-bub-bub, bub-bub-bub-bub – whose call?

SECOND LADY: Your callikins.

FIRST LADY (*still engrossed in her cards*): My little callikins, well, well, well – *my* little callikins. Let me see, then, let me see – I think – I think – I think-a-pink-a-pink – no bid.

SECOND LADY: Tch-tch-tch, tch-tch-tch, tch-tch, tch-tch, tch-tch-tch, tch-tch-tch – no bid.

FIRST MAN: One cloob.

SECOND MAN (*dropping into Irish*): Did ye say one cloob?

FIRST MAN (*dropping into Irish*): I did that.

SECOND MAN: *Er hat ein cloob gesagen.* (*Singing*) *Er hat ein cloob gesagen, er hat ein cloob* ... One hearty-party.

FIRST LADY: Two diminx.

SECOND LADY: No bid, no bid.

FIRST MAN: No bid-a-bid-bid.

SECOND MAN: Two diminx, is it? Two naughty leetle diminx. This, I think demands a certain amount of *considération.* (*Drums fingers on table.*) Yes, yes, my friends, *beaucoup de considération.*

SECOND LADY (*after a pause*): Your *call*, partner.

SECOND MAN: I know it, I know it, I know it, I know it, I know it, indeed, indeed, I know it. (*Clacks tongue*) I know it, I know it, I double two diminx.

SECOND LADY: He doubles two diminx.

FIRST MAN: He doubles two diminx.
SECOND MAN: I double, I double, I double two diminx.
FIRST LADY: Very well, then, have at you. Two no trumpets.
FIRST MAN: Ha, ha!
SECOND MAN: Ho, ho!
FIRST LADY: He, he!
SECOND LADY: H'm, h'm!

They revert to their pet noises as they consider their hands.

1938   *Nine Sharp*

FROM THE BONDS OF GRAVITY AND FORMULA

ANON

The Dying Aviator

A handsome young airman lay dying,	(CHORUS): *lay dying,*
And as on the aer'drome he lay,	*he lay,*
To the mechanics who round him came sighing,	*came sighing,*
These last dying words he did say,	*he did say:*
'Take the cylinder out of my kidneys,'	*of his kidneys,'*
'The connecting rod out of my brain,'	*'of his brain,'*
'The cam box from under my backbone,'	*'his backbone,'*
'And assemble the engine again,'	*'again.'*
'When the court of inquiry assembles,'	*'assembles,'*
'Please tell them the reason I died,'	*'he died,'*
'Was because I forgot twice iota,'	*'twice iota,'*
'Was the minimum angle of glide,'	*'of glide.'*

World War I

SAMUEL BUTLER

(*Unpleasantness of Youth*)

To me it seems that youth is like spring, an overpraised season – delightful if it happen to be a favoured one, but in practice very rarely favoured and more remarkable, as a general rule, for biting east winds than genial breezes ... Fontenelle at the age of ninety, being asked what was the happiest time of his life, said he did not know that he had ever been much happier than he then was, but that perhaps his best years had been those when he was between fifty-five and seventy-five, and Dr Johnson placed the pleasures of old age far higher than those of youth.

1872–85   *Way of all Flesh*

The Lost Chord

It should be 'The Lost Progression' for the young lady was mistaken in supposing she had ever heard any single chord 'like the sound of a great Amen'.   *Notebook*

EDWARD LEAR

Self-Portrait of the Laureate of Nonsense

How pleasant to know Mr Lear!
  Who has written such volumes of stuff!
Some think him ill-tempered and queer,
  But a few think him pleasant enough.

His mind is concrete and fastidious,
  His nose is remarkably big;
His visage is more or less hideous,
  His beard it resembles a wig.

He has ears, and two eyes, and ten fingers,
  Leastways if you reckon two thumbs;
Long ago he was one of the singers,
  But now he is one of the dumbs.

He sits in a beautiful parlour,
  With hundreds of books on the wall;
He drinks a great deal of Marsala,
  But never gets tipsy at all.

He has many friends, laymen and clerical;
  Old Foss is the name of his cat;
His body is perfectly spherical,
  He weareth a runcible hat.

When he walks in a waterproof white,
    The children run after him so!
Calling out, 'He's come out in his night-
    Gown, that crazy old Englishman, oh!'

He weeps by the side of the ocean,
    He weeps on the top of the hill;
He purchases pancakes and lotion,
    And chocolate shrimps from the mill.

He reads but he cannot speak Spanish,
    He cannot abide ginger-beer:
Ere the days of his pilgrimage vanish,
    How pleasant to know Mr Lear!

NASTICREECHIA KRORLUPPIA
Edward Lear's Botany

Cockney Humour

(MARIE LLOYD'S HEART)

The Marie Lloyd story is lovely – and so like her. The bookie's
'A heart the size of Waterloo Station' is still her best epitaph!
1942   James Agate. *Ego* 5

Mrs Boss (who was Samuel Butler's friend's char)
'Bell? Bald? Why I've seen better hair on pork. And then he goes to chapel, and his mother's prepared to meet Jesus, and all that muck to me, and now she ain't a going to die, and drinks half a bottle of champagne a day.

'And then Grigg asks Bell if I really was a gay woman; still, when I was young, I would snap my fingers at any ooar in Holborn, and if I was togged out and had my teeth I would hold my own now with any fly-b'-night of them all. I lost my poor dear Watkins, but that of course could not be helped, and then I lost my dear Rose.

'I can't bear anyone so whitelivered in the face as Bell, though he is very civil to me and say good morning. He hasn't an upright vein in his whole body; and now he's going to send away the servant – and what if she is an ooar, she ain't no wuss for that, is she?'

*

'Oh Lor, Mr Worsley, what shameful words you do learn me to be sure; I never knew no bad words at all till I came to live with you. When you say "bloody" it makes my backbone curdle, and my heart jump out of its socket, and then I goes and tells it all to Tom.'

She says her son Tom calls her 'Gray's Inn ooar,' and she complains to my cousin that he and his bigamous wife, Topsy, are corrupting the baby's morals by teaching it to swear. 'And it do swear', she said, 'awful.' All the time she is delighted.

Boss complains to Mrs Pillinger of the way in which my cousin treats her.

She says: 'He calls me a rotten old ooar. "Well," say I to him, "if I am a ooar it ain't no thanks to you at any rate," and I did look at him scornful. But then you know there's his dear eyes.' To which Mrs Pillinger rejoined, 'Oh, you bloody old fool, you ought to be pole-axed.'

*

Mrs Boss during the cold weather applied to the church-warden for a ticket for coals. The churchwarden, who like every one else knows her exceedingly well, told her she was not a churchgoer. Mrs Boss said she couldn't look him in the face and say she had been a regular churchgoer. (She had, of course, never been inside the church at all.)

She said: 'Mrs Sloper don't know what to do. Sloper won't lay on his bed and die, and if any one comes to the door there is Sloper behind her. What with the girl with St Pancras dance, don't you call it, and Sloper, she does not know which way to turn.'

1890s   *Butleriana*

CHAPTER 3

Humour in Criticism

CRITICISM DIRECT

The criticisms of Coleridge, Hazlitt, and more surprisingly Charles Lamb tend to be serious, no doubt because as with all great or considerable critics they heighten far more often than they lessen. But the two celebrated destructive criticisms of this period, by Jeffrey and Macaulay respectively, still seem to me funny, not unfair, and always worth requoting. A hundred years later the great age of humour had produced its great humorous critics. Now the general level of critical wit seems higher, though the greatness has departed.

FRANCIS JEFFREY

on Wordsworth's 'The Excursion'

This will never do! It bears no doubt the stamp of the author's heart and fancy: but unfortunately not half so visibly as that of his peculiar system. His former poems were intended to recommend that system, and to bespeak favour for it by their individual merit; – but this, we suspect, must be recommended by the system – and can only expect to succeed where it has been previously established. It is longer, weaker, and tamer, than any of Mr Wordsworth's other productions; with less boldness of originality, and less even of that extreme simplicity and lowliness of tone which wavered so prettily, in the *Lyrical Ballads*, between silliness and pathos. We have imitations of Cowper, and even of Milton here; engrafted on the natural drawl of the Lakers – and all diluted into harmony by that profuse and irrepressible wordiness which deluges all the blank verse of this school of poetry, and lubricates and weakens the whole structure of their style.

Though it fairly fills four hundred and twenty good quarto

pages, without note, vignette, or any sort of extraneous assistance, it is stated in the title – with something of an imprudent candour – to be but 'a portion' of a larger work; and in the preface, where an attempt is rather unsuccessfully made to explain the whole design, it is still more rashly disclosed, that it is but '*a part of the second part*, of a *long* and laborious work' – which is to consist of three parts!

What Mr Wordsworth's ideas of length are, we have no means of accurately judging: but we cannot help suspecting that they are liberal to a degree that will alarm the weakness of most modern readers. As far as we can gather from the preface, the entire poem – or one of them (for we really are not sure whether there is to be one or two), is of a biographical nature; and is to contain the history of the author's mind, and of the origin and progress of his poetical powers, up to the period when they were sufficiently matured to qualify him for the great work on which he has been so long employed. Now the quarto before us contains an account of one of his youthful rambles in the vales of Cumberland, and occupies precisely the period of three days! So that, by the use of a very powerful *calculus*, some estimate may be formed of the probable extent of the entire biography.

This small specimen, however, and the statements with which it is prefaced, have been sufficient to set our minds at rest in one particular. The case of Mr Wordsworth, we perceive, is now manifestly hopeless; and we give him up as altogether incurable, and beyond the power of criticism. . . .

1814   *The Edinburgh Review*

LORD MACAULAY
on the Poems *of Robert Montgomery*

. . . We have of late observed with great pleasure some symptoms which lead us to hope that respectable literary men of all parties are beginning to be impatient of this insufferable nuisance [of puffing]. And we purpose to do what in us lies for the abating of it. We do not think that we can more usefully assist in this good work than by showing our honest countrymen what that sort of poetry is which puffing can drive through eleven editions, and how easily any bellman might, if a bellman would stoop to the necessary degree of meanness, become a 'master-spirit of the age'. We have no enmity to Mr Robert Montgomery. We know nothing whatever about him, except what we have learned from his books, and from the portrait prefixed to one of them, in which he appears to be doing his very best to look like a man of genius and sensibility, though with less success than his strenuous exertions deserve. We select him, because his works have received more enthusiastic praise, and have deserved more unmixed contempt, than any which, as far as our knowledge extends, have appeared within the last three or four years. His writing bears the same relation to poetry which a Turkey carpet bears to a picture. There are colours in the Turkey carpet out of which a picture might be made. There are words in Mr Montgomery's writing which, when disposed in certain orders and combinations, have made, and will again make, good poetry. But, as they now stand, they seem to be put together on principle in such a manner as to give no image of anything 'in the heavens above, or in the earth beneath, or in the waters under the earth'.

The poem on the *Omnipresence of the Deity* commences with a description of the creation, in which we can find only one thought which has the least pretension to ingenuity, and that one thought is stolen from Dryden, and marred in the stealing. The all-pervading influence of the Supreme Being is then described in a few tolerable lines borrowed from Pope, and a great many intolerable lines of Mr Robert Montgomery's own. The following may stand as a specimen:

> 'But who could trace Thine unrestricted course,
> Though Fancy followed with immortal force?
> There's not a blossom fondled by the breeze,
> There's not a fruit that beautifies the trees,
> There's not a particle in sea or air,
> But nature owns thy plastic influence there!
> With fearful gaze, still be it mine to see
> How all is fill'd and vivified by Thee;
> Upon thy mirror, earth's majestic view,
> To paint Thy Presence, and to feel it too.'

The last two lines contain an excellent specimen of Mr Robert

Montgomery's Turkey carpet style of writing. The majestic view of earth is the mirror of God's presence; and on this mirror Mr Robert Montgomery paints God's presence. The use of a mirror, we submit, is not to be painted upon. ...

We would not be understood, however, to say, that Mr Robert Montgomery cannot make similitudes for himself. A very few lines further on, we find one which has every mark of originality, and on which, we will be bound, none of the poets whom he has plundered will ever think of making reprisals:

> 'The soul, aspiring, pants its source to mount,
> As streams meander level with their fount.'

We take this to be, on the whole, the worst similitude in the world. In the first place, no stream meanders, or can possibly meander, level with its fount. In the next place, if streams did meander level with their founts, no two motions can be less like each other than that of meandering level and that of mounting upwards. ...

1830   *The Edinburgh Review*

GEORGE BERNARD SHAW
on Irving in Walerloo

MR IRVING TAKES PAREGORIC

... Before the curtain rises, you read the playbill; and the process commences at once with the suggestive effect on your imagination of 'Corporal Gregory Brewster, age eighty-six, a Waterloo veteran,' of 'Nora Brewster, the corporal's grandniece,' and of 'Scene – Brewster's lodgings'. By the time you have read that, your own imagination, with the author pulling the strings, has done half the work you afterwards give Mr Irving credit for. Up goes the curtain; lodgings are before you, with the humble breakfast table, the cheery fire, the old man's spectacles and Bible and a medal hung up in a frame over the chimney piece. Lest you should be unobservant enough to miss the significance of all this, Miss Annie Hughes comes in with a basket of butter and bacon, ostensibly to impersonate the grandniece, really to carefully point out all these things to you. Mr Fuller Mellish enters in the uniform of a modern artillery sergeant, with a breech-loading carbine. You are touched: here is the young soldier come to see the old – two figures from the Seven Ages of Man. Miss Hughes tells Mr Mellish all about Corporal Gregory. She takes down the medal, and describes the feat for which the medal was given. In short, the pair work at the picture of the old warrior until the very dullest dog in the audience knows what he is to see, or to imagine he sees, when the great moment comes. Thus is Brewster already created, though Mr Irving has not yet left his dressing room. At last, everything being ready, Mr Fuller Mellish is packed off so as not to divide the interest. A squeak is heard behind the scenes: it is the childish treble that once rang like a trumpet on the powder-wagon at Waterloo. Enter Mr Irving, in a dirty white wig, toothless, blear-eyed, palsied, shaky at the knees, stooping at the shoulders, incredibly aged and very poor, but respectable. He makes his way to his chair, and can only sit down, so stiff are his aged limbs, very slowly and creakily. This sitting down business is not acting: the callboy could do it; but we are so thoroughly primed by the playbill, the scene-painter, the stage-manager, Miss Hughes and Mr Mellish, that we go off in enthusiastic whispers, 'What superb acting! How wonderfully he does it!' He gets a bronchial attack and gasps for paregoric, which Miss Hughes administers with a spoon, whilst our faces glisten with tearful smiles. 'Is there another living actor who could take paregoric like that? ...'

1895   *Saturday Review*

MAX BEERBOHM
on Duse

I have often wondered why Sydney Smith said he 'would as soon speak disrespectfully of the Equator.' After all, the Equator is a mere geographical expression. It casts no weird spell of awe over mankind. On the contrary, seafarers, when they come to it, put on false noses and play practical jokes. For 'Equator' read 'Duse', and then the remark has point. There never was an influence so awe-inspiring as Duse. At her coming, all voices of the critics are hushed. Or rather, they are uplifted in unisonant dithyrambus.

1900   *Saturday Review*

(*on* The Passing of the Third Floor Back)

'A DEPLORABLE AFFAIR'

In the course of a theatrical season, the critic's proud spirit is gradually subdued. Twaddling play succeeds twaddling play, and, as the wearisome procession goes by, the critic's protests become fainter: he begins to acquiesce in what cannot apparently be stopped. But when he comes back after a holiday, with a fresh eye, with a soul invigorated by contact with real things and lovely things and things that matter, and comes just in time to see the same old procession starting placidly forth on the same old route, then, oh then, it needs a very great effort in him to control his temper. Why should he try? I shall *not* try. All for art, and the temper well lost, I say. How can Mr Forbes-Robertson expect me to be polite about his production at the St James'? In the provinces, recently, he produced a play by Mr Henry James – a play that was reported to be a great success. It would be a privilege to produce a play by Mr Henry James, even though the play failed utterly. In its failure, it would be more interesting, and would bring higher esteem to its producer, than any number of successful plays by second-rate men. Having produced Mr James' play with success, what does Mr Forbes-Robertson do so soon as he comes to London? Apparently in doubt whether Mr James be good enough for the metropolis, he gives us Mr Jerome Klapka Jerome. This tenth-rate writer has been, for many years, prolific of his tenth-rate stuff. But I do not recall, in such stuff of his as I have happened to sample, anything quite so vilely stupid as 'The Passing of the Third Floor Back'. I do not for a moment suppose that Mr Forbes-Robertson likes it one whit more than I do. And I wish his pusillanimity in prostituting his great gifts to it were going to be duly punished. The most depressing aspect of the whole matter is that the play is so evidently a great success. The enthusiasm of a first-night audience is no sure gauge of success. Nor is the proverbial apathy of a second-night audience a sure gauge of failure. It was on the second night that I saw 'The Passing of the Third Floor Back'; and greater enthusiasm have I seldom seen in a theatre. And thus I am brought sharply up against that doubt which so often confronts me: what can be hoped of an art which must necessarily depend on the favour of the public – of such a public, at least, as ours? Good work may, does sometimes, succeed. But never with the degree of success that befalls twaddle and vulgarity unrelieved. Twaddle and vulgarity will have always the upper hand.

The reformation of a bad person by a supernatural visitor is a theme that has often been used. Mr Jerome, remembering the converted miser in 'A Christmas Carol', and the converted egoist in 'A Message from Mars', and many a similar convert, was struck by the bright idea that the effect would be just a dozen times as great if there were a dozen converts. So he has turned a supernatural visitor loose in a boarding-house inhabited by a round dozen of variously bad people –'A Satyr', 'A Snob', 'A Shrew', 'A Painted Lady', 'A Cheat', and so on. Now supposing that these characters were life-like, or were amusing figments of the brain, and supposing that we saw them falling, little by little, under the visitor's spell, till gradually we were aware that they had been changed for the better, the play might be quite a passable affair. But to compass that effect is very far beyond Mr Jerome's power. He has neither the natural talent nor the technical skill that the task requires. There is not a spark of verisimilitude in the whole dozen of characters. One and all, they are unreal. Mr Jerome shows no sign of having ever observed a fellow-creature. His characters seem to be the result solely of a study of novelettes in the penny weekly papers, supplemented by a study of the works of Mr Jerome K. Jerome. Take Major Tompkins, and his wife and daughter, for example. Could anything be more trite and crude than their presentment? Major and Mrs Tompkins are anxious to sell their daughter for gold to an elderly man. 'His very touch,' says the daughter, according to custom, 'is loathsome'. The Major persists and says – what else could a stage-major say? – 'Damn your infernal impudence!' The unnatural mother tries to persuade the unwilling daughter to wear a more décolleté dress. The daughter, of course, loves a young painter in a brown velveteen jacket; but she is weak and worldly, and she is likely to yield to the importunities of the elderly man. The young painter – but no, I won't bore you by describing the other characters: suffice it that they are all ground out of the same old rusty machine that has served *The Family Herald* and similar publications for so many weary years. Mr Jerome's humour, however, is his own, and he plasters it about with a liberal hand. What could be more screamingly funny than the doings at the outset? The landlady pours tea into the decanter which is supposed to hold whisky, on the chance that the drunken boarder won't notice the difference. Then she goes out, and the servant drinks milk out of the jug and replenishes the jug with water. Then *she* goes out, and the 'Painted Lady' comes in and steals a couple of fresh candles from the sconces on the piano and substitutes a couple of candle ends. Then *she* goes out, and the Major comes in and grabs the biscuits off the plate and drops them into his hat. Then *he* goes out, and the 'Cad' and the 'Rogue' come in and unlock the spirit-case with an illicit key and help themselves to what they presently find is tea. He's inexhaustibly fertile in such sequences is Mr Jerome K. Jerome. When the 'Passer-By' knocks at the front-door, and is admitted with a limelight full on his (alas, Mr Forbes-Robertson's) classic countenance, the sequences set in with an awful severity. The beneficent stranger has one method for all evildoers, and he works it on every one in turn, with precisely the same result. He praises the landlady for her honesty; then the landlady is ashamed of her dishonesty and becomes honest. He praises the Major for his sweet temper; then the Major is ashamed of his bad temper, and becomes sweet-tempered. He praises the 'Painted Lady' for her modesty in not thinking herself beautiful without paint; then the 'Painted Lady' is ashamed of her paint, and reappears paintless. He praises – but again I won't bore you further. You have found the monotony of the foregoing sentences oppressive enough. Picture to yourselves the monotony of what they describe! For a period of time that seemed like eternity, I had to sit knowing exactly what was about to happen, and how it was about to happen, and knowing that as soon as it had happened it would happen again.

The art of dramaturgy, someone has said, is the art of preparation. In that case Klapka is assuredly the greatest dramatist the world has ever known. It is hard to reconcile this conclusion with the patent fact that he hasn't yet mastered the rudiments of his craft.

The third and last act of the play, like the second, consists of a sequence of interviews – next man, please! – between the visitor and the other (now wholly reformed) persons of the play. Steadily, he works through the list, distributing full measure of devastating platitudes, all the way. The last person on the list, the Major's daughter, says suddenly 'Who are you?' The visitor spreads his arms, in the attitude of 'The Light of the World.' The Major's daughter falls on her knees in awe. When the visitor passes out through the front-door, a supernatural radiance bursts through the fan-light, flooding the stage; and then the curtain comes slowly down. Well, I suppose blasphemy pays.

1908   *Saturday Review*

H. G. WELLS

on the First Night of Henry James's Guy Domville

Alexander at the close had an incredibly awkward exit. He had to stand at a door in the middle of the stage, say slowly, 'Be keyned to Her . . . *Be* keyned to Her' and depart. By nature Alexander had a long face, but at that moment, with audible defeat before him, he seemed the longest and dismallest face, all face, that I have ever seen. The slowly closing door reduced him to a strip, to a line, of perpendicular gloom. The uproar burst like a thunderstorm as the door closed and the stalls responded with feeble applause. Then the tumult was mysteriously allayed. There were some minutes of uneasy apprehension. 'Author,' cried voices. 'Author!' The stalls, not understanding, redoubled their clapping.

Disaster was too much for Alexander that night. A spasm of hate for the writer of those fatal lines must surely have seized him. With incredible cruelty he led the doomed James, still not understanding clearly how things were with him, to the middle of the stage, and there the pit and gallery had him. James bowed;

he knew it was the proper thing to bow. Perhaps he had selected a few words to say, but if so they went unsaid. I have never heard any sound more devastating than the crescendo of booing that ensued. The gentle applause of the stalls was altogether overwhelmed. For a moment or so James faced the storm, his round face white, his mouth opening and shutting, and then Alexander, I hope in a contrite mood, snatched him back into the wings.

1915   *Boon*

JAMES AGATE
on Mozart

Myra Hess in Mozart's B flat Piano Concerto (K.595). The shallowest water by this melodious bird ever madrigalised. Then Tschaikowsky No. 5. Drenched with self-pity. But I like listening to it just as I like looking at a fuchsia drenched with rain.

1945   *Ego 8*

C. A. LEJEUNE
Dietrich as an Angel

The first moment that Miss Marlene Dietrich sweeps up to the reception desk of a Paris hotel in *Angel*, you feel sure that you are looking at a mystery woman. It is something about the highlight on her lip-rouge, the way her eyes peek from side to side, and the dashing way in which she tosses off the signature 'Mrs Brown' in the register. You know, of course, that she isn't Mrs Brown, but beyond that you have no notion who she may be, except possibly Miss Marlene Dietrich, the film star, practising acting. In point of fact, she is the wife of a British Cabinet Minister, who is currently engaged in representing his country at Geneva. Oh, you move in exalted circles in *Angel*, and meet the most wonderful people. There is no house with less than four upper servants kept in the whole of the film.

It is Mr Melvyn Douglas, whom she meets in Paris at a gaming-house, who thinks up the cosy name of 'Angel' for Miss Dietrich. As an upper-class Englishman 'recently returned from Government service in India', he would have these bright thoughts, naturally. Quite naturally, too, and with a well-bred charm that robs the idea of any crudeness, he suggests to his mysterious lady that they should 'get together for the evening'. They get together. A perambulating violinist plays for them, tenderly, suggestively, right in the eardrum. Under his influence, Miss Dietrich, dismissing the trifling thought of her husband, the Cabinet Minister, indicates that they might meet again, and elope, next Wednesday, at five-thirty. It is Paris, *mon Dieu*, and cinema, and spring.

The next day, in England, Sir Frederick Barker, brilliant statesman, fresh from his round-table conquest of twenty-one nations, arrives home from Geneva. The papers are full of it. There is nothing else but Barker in the evening editions. Crowned with a weary charm that only Mr Herbert Marshall can achieve, he retires to his country seat just outside London. A real regular English home it is, just like yours or mine, or Mr Anthony Eden's, with a Great Dane on the hearthrug, yards of mullion round the windows, and Miss Marlene Dietrich sleeping in the best bedroom. Only, just to remind you that this is an important picture, Miss Dietrich, in swansdown, presently tiptoes in to her husband with a telegram. He reads it, and frowns, looking frightfully political. 'What's worrying you darling?' asks Miss Dietrich. 'Is it France?' 'No,' says Mr Marshall briefly, 'Jugo-Slavia'. 'Oh,' replies Miss Dietrich, with a whole leading article in the inflection, 'I see'.

The problem of Jugo-Slavia being settled, presumably by breakfast time, life at Barker Hall resumes its proper serenity. The Cabinet is quiescent. Sir Frederick and lady attend the races. I have forgotten why they do this, but I am quite clear why they also attend the opera. It is so that Mr Marshall may murmur to Miss Dietrich, in that rich indifferent voice which has thrilled thousands, 'Look, my dear, there's the Duchess of Loamshire on your left.'

Since it is essential, by this time, that Mr Melvyn Douglas should come back into the story, Mr Marshall meets him, quite by accident, at Lord Davington's place after luncheon. Finding that one of them was called Snooky and the other Poochy by the same Paris sempstress during the war, the two men just naturally get together. Mr Marshall asks Mr Douglas to luncheon next day at Barker Hall. That's natural, too, and Etonian. 'You know,

I've only known you for a day, and yet I feel – ' 'I know, old man, I feel it, too.' 'You forget, Barker – ' 'Frederick,' 'Of course, Frederick.' 'Gin and tonic?' 'Thanks. Just a spot.'

They have veal for lunch that day, at the great reunion. Angel, Lady Barker, doesn't eat the veal, but she carries off the reunion superbly. Not an eyelash flickers when she is left alone with Mr Douglas. 'Angel,' he murmurs. 'I don't understand you,' she replies, with that *savoir faire* that is only learnt in Downing Street and Hollywood. 'The lampshade may be blue,' he whispers, wildly and irrelevantly, 'but when you light it up, it's the greenest green in the world. I'll be waiting for you in Paris at 5.30 on Wednesday,' 'I shall not be there,' says Miss Dietrich firmly. Meanwhile, Mr Marshall is on the telephone to the Foreign Office. His face is again grimly political. 'Anderson?' he listens. 'Dear, dear, what's the trouble? Oh, t-t-t-t-t.'

'I'm afraid,' says Mr Marshall, sadly, to his wife over the whisky, 'that I shall have to go back to Geneva.' 'Can't Anderson do it?' 'He could, of course, but – ' Miss Dietrich is huffed at this. She has been counting, God knows why, on a second honeymoon in a little place in Vienna, up six flights of stairs and no elevator. That seems heaven to her, after the Barker place, and somehow terribly, psychologically important. 'Oh, very well,' she says in a pique, 'if we can't go to Vienna, take me with you as far as Paris. I haven't bought any clothes in ages.' I'll do a bit of shopping, she seems to hint, like any suburban housewife. Just drop me off at the Rue de la Paix and I'll make my own way home.

In the end it's the manager of Croydon Airport who tips Mr Marshall off to the domestic situation. In a scene that is all English and stiff upper lip, the three meet in the gaming-house in Paris. Nothing is said that can be regretted. Nothing is said that can even be remembered. Angel, Lady Barker, and Sir Frederick entrain for their inadequate hotel in Vienna, leaving Mr Douglas repentant and the English Cabinet to go to the devil.

This film, which you may care to add to your collection, was directed and produced by Ernst Lubitsch. It is intended, I am told, for 'the young, the gay, and the sophisticated'. It is also 'Dietrich as You Desire Her'. Finding that none of these qualifications concerns me deeply, I might have tossed off the film in a couple of paragraphs. Courtesy, however, compels me to give it a column, in view of the Chinese proverb printed so neatly on the front of the programme. 'One picture,' this states succinctly, though rather optimistically, even for weekly journalism, 'is worth ten thousand words'.

1936

Evening Dress Compulsory

The Spanish Main, which is not meant to be funny, seems to me a much funnier pirate picture than *The Princess and the Pirate*, which was. It is an incredibly genteel account of the adventures of a Mexican heiress with an Irish Accent (Maureen O'Hara), who is betrothed to a Spanish Governor with an Austrian accent (Walter Slezak). On her way to her wedding she is abducted and married by a Dutch pirate with another Austrian accent (Paul Henreid). Since the lady has brought her trousseau, her vanity case, and her hairdresser with her, she is able to dress for dinner with some formality aboard the pirate ship, and lend quite a tone to the captain's table. Unhappily, the sight of her deep *décolletage* and the blue baby ribbons she affects in her hair proves too much for the pirate's ex-fiancée (Binnie Barnes), an outdoor type with a wardrobe confined to two crisply laundered blouses and a couple of golfing outfits. With her eye on a Brussels lace nightgown, she betrays the married couple to the jilted governor, and it is then that the heroine's fully-fashioned, non-austerity models prove really useful. For she manages to secrete in their folds (1) a dagger, (2) a horse pistol, (3) a rapier, and (4) the keys to all the cells in the local prison. With a hurried plea, for she is a tenderhearted girl, that the apoplectic governor shall be allowed to live and 'find a way to do some useful work', she puts out to sea again with her pirate husband, prudently reappropriating the nightgown, still incredibly free from signs of wear and tear. The last shot shows the happy couple sailing away towards the Carolinas, into a Technicolour sun rising boldy and bloodily in the west.

NOTE: Herodotus records the same phenomenon on the authority of the Egyptian priests. In eleven thousand three hundred and forty years, he declares, 'they related that the sun had four times risen out of his usual quarter, and that he had twice risen where he now sets, and twice set where he now rises'. On none of these occasions he adds, had the phenomenon been accompanied by other curious manifestations; a point in which superiority must be allowed to *The Spanish Main*.

1946   *The Observer*

PAUL JENNINGS
(on Beatrix Potter Translated)

It is difficult to decide whether translators are heroes or fools. They are surely aware that the Afrikaans for 'Hamlet, I am thy father's ghost' sounds something like '*Omlet, ek is de papap spook*,' and that an intense French actor, beginning Hamlet's speech to Gertrude with '*Mère, mère*,' sounds exactly like a sheep. In Denmark the film *King Kong* had to be called *Kong King* because *Kong* means 'King' in Danish. Seeing a book in shops all over France with the title '*Ainsi en emporte le vent*', like a line from Lamartine, I took a long time to realize it was 'Gone with the Wind'.

The racial realities of language have become mere intellectual concepts to the translator. He floats over the world in a godlike balloon. The babble of voices under the arches of teeming cities, the infinite variations of uvula and hard palate, the words formed in tribal battles and in tales over the winter hearth, float up to him in a vague, jumbled unity, rich but disembodied, like a distant cooking smell.

*

Paradoxically, the more a work expresses some special national genius, the more it attracts translators. Until recently I had thought the supreme example of this was *Jabberwocky* done into French, German, and even Latin (*ensis vorpalis persnicuit persnacuitque*). But now I perceive that something even more secret and English has attracted them; the children's books of Beatrix Potter.

Quite apart from their literary style, these have the same 'central' symbolic appeal as Jane Austin. Jemima Puddle-Duck, Mrs Tiggy-Winkle, Ribby, Duchess and the rest of them live in a transcendentalized English village, where shops with bottle-glass windows doze in an endless summer afternoon, and nothing changes. No one has heard of foreigners, just as the Napoleonic Wars are never mentioned in Jane Austen.

The moment even the titles are translated we are very much aware indeed of foreigners, of Europe. Here are some:

FRENCH

Sophie Canetang (Jemima Puddle-Duck).
Noisy-Noisette (Squirrel Nutkin).
La Famille Flopsaut (Flopsy Bunnies).
Jeremie Péche-à-la-Ligne (Jeremy Fisher).

DUTCH

Tom Het Poesje (Tom Kitten).
Jeremias de Hengelaar (Jeremy Fisher).

WELSH

Hanes Dili Minllyn (Jemima Puddle-Duck).
Hanes Meistres Tigi-Dwt (Mrs Tiggy-Winkle).

ITALIAN

Il Coniglio Pierino (Peter Rabbit).

SWEDISH

Sagan Om Pelle Kanin (Peter Rabbit).

GERMAN

Die Geschichte von Frau Tigge-Winkel.
Die Geschichte der Hasenfamilie Plumps (Flopsy Bunnies).

*

Who *are* these characters, we ask? Well may the inhabitants of the Potter village peep from behind their dimity curtains as this babbling procession pours down the quiet street. Here comes Sophie Canetang, a Stendhal heroine, acutely analysing love with a cavalry officer and a *petit bourgeois* – but respectable compared with the awful Mauriac Famille Flopsaut, festering with hate, ruining the brilliant son who will never get to Paris; compared with the gaudy career of Noisy-Noisette, the Mata Hari of the twenties, as depicted by Colette, or the Maupassant Péche-à-la-Ligne, the quiet angler who pushes his mistress's husband into the trout pool.

Behind these comes Tom Het Poesje, a kind of Dutch Till Eulenspiegel, half jester, half highwayman, a doubtful figure in leather jerkin, plaguing the burghers with rather unfunny practical jokes. Then there is a momentary silence as Jeremias de Hengelaar, the fourteenth-century mystic, shuffles by, pondering on the One.

*

What on earth does Dili Minllyn, thinking of the April clouds sweeping over her white farmhouse on the green Welsh hill, of the clock ticking on the silent dresser, have to say to Il Coniglio Pierino, the swarthy Sicilian bandit, or to the Nordic hero Pelle Kanin, seen through smoke and fire, howling songs against the northern wind on long-prowed ships?

And who, in this village, is going to be interested in the story of Frau Tigge-Winkel, the widow of a Prussian general who revolutionized something or other in 1874? To say nothing of the Hasenfamilie Plumps I.G., a lesser version of the Krupp dynasty, an endless succession of stern characters extending the family factories in the Ruhr . . .

Almost it is unfortunate that the children in the village, who have one language and one vision, will not see them.

1953   *The Observer*

JOHN CROW

on The Oxford Dictionary of Quotations, *Second Edition*

O for a life of reference-books rather than of literature! It is pleasant to welcome a new and much better edition of one of the most readable books of our century. This edition adds about 1,300 quotations to the 1941 stock and purges some which, presumably, we have now ceased to quote. I can, after some search track two of these purgings: we no longer quote 'as right as rain' from *Love and a Quiet Life* by Walter Raymond (1851–1931) – I should hope not; we now look for it in the *Oxford Dictionary of Proverbs* and find it referred to Plautus (though it is odd to find no earlier English example than Raymond's 1894 book). Our conversation now does without a repugnant couplet, 'Only a baby small Dropt from the skies,' which can be laid on the doorstep of Matthias Barr (fl. 1870 – *floruit* wouldn't be my word). If other purgings are similar, I rejoice. I welcome also a better index and the numbering of every quotation on its page.

What improvements do I desire for a Third Edition? These things are much a matter of whim. We depend, as we are told, upon what we heard at the nursery table and at school – and feel surprise when pet phrases are absent. Some of the included also surprise: there are, for me, too many uplifting little things from the School of Ella Wheeler Wilcox, a school which would appear to include here Grantland Rice ('When One great Scorer'), Mr John Pudney (a new acquisition), Mr Stephen Spender, Dorothy Frances Gurney, and, splendidly emetic, Phoebe Carr. We quote, it seems, the modern poets but little. Not a word from Auden, MacNeice, Roy Campbell, Dylan Thomas, Empson. We repeat no quips of Waugh, Greene, Dorothy Parker. From Virginia Woolf and Robert Graves we use no more than *A Room of One's Own* and *Goodbye to All That*. There are thirty-three things from Mr Eliot on our lips; there were only nineteen in 1941.

I should be for adding phrases from some of the dimmish hymns of my youth – 'Dare to be a Daniel' and 'You in your small corner and I in mine' and a nauseous recitation 'Pappa's letter is with God'. Clearly, also, at the Crow nursery table far too many extracts from *Eric, or Little by Little* flew around.

We are given 'a louse in the locks of literature', but not (naturally, I suppose) the current Oxford variant, 'a***** on the rocks of literature'. And where shall I find such little favourites of mine as the first alleged cancelled stanza of 'In Memoriam'?

> (a) The sun goes down upon the west
> And ever rises in the east;
> That much, we know is true, at least,
> And hope and trust 'tis for the best.

*

I boggle at a few other matters. The 'Anon' quotation 'The Sun himself cannot forget his fellow-traveller' is a translation from John Owen; the 'Harington' quotation about pleasing guests not cooks is a translation from Martial. I grumble at the allotting to Porson and Suckling of two straight Shakespeare quotations. I can't see why 'Since first I saw your face' is Anon and 'I did but see her passing by' is Thomas Ford when both are from Ford's songbook and neither is by Ford. Four words seem to be missing from the second Sophocles quotation. Two people are credited with saying that beauty is in the eye of the beholder. 'Go West, young man' is here given to J. B. L. Soule (1815–91) in the 1941 edition it was in the index and not, apparently, in the text. Why are we told that Mr A. C. McAuliffe said 'Nuts' to some Germans? Why are there no post-1904 *Punch* quotations? Is it a matter of copyright, or something like the scent of musk? There are, anyway, they tell us, 'well over 40,000 quotations' in this splendid book, which moved my heart more than a trumpet and held me long at the chimney corner. I'm happy and thankful about it and please do not take my bogglings too seriously.

1953   *The Listener*

CRITICISM BY PARODY

This section is disproportionately long because of my disproportionate liking for this form of humour and my enjoyment of this richest yet most compressed form of negative criticism. Successful parody entails a truly wide, if not a deep, knowledge of the victim. Perhaps my favourite sentence in all parody is Max's summary of Galsworthy's attitude to his Forsyte heroine Irene, whose entrance is 'heralded by that almost unseizable odour that uncut turquoises have' (p. 115). Here again, my choice is from my personal favourites of the moment. I remind the reader that there are wonderful parodies in Chaucer, Shakespeare, and Lewis Carroll, and that the pioneers, like James and Horace Smith, were men of the highest talent.

I begin with my favourite paragraph from the works of Swift:

The Verisimilitude of Travellers' Tales
(GULLIVER SAYS FAREWELL TO THE HOUYHNHNMS)

When all was ready, and the day came for my departure, I took leave of my master and lady, and the whole family, mine eyes flowing with tears, and my heart quite sunk with grief. But his honour, out of curiosity, and perhaps (if I may speak it without vanity) partly out of kindness, was determined to see me in my canoo; and several of his neighbouring friends to accompany him. I was forced to wait above an hour for the tide, and then observing the wind very fortunately bearing towards the island, to which I intended to steer my course, I took a second leave of my master: but, as I was going to prostrate myself to kiss his hoof, he did me the honour to raise it gently to my mouth. I am not ignorant how much I have been censured for mentioning this last particular. Detractors are pleased to think it improbable, that so illustrious a person should descend to give so great a mark of distinction to a creature so inferior as I. Neither have I forgot, how apt some travellers are to boast of extraordinary favours they have received. But, if these censurers were better acquainted with the noble and courteous disposition of the Houyhnhnms, they would soon change their opinion.

1726   *Travels of Lemuel Gulliver*

MAX BEERBOHM

Galsworthy's 'Forsyte Saga'

... Adrian Berridge paused on the threshold, as was his wont, with closed eyes and dilated nostrils, enjoying the aroma of complex freshness which the dining-room had at this hour. Pathetically a creature of habit, he liked to savour the various scents, sweet or acrid, that went to symbolize for him the time and place. Here were the immediate scents of dry toast, of China tea, of napery fresh from the wash, together with that vague, super-subtle scent which boiled eggs give out through their unbroken shells. And as a permanent base to these there was the scent of much polished Chippendale, and of bees' waxed parquet, and of Persian rugs. Today, moreover, crowning the composition, there was the delicate pungency of the holly that topped the Queen Anne mirror and the Mantegna prints.

Just at that moment, heralded by a slight fragrance of old lace and of that peculiar, almost unseizable odour that uncut turquoises have, Mrs Berridge appeared.

'What is the matter, Adrian?' she asked quickly. She glanced sideways into the Queen Anne mirror, her hand fluttering, like a pale moth to her hair, which she always wore braided in a fashion she had derived from Pollaiuolo's St Ursula.

1912   *A Christmas Garland*

MAX BEERBOHM
of Kipling

(1) P.C. X 36

Then it's collar 'im tight,
  In the name o' the Lawd!
'Ustle 'im, shake 'im till 'e's sick.'
  Wot, 'e *would*, would 'e? Well,
  Then yer've got ter give 'im 'Ell,
An' it's trunch, trunch, truncheon does the trick.

Police Station Ditties

(2) SLUSHBY

I had spent Christmas Eve at the Club, listening to a grand pow-wow between certain of the choicer sons of Adam. Then Slushby had cut in. Slushby is one who writes to newspapers and is theirs obediently 'HUMANITARIAN'. When Slushby cuts in, men remember they have to be up early next morning.

Sharp round a corner on the way home, I collided with something firmer than the regulation pillar-box. I righted myself after the recoil and saw some stars that were very pretty indeed. Then I perceived the nature of the obstruction.

'Evening, Judlip,' I said sweetly, when I had collected my hat from the gutter. 'Have I broken the law, Judlip? If so, I'll go quiet.'

1912   *The Christmas Garland*

G. K. CHESTERTON
of The Poets as they might have re-written 'Ole King Cole'

TENNYSON:
  Cole, that unwearied prince of Colchester,
  Growing more gay with age and with long days

127

Deeper in laughter and desire of life,
As that Virginian climber on our walls
Flames scarlet with the fading of the year;
Called for his wassail and that other weed
Virginian also, from the western woods
Where English Raleigh checked the boast of Spain ...

W. B. YEATS:

Of an old King in a story
From the grey sea-folk I have heard,
Whose heart was no more broken
Than the wings of a bird ...

BROWNING:

Who smoke-snorts toasts o' my Lady Nicotine,
Kicks stuffing out of Pussyfoot, bids his trio
Stick up their Stradivarii (that's the plural)
Or near enough, my fatheads; *nimium
Vicina Cremonae;* that's a bit too near.
Is there some stockfish fails to understand?
Catch hold o' the notion, bellow and blurt back 'Cole'?
Must I bawl lessons from a horn-book, howl,
Cat-call the cat-gut 'fiddles'? Fiddlesticks!

WALT WHITMAN:

Me clairvoyant,
Me conscious of you, old camarado,
Needing no telescope, lorgnette, field-glass, opera-glass myopic
pince-nez,
Me piercing two thousand years with eye naked and not ashamed;
The crown cannot hide you from me;
Musty old feudal-heraldic trappings cannot hide you from me,
I perceive that you drink.
(I am drinking with you. I am as drunk as you are.)
I see you are inhaling tobacco, puffing, smoking, spitting
(I do not object to your spitting),
You prophetic of American largeness,
You anticipating the broad masculine manners of these States;
I see in you also there are movements, tremors, tears, desire for the
melodious

I salute your three violinists, endlessly making vibrations,
Rigid, relentless, capable of going on for ever;
They play my accompaniment; but I shall take no notice of any
accompaniment;
I myself am a complete orchestra.
So long.

J. C. SQUIRE

G. K. Chesterton

When I leapt over Tower Bridge
   There were three that watched below,
A bald man and a hairy man,
   And a man like Ikey Mo.

When I leapt over London Bridge
   They quailed to see my tears,
As terrible as a shaken sword
   And many shining spears.

But when I leapt over Blackfriars
   The pigeons on St Paul's
Grew ghastly white as they saw the sight
   Like an awful sun that falls;

And all along from Ludgate
   To the wonder of Charing Cross,
The devil flew through a host of hearts –
   A messenger of loss.

With a rumour of ghostly things that pass
   With a thunderous pennon of pain,
To a land where the sky is as red as the grass
   And the sun as green as the rain.

1917
                                          Tricks of the Trade

W. C. SELLAR AND R. J. YEATMAN

Test Paper II

UP TO THE END OF HENRY III

*1. Give the dates of at least *two* of the following:
   (1) William the Conqueror.
   (2) 1066.

*2. What is a Plantagenet? Do you agree?

*3. Trace by means of graphs, etc.:
   (1) The incidence of scurvy in the Chiltern Hundreds during the reign of Rufus.
   (2) The Bosom of the Pope.
   (Squared paper, compasses, etc., may be used.)

*4. Expostulate (chiefly) on:
   (*a*) The Curfew.
   (*b*) Gray's Energy in the Country Churchyard.

*5. Estimate the size of:
   (1) Little Arthur.
   (2) Friar Puck.
   (3) Magna Charta.

6. Fill in the names of at least some of the following:
   (1) ....
   (2) ....
   (3) Simon de Montfort.

7. King John had no redeeming features. (Illustrate).

8. Arrange in this order:
   (1) Henry I.
   (2) Henry II.
   (3) Henry III.
   (Do not attempt to answer more than once.)

*9. (*a*) How far did the Lords Repellent drive Henry III into the arms of Pedro the Cruel? (Protractors may *not* be used.)
   (*b*) Matilda or Maud? (Write on *one* side of the paper only.)

*10. How would you dispose of:
   (*a*) A Papal Bull?
   (*b*) Your nephews?
   (*c*) Your mother? (Be brutal.)

*11. Which would you rather be:
    (1) The Sheriff of Nottingham?
    (2) A Weak King?
    (3) Put to the Sword?

*N.B. Candidates over thirty need *not* attempt questions 10, 2, 5, 3, 4, 11, 9 or 1.

Preface to a Second Edition.

A first edition limited to 1 copy and printed on rice paper and bound in buck-boards and signed by one of the editors was sold to the other editor, who left it in a taxi somewhere between Piccadilly Circus and the Bodleian.
                                   W. C. S.
                                   R. J. Y.

Of Errata

P. 43. *For* Pheasant *read* Peasant, throughout.
P. 44. *For* sausage *read* hostage.
1930
                                     1066 and All That

J. B. MORTON ('BEACHCOMBER')
'*Little-Known-Facts*' column

Today the little Essex town of Manningtree celebrates the traditional suet-fair. Soon after dawn the suet-men, each armed with a ladder and a lump of suet, proceed through the town. They place their ladders against houses, mount them and present the suet to the girl of their choice, in return for a kiss. Later, the girls bring the suet on wheel-barrows to the old chafing-ground outside the Muniment Room in Castle Street, where the dolmonnies, in doublet and hose, bore holes in each lump and stick it on a painted post set up in the cattle-pen. Coloured ribbons are attached to the posts, and the dolmonny dance begins, with its quaint old words:

> Give thee good cheer of thy suet,
> With a rumby-o and a dumby-o,
> Give the good cheer of thy suet
> And a fair sueting, good lack,
> And who shall trool the suet-man?

The suet is then removed from the posts and thrown about in the market-place until dusk. Every townsman takes a piece

home with him, and every girl who has been kissed is presented
with a rung of one of the ladders by the mayor.

Daily Express

D. B. WYNDHAM LEWIS
Leader Page in a National Daily

Smash-O. Another little smash on the South-North-
Western line. Couple of folks killed. Couple more
maybe injured for life. One of them was a registered
reader of the 'Daily X' gets £300. That's commonsense.

It isn't commonsense for the railway to smash them
up. It isn't good business. The railways are up against
enough competition already without making things
worse by having smashes. Look at it from the commonsense angle. A grocer doesn't get more trade by
beaning his customers with an axe. He gets less, and
for why? Because he frightens folks away. That goes
for every other line of business, too. We are a nation
of shopkeepers, as Shakespeare said, and it's up to us
to act business-like. Look at Canada. Look at America. Here's trade booming and everything all set for
prosperity, and the railways either can't kick in or
won't. Not so good.

Give Youth a Chance

Because his aunt reproved him for calling his mother
a cross-eyed haybag, a ten-year-old boy did her in
with a meat-axe. This is a crime. The Daily X is
against crime. But the Daily X believes in youth.
Believes in giving youth a chance. Too many grey-
beards about. Youth will be served.

Maybe if that young boy's aunt had let him express
himself he wouldn't have beaned her. Modern Youth
demands the right to self-expression. You can't get
over that. The eaglets of today are tomorrow's lions.
Don't treat them as if they were saps. The Empire
looks to youth today.

1937   *Press Gang*

HUGH KINGSMILL
Lytton Strachey

EMINENT EGYPTIANS

If we take the trouble to examine our general impression of
Joseph's character, we shall make a rather startling discovery.
The ex-convict, the member of an outcast, desert tribe, whose

infinitely patient, and infinitely discreet, manipulation of men and circumstances elevated him to the position of virtual ruler over the 'proudest and most powerful of States, is entirely overshadowed in our imagination by the naive boy of seventeen. Do we, when we think of Joseph, see the subtle autocrat with drooping eyelids and immobile face, moving in unheeding majesty down the long lane of beseeching suppliants? Or, do we not rather see a foolish, charming boy, parading before his envious brothers an ill-fitting, parti-coloured jacket, stitched by a doting father with a hand that trembled in the last agitations of affection and the first approaches of senility?

1933   *The Table of Truth*

HENRY REED
Thomas Hardy

STOUTHEART ON THE SOUTHERN RAILWAY

What are you doing, oh high-souled lad,
  Writing a book about me?
And peering so closely at good and bad,
  That one thing you do not see:
A shadow which falls on your writing-pad;
It is not of a sort to make men glad.
  It were better should such unbe.

No: though you look up, but you do not chance
  To see in the railway-train,
Amid pale trackfarers with listless glance,
  One who enghosts him plain.
You throw him not even a look askance,
And your mind toils on, in a seeming trance,
  To unearth some hap or twain.

No: the wistful hand you do not mark,
  Laid weightless upon your sleeve;
To a phasmal breath you give no hark –
  To a disembodied heave,
That at memories wakened of bliss or cark
Goes sighing across the gritty dark
  In an iterate semi-breve.

THE SENSE OF HUMOUR

No : you don't see the one the night-time-brings
   To thuswise hover above
Your pages of quizzings and questionings
   Undertaken (say you) for love,
No : you don't see the shadow the lamp downflings.
But I've come to make sure there are just a few
    things
   You still are unwotful of.

Manuscript

LIONEL MILLARD
Elizabethan Prose

(FOR ADULTS ONLY)

... The other of the twain is an ancient crone, nurse to Juliet, forever harping on the amorous delights now beyond her save by proxy, who continuously disparages the blessed state of virginity in despite of Christ's holy Mother and the dazzling example of our Sovereign Lady: ... There is, moreover, an old lecher, father to Juliet, whose mammerings show how his youth was spent, misspent I would say, Master Kemp too, as a foolish follower, sounds with no abridged plummet all the depths of scurrility. And the very centre of this nastiness, the young Romeo himself, is shown at the outset as mistressed (albeit lightly enough), and is continually comforted in his concupiscence by a Papistical and prolixious friar. Nay more and to conclude, we were presented to the lovers hot from their (scarce can I term it so) nuptial bed.   *New Statesman* Competition
1934

STEPHEN POTTER
Script of a B.B.C. Regional Literary Feature, period 1940

ANNOUNCER: One hundred years ago this month, the memorial tablet to Thomas Cobbleigh, the Dartmoor poet, was erected at Worlby Chapel in Ipswich, town of his birth. From the East Coast Regional Wavelength, therefore, we present this evening THOMAS COBBLEIGH, POET. A PORTRAIT.

(*Seven bars of Waltz theme, Dohnányi's 'Variations on a Nursery Tune', quietly wells and fades behind:*)

NARRATOR: Back, now. Back to 1799 and its quiet streets, time of leisure. In the depths of the Devonshire country, and its quiet rills, a boy sits.

(*Rill effect.* ADP 99 *band* 3 – *Walthamstow effluent.*)

NARRATOR: Ostensibly he is guarding kine.

(*Cow effect.* B396 *band iv.*)

NARRATOR: But elbows on knees he is deep in a book.

(*fade-up*)

MRS COBBLEIGH (*distant*): Timmus! Timmus!

NARRATOR: But his mother, old Mrs Cobbleigh, approaches furiously.

MRS COBBLEIGH: Timmus! Timmus! Where be thy wits, rattle brain? Yon coo is almost into the bog –

(*Cow:* B396 *band v*)

MRS COBBLEIGH: – and half thy flock is turnty scattered.

THOMAS: I know, mother.

MRS COBBLEIGH: What is it you know, poring alone all day over the printed stuff? It's – it's not like other boys.

THOMAS: I know, mother . . . but old Mr Dollington says that 'Books ope doors where Begging fails'.

(*fade sharply*)

NARRATOR (*Brighter, clearer*): On, now, to 1815. It would surely take more than books to open the doors of (*bring out*) Holland House, seat of London's wealth and fashion.

(*Music:* Henry VIII *dances.* C.B.1029, *2nd blue mark on disk.*)

NARRATOR: Fame and fortune and beauty are present tonight. Eagerly they talk together.

(*Cross-fade music to social chatter,* GF 830028)

(*fade up*)

FOOTMAN (*Distant*): Lord Davenport . . . The Duke of Argyll. Mr Percy Bysshe Shelley.

(*mix in studio chatter*)

FIRST LADY (*Artificial – close to mike*): La, my dear, look. Shelley, the scribbler.

SECOND LADY (*Also artificial*): What, that renegade?

FIRST LADY: He.

FOOTMAN: Mr William Wordsworth ... Lord Byron.
(*Flash up and down, of Henry VIII*)

SECOND LADY: Wordsworth. His poem, *We are Seven*, is just out, they say.

FIRST LADY (*close to mike*): Look, my dear, Byron.

SFCOND LADY: How pale he looks ...

FIRST LADY: Byron! (*Very close*)

FOOTMAN: His Grace the Archbishop of York. Mr John Keats.

FIRST LADY: Look, Keats.

GENTLEMAN: }
SECOND LADY: } What Keats the scribbler?

GENTLEMAN: Keats is speaking now.

SECOND LADY: Yes, and somebody's speaking to him.

BEAU BRUMMEL (*Artificial*): You are John Keats.

KEATS (*Sincere*): You are Beau Brummel.

BRUMMEL: Would I had thy power of versing, Keats.

KEATS: And I thy wit, Brummel.

FOOTMAN: The Duke of Wellington. Mr Thomas Cobbleigh.

KEATS: Look – Cobbleigh!

FIRST LADY: Thomas Cobbleigh?

ALL: What, – that –
(*Music: bring broadly up Pomp and Circumstance 2*)

ANNOUNCER: And now we must leave the biography of Cobbleigh (written and produced by Stephen Pinker) for Harry Hasmussen and his Happy Hobbledehoys ...

1946   *How to Listen*, Stephen Potter and Joyce Grenfell

PETER USTINOV

(*on Stage Dialogue We Cannot Do Without*)

John, d'you think it's going to be all right ... about us, I mean?

*

O God, Mary, what a blind fool I've been all along.

*

But Clive, that's ... that's nothing short of blackmail!

Oh come, my dear, that's a very nasty word.

Oh Clive, don't you see – I'm trying to help you, but you won't let me.

*

You were always the lucky one, John. It's been like that as long as I can remember. It was you who was sent to St Paul's, while I ... what's the use of talking about it?

*

Mary, do you think you are being very fair to your mother? You know what she feels about lipstick and all this newfangled gallivanting and ... what d'ye call the stuff ... boogie-woogie and so on ...

*

I was in love with an artist once, Mary ... *before* I met your father ... in Paris ... we had the maddest time in the Artists' Balls in the Latin Quarter, dancing all through the night, ... life was one long glorious dream ... and yet, I'm glad I didn't marry Gaston ... I'm glad I came to live in Alperton.

1947   *The Author*

OSBERT LANCASTER

the Literary Guidebook (*in Leisurely Prose*) '*Drayneflete Revealed*'

POETS' CORNER

The second Earl, 'Sensibility Littlehampton' as he was known, at the time of the second rebuilding of Drayneflete Castle conceived the kindly idea of building a small Gothic Lodge at this corner of his estate for his friend and protégé, the poet Jeremy Tipple. It was the long residence of this celebrated bard in this villa which first gained for the cross-roads the appellation 'Poet's Corner', and it was here that he wrote his immortal *The Contemplative Shepherd*, a poem of some fifteen thousand lines of which we can, alas, only quote a small selection. The passage chosen is of particular topographical interest as the landscape described is today almost entirely covered by the municipal sewage farm.

Th' enamelled meadows that can scarce contain
The gentle windings of the limpid Drayne
Full oft have seen me, wandering at dawn
As birds awaken and the startled fawn
Leaps from her mossy bed with easy grace
On catching sight of my indulgent face.
Deep in some crystal pool th' enamoured trout
Frolics and wantons up a lichened spout
By which the stream, in many a sparkling rill,
Is made by art to turn a water-mill.
At last the sluggard Phoebus quits his bed
And bares the glory of his fiery head;
Now all the world assumes an aspect new
And Nature blushes 'neath the mantling dew.
E'en yonder mossy walls and em'rald sward
The home of Littlehampton's puissant lord,
The ancient fastness of a warrior race
Regards these marches with a kindlier face . . .

The Gothic Villa itself was now in the possession of Miss Amelia de Vere, the only child of the poet's married sister, Sophonisba, who had long kept house for her brother. Along with the house Miss Amelia had inherited much of her uncle's poetic gift, although at first this was only revealed to a small circle of intimate friends. After, however, the anonymous publication of her *Lines on the Late Massacre at Chios*, which sounded like a tocsin throughout Liberal Europe, her fame was assured. It is not, alas, possible, nor indeed is it probably necessary, to quote this celebrated work in full, but the two opening verses will serve to demonstrate both the fearless realism of the gentle poetess and her exceptional command of local colour, a command the more extraordinary in that she never, save for a brief visit to Tunbridge Wells, travelled more than ten miles from Drayneflete in all her life.

O hark to the groans of the wounded and dying,
Of the mother who casts a last lingering look
At her infant aloft, understandably crying,
Impaled on the spear of a Bashi Bazook.

O see where the vultures are patiently wheeling
As the scimitars flash and the yataghans thud

CASIMIR DE VERE-TIPPLE, ESQ. FROM A DRAWING BY JACQUES
EMILE BLANCHE. REPRODUCED BY KIND PERMISSION OF THE
TATE GALLERY.

On innocent victims, vainly appealing
To dreaded Janissaries lusting for blood.

*

On the death of Miss de Vere, Poet's Corner passed to her nephew, Mr Casimir de Vere-Tipple, in whom the poetic gift, so constant in this remarkable family, burnt, if not with renewed vigour, certainly with a 'hard gem-like flame'. His contributions appeared regularly in *The Yellow Book*, and were published in a slim volume by the Bodley Head under the title *Samphire and Sardonyx*. Unfortunately he did not long enjoy his property as he was forced, for private reasons, to live abroad from 1895 onwards and thenceforth resided on Capri in a charming villa where his great social gifts and exquisite hospitality will still be remembered by many visitors.

After the departure of Mr de Vere-Tipple the Poet's Corner was let on a long lease to a firm of monumental masons. A further great change in the appearance of the neighbourhood occurred when, shortly before the 1914 war, Messrs Pinks, the drapers, entirely rebuilt their premises and a confectioner's acquired the space between them and the Poet's Corner. The secluded quiet of this once shady nook was further interrupted by the substitution of trams for horsebuses at the turn of the century, and the subsequent increase in traffic due to the coming of the internal combustion engine.

However, the poetic tradition of the locality was not even yet extinct. On his death in 1929 Mr de Vere-Tipple left this valuable site to his favourite nephew, then at Oxford, Guillaume de Vere-Tipple, who had already made a name for himself by the publication of *Feux d'artifice* (Duckworth 1927), a collection of verse astonishing in its maturity, from which we quote a single poem, *Aeneas on the Saxophone*.

... Delenda est Carthago!
(ses beins de mer, ses pláges fleuries,
And Dido on her lilo à sa proie attachée)
And shall we stroll along the front
Chatting of this and that and listening to the bands?
The plumed and tufted sea responds
Obliquely to the trombone's call

    The lecherous seaweed's phallic fronds
    Gently postulate the Fall.
But between the pebble and the beach rises the doubt, ... Delenda
Between the seaside and the sea the summons, ... est
Between the *wagon* and the *lit* the implication, ... Carthago.

In the years between the wars the whole character of the district was still further altered. In 1930 Messrs Watlin acquired the *Duke of York*, which was at once rebuilt in a contemporary style which, although it at first struck those accustomed to the brassy vulgarity of the old 'pub' as strangely austere, was soon generally agreed to be both socially and aesthetically an immense improvement. Two years later another even more daring example of 'the Modern Movement', as it had come to be known, arose in the shape of the Odium Cinema. While some of the more old-fashioned residents might find fault with the functional directness of this great building, nothing but praise could be accorded to the modified Georgian style in which the new Council flats across the road were built at much the same date.

The coming of a new age, of which the buildings round Poet's Corner were a portent, found a reflection in the poet's verse. Guillaume de Vere-Tipple was socially conscious to a remarkable degree and had long entertained doubts as to the security of capitalist society, doubts which received striking confirmation when International Nickel, in which he had inherited a large holding, slumped to $11\frac{1}{2}$. Making a clean break with the past, his next volume of poetry, *the liftshaft* (Faber and Faber 1937) appeared above the signature Bill Tipple, and, as may be seen from the poem quoted below, this re-orientation is reflected in the contents:

crackup in barcelona

among the bleached skeletons of the olive-trees
stirs a bitter wind
and maxi my friend from the mariahilfer strasse
importunately questions a steely sky
his eyes are two holes made by a dirty finger
in the damp blotting paper of his face
the muscular tissues stretched tautly across the scaffolding of bone
are no longer responsive to the factory siren

and never again will the glandular secretions react
to the ragtime promptings of the palais-de-danse
while I am left balanced on capricorn
the knife-edged tropic between anxiety and regret
while the racing editions are sold at the gates of football grounds
and maxi lies on a bare catalan hillside
knocked off the tram by a fascist conductor
who misinterpreted a casual glance.

Today Poet's Corner is up for sale: its owner, Bill Tipple, who
on the outbreak of war had been a conscientious objector, but
who, on hearing the news of the invasion of Russia, experienced
a complete change of heart and immediately joined the Drayne-

flete section of the National Fire Service, is absent for long periods abroad in his capacity of organizing secretary of the World Congress of International Poets in Defence of Peace. The long Littlehampton connexion with the town is now a thing of the past; the great race of Ffidgets is extinct. But their spirit lives on and their successors on the Borough Council are determined that the Drayneflete tradition shall at all costs be maintained. But, whatever the future may hold in store, let the visitor reflect as he goes round the Museum, as he inspects the magnificent collection of Ffidget portraits in the Art Gallery (bequeathed to the town in 1948 by the late Miss Dracula Parsley-ffidget), as he wanders in the old-world Market Place, as he paces the banks of the 'limpid Drayne', let him reflect on the men and women who through the ages have all played their part in making Drayneflete what it is today, and see to it that we, their heirs, shall prove ourselves worthy of so goodly a heritage.

1949   *Drayneflete Revisited*

CHAPTER 4

The Humour of Satire

No department of the Comic is less exclusively English than
Satire. It would be out of place in this book to make excerpts
from the hard words of Jonson and Dryden, Swift and
Pope, or of the great, grim and not always totally un-
humorous *Piers Plowman*. But except in Puritan and anti-
Puritan times and the Regency period, our satire has usually
been tinged with a national flavour of the humane – or so it
seems to me when I read these few extracts of my choice.

ALEXANDER POPE
Chloe

'Yet Chloe sure was form'd without a spot' –
Nature in her then err'd not, but forgot.
'With ev'ry pleasing, ev'ry prudent part,
Say, what can Chloe want?' – She wants a Heart.
She speaks, behaves, and acts just as she ought;
But never, never, reach'd one gen'rous Thought.
Virtue she finds too painful an endeavour,
Content to dwell in Decencies for ever.
So very reasonable, so unmov'd,
As never yet to love, or to be lov'd.
She, while her Lover pants upon her breast,
Can mark the figures on an Indian chest;
And when she sees her Friend in deep despair,
Observes how much a Chintz exceeds Mohair.
Forbid it Heav'n, a Favour or a Debt
She e'er should cancel – but she may forget.
Safe is your Secret still in Chloe's ear;
But none of Chloe's shall you ever hear.
Of all her Dears she never slander'd one,
But cares not if a thousand are undone.

Would Chloe know if you're alive or dead?
She bids her Footman put it in her head.
Chloe is prudent – Would you too be wise?
Then never break you heart when Chloe dies.

1735   *Moral Essays*

CHARLES LAMB
on Stage Morality

A Puritanical obtuseness of sentiment, a stupid infantile goodness, is creeping among us, instead of the vigorous passions, and
virtues clad in flesh and blood, with which the old dramatists
present us. Those noble and liberal casuists could discern in the
differences, the quarrels, the animosities of men, a beauty and
truth of moral feeling no less than in the everlastingly inculcated
duties of forgiveness and atonement. With us, all is hypocritical
meekness. A reconciliation-scene, be the occasion never so
absurd, never fails of applause. Our audiences come to the theatre
to be complimented on their goodness.

1808   *Specimens of English Dramatic Poets*

(Lamb suggests an emendation to a passage in Coleridge's
'Christabel')

> Sir Leoline the Baron Rich
> Hath a toothless mastiff bitch;

All the printed versions except 1834 print the following Tenny-
sonian variant to this line (made in response to the wishes of an
'honoured friend'):

> Hath a toothless mastiff which

A first tentative alteration was:

> Sir Leoline the Baron bold
> Hath a toothless mastiff old;

Charles Lamb suggested:

> Sir Leoline, the baron round
> Hath a toothless mastiff hound.

The Nonesuch Coleridge

BYRON

(*Sweetness*)

'Tis sweet to hear the watch-dog's honest bark
   Bay deep-mouth'd welcome as we draw near home;
'Tis sweet to know there is an eye will mark
   Our coming, and look brighter when we come;
'Tis sweet to be awaken'd by the lark,
   Or lull'd by falling waters; sweet the hum
Of bees, the voice of girls, the song of birds,
The lisp of children, and their earliest words.

Sweet is the vintage when the showering grapes
   In Bacchanal profusion reel to earth,
Purple and gushing; sweet are our escapes
   From civic revelry to rural mirth;
Sweet to the miser are his glittering heaps,
   Sweet to the father is his first-born's birth,
Sweet is revenge – especially to women,
Pillage to soldiers, prize-money to seamen.

Sweet is a legacy, and passing sweet
   The unexpected death of some old lady
Or gentleman of seventy years complete,
   Who've made 'us youth' wait too – too long already
For an estate, or cash, or country seat,
   Still breaking, but with stamina so steady
That all the Israelites are fit to mob its
Next owner for their double-damn'd post-obits.

'Tis sweet to win, no matter how, one's laurels,
   By blood or ink; 'tis sweet to put an end
To strife; 'tis sometimes sweet to have our quarrels,
   Particularly with a tiresome friend:
Sweet is old wine in bottles, ale in barrels;
   Dear is the helpless creature we defend
Against the world; and dear the schoolboy spot
We ne'er forget, though there we are forgot.

But sweeter still than this, than these, than all,
  Is first and passionate love – it stands alone,
Like Adam's recollection of his fall;
  The tree of knowledge has been pluck'd – all's known –
And life yields nothing further to recall
  Worthy of this ambrosial sin, so shown,
No doubt in fable, as the unforgiven
Fire which Prometheus filch'd for us from heaven.

(*Age of Inventions*)

This is the patent age of new inventions
  For killing bodies, and for saving souls,
All propagated with the best intentions;
  Sir Humphrey Davy's lantern, by which coals
Are safely mined for in the mode he mentions,
  Tombuctoo travels, voyages to the Poles,
Are ways to benefit mankind, as true,
Perhaps, as shooting them at Waterloo.

1819   *Don Juan*

CHARLES DICKENS

*(A Letter from Fanny Squeers, Nicholas Nickleby having
thrashed her Father)*

Dotheboys Hall,
Thursday Morning.

SIR, My pa requests me to write to you, the doctors considering
it doubtful whether he will ever recuvver the use of his legs which
prevents his holding a pen.

We are in a state of mind beyond everything, and my pa is one
mask of brooses both blue and green likewise two forms are
steepled in his Goar. We were kimpelled to have him carried
down into the kitchen where he now lays. You will judge from
this that he has been brought very low.

When your nevew that you recommended for a teacher had
done this to my pa and jumped upon his body with his feet and
also langwedge which I will not pollewt my pen with describing,
he assaulted my ma with dreadful violence, dashed her to the

147

earth, and drove her back comb several inches into her head. A very little more and it must have entered her skull. We have a medical certifiket that if it had, the tortershell would have affected the brain.

Me and my brother were then the victims of his feury since which we have suffered very much which leads us to the arrowing belief that we have received some injury in our insides especially as no marks of violence are visible externally. I am screaming out loud all the time I write and so is my brother which takes off my attention rather and I hope will excuse mistakes.

The monster having sasiated his thirst for blood ran away, taking with him a boy of desperate caracter that he had excited to rebellyon, and a garnet ring belonging to my ma, and not having been apprehended by the constables is supposed to have been took up by some stage-coach. My pa begs that if he comes to you the ring may be returned, and that you will let the thief and assassin go, as if we prosecuted him he would only be transported, and if he is let go he is sure to be hung before long which will save us trouble and be much more satisfactory. Hoping to hear from you when convenient

I remain
Yours and cetrer
Fanny Squeers.

'P.S. – I pity his ignorance and despise him.'

1838   *Nicholas Nickleby*

W. R. SICKERT
(*The Royal Academician*)

Though Millais called George Moore and me 'insolent disturbers' for writing to *The Times* to say that we didn't see why the nation should pay for a site on which to house Mr Tate's bad pictures, I can testify that Holman Hunt was right when he said that Millais had the face of an angel – an angel, perhaps, with whom one would not care to discuss one's right of re-entry into Paradise.

I have sometimes seen him sitting with a friend on the bench which, I hope, still stands by the Kensington entrance of the Gardens facing up the Broad Walk. It was a touching and majestical presence, and we should do wrong to offer to its shade a show of violence. He was an angelic and blustering personification of John Bull, what the Germans call *der Stock-Englander*. He answered to the *stage* idea of the superior officer, although the superior officer is characterized rather by the gentleness, the tact and the scrupulous sympathy which command by persuasion. Millais was a man who – there is no English equivalent, my dear Moore – *ne se doutait de rien.*

There was one person whose name seems to have sent a shiver down the spine of Millais. Where Vergil said '*Guarda e passa*' to Dante, where Ingres said to his students, in passing by some paintings by Delacroix, '*Saluez, mais ne regardez pas,*' Millais said to Archie Wortley, in front of Whistler's pictures at the Grosvenor, 'It's damned clever; it's a damned sight too clever!' 'And,' said Archie, 'he dragged me on.' To Millais, Frith, and many others, Whistler was a sort of Gorgon's head, and in their speeches and writings he was also the head of Charles the First. But they never mentioned him by name. They always circumlocuted him. That terrible straight and ineluctable conscience of Whistler's was intolerable to them. He made them feel like Saul when he woke in the cave of En-gedi.

Millais did not know how to spell ichthyosaurus, and he believed that painting was a 'profession', and spoke of 'throwing it up' when a picture of his remained unsold for a few weeks. He cried out in his anguish that only after his death would he be appreciated! We have it on the authority of his son and biographer that Millais had 'long held' that a baronetcy was 'an encouragement to the pursuit of Art in its highest and noblest form'. Velasquez he called 'my favourite Velasquez'. He never went to Spain, but he paid his favourite the compliment of calling one of his own paintings *Souvenir of Velasquez*, for all the world to see. His unique literary effort was an article on 'Time as the Great Old Master'. The article opened: 'I am strongly of opinion'.

A lady I had the honour of knowing used to say, 'When I say "religion" I mean of course, "Christianity", and when I say "Christianity" I mean, of course, the Church of England'. When Millais said 'Art', he meant British Art. And when he said 'British Art', he meant the painting of John Everett Millais. And we loved him so greatly that nobody so much as squeaked. Like his friend Henry Irving, Millais was always called 'the head of the profession', whatever that may mean. Like Sir Henry, he believed that the 'status of Art', whatever that may mean, was raised by bestowal, in geometrical progression, of knighthood, baronetcy, or even peerage, if a bachelor, on the mysterious entity 'the head of the profession'. They neither of them differed from the rest of us in believing devoutly that 'the head of the profession' was *bibi*, as the French translate 'number one'. They differed only in the frankness with which they proclaimed their belief, and the sense of economy that enabled them to offer it as a good and sufficient substitute for discourses on art. Nor did anybody squeak – except my mother's cook, Elizabeth, who poured cold water on the Irving delirium of the Slade students of 1877 by the reminder: 'After all, Irving's only *a man* when all's said and done.' Which, I believe, came as a shock to Margery May, and certainly to me.

But a mere century changes nothing. I sat not long ago at a private dinner next to, perhaps, the only peer who is not a high-brow. Always, even in Society, the pedagogue, I was murmuring eloquently of Millet. I saw MacEvoy giggling and egging me on discreetly. 'I still have,' said the peer, 'a splendid copy of *Bubbles*.' (It has since been explained to me that very elementary classes in French are now taught to pronounce the double 'l' in Millet as a *y*, on the analogy of Caillaux. Just as 'Degas' is now, beyond remedy, pronounced in England by some peers, all professors of Art, neo-curators, and even some picture dealers, as if the name were Des Gas, like Desboutin, Desmarolles, Desanges, etc., instead of like De La Calprenede, De Musset, De Neuville, De Ste Croix, etc. Degas ran the two syllables of his name together on his canvases because he did not wish to emphasize the particle in his trade signature, just as Henry Irving did not print the 'Sir' in his programmes. ('How different from us!').)

The quite young men among us today are rather prone to

touch what Millais used to call 'devotional subjects' in a guying spirit without, as yet, much result in wit – just as the mention of Queen Victoria automatically gets a forced laugh in a flagging scene, or as the Albert Memorial is jeered at by a generation that is certainly ignorant of the fact that the Prince Consort initiated the piece of legislation known as the Truck Act. But the later 'devotional' pictures of Millais are beyond all believable bounds of flippant ineptitude, coming, as they do, from a grown-up member of a State from whose Head, apex also of the Church, he was content to accept honours. Donovan, the phrenologist, after having read the bumps of Millais, who was incognito, pronounced him utterly deficient in imagination. After a century in which to consider the verdict, the world is probably now of the opinion of Donovan, and is no longer amused. When we look at his *Jephthah's Daughter* and his *Martyrdom of St Stephen* it is difficult to believe that he can have read the stories in the Authorized Version. He is better in *The Enemy Sowing Tares*, because his brush was winged by indignation with the 'wicked clique' in the Academy who did not like his pictures. It would be interesting to know who was the handsome old Jewish R.A. (was it Solomon Hart?) whose alleged resemblance to the portrait of Satan caused the Hanging Committee to hover on the verge of rejection in 1865 . . .

Millais' practice, like that of many of his contemporaries, was vitiated by the accursed theory of painting his pictures from nature. It led him, as it has led thousands at home and abroad, as far from nature as possible. The masters to whom we all pay lip-service did not produce in this manner. The *St Helena* of the *Vision* is asleep, and you cannot paint a life-sized figure in the time of a woman's slumber. The art of oil-painting in its excellence demands execution in several stages with, in northern climates, long intervals for drying. Cézanne has been of the greatest utility by reducing the painting from nature method to the crowning absurd in his men playing cards. A laborious copy of four models sitting for hours, day after day, for weeks, pretending to play cards is the cumulation of lifelessness and ennui, the priceless classic of how not to do it. It should hang in the National Gallery. Hogarth's *Modern Midnight Conversation* was not done from eleven men simultaneously drunk in the studio from 10 a.m. to 4 p.m., with an interval for luncheon. We have Leighton's admirable example in our own lifetime. Millais had the benefit of Leech's friendship, but his example taught him nothing, no more than did that of Keene. If we would only all go to school to the black-and-white men! Painting and drawing were, for such as he and Frith, in watertight compartments. Millais summed up the spirit of the *Derby Day* in a drawing (1853) entitled *The Race Meeting*. Weeping and bitterly humiliated women, drunken whiskered Champagne Charlie, and all, in the barouche, compared with which Frith's *Derby Day* is a population entirely consisting of a wilderness of recurring and quite nice Eugene Wrayburns. If Millais had simply facsimiled in paint his ripping drawing of *The Romans leaving Britain*, we should have had at least a startling melodrama of history instead of the dullest, dreariest, and grosvenorest of his duller work. For all men kill the things they love when they superimpose on a perfect and finished design a palimpsest of oil-paint done from imported irrelevant models in a box 40 feet by 20 feet, with a north light in Palace Gate or Fitzroy Street.

'*Aimer ce que jamais on ne verra deux fois*' is the painter's golden rule.

1929   *Fortnightly Review*

BERNARD SHAW
(*Don Juan in Hell*)

DON JUAN (*to the Devil*): Your friends are all the dullest dogs I know. They are not beautiful: they are only decorated. They are not clean: they are only shaved and starched. They are not dignified: they are only fashionably dressed. They are not educated: they are only college passmen. They are not religious: they are only pewrenters. They are not moral: they are only conventional. They are not virtuous: they are only cowardly. They are not even vicious: they are only 'frail'. They are not artistic: they are only lascivious. They are not prosperous: they are only rich. They are not loyal, they are only servile; not dutiful, only sheepish; not public spirited, only patriotic; not courageous, only quarrelsome; not determined, only obstinate; not masterful, only domineering; not self-controlled, only obtuse; not self-respecting, only vain; not kind, only sentimental; not social, only gregarious; not considerate, only polite; not intelligent, only opinionated; not progressive, only factious; not imaginative, only superstitious; not just, only vindictive; not generous, only propitiatory; not disciplined, only cowed; and not truthful at all – liars every one of them, to the very backbone of their souls.

1901–3   *Man and Superman*

D. H. LAWRENCE
Don'ts

Fight your little fight, my boy
   fight and be a man.
   Don't be a good little, good little boy
   being as good as you can
   and agreeing with all the mealy-mouthed, mealy-mouthed
   truths that the sly trot out
   to protect themselves and their greedy-mouthed, greedy-
                              mouthed
   cowardice, every old lout.

Don't live up to the dear little girl who costs
   you your manhood, and makes you pay.
   Nor the dear old mater who so proudly boasts
   that you'll make your way.

Don't earn golden opinions, opinions golden,
   or at least worth Treasury notes,
   from all sorts of men; don't be beholden
   to the herd inside the pen.

Don't long to have dear little, dear little boys
   whom you'll have to educate
   to earn their living; nor yet girls, sweet joys
   who will find it so hard to mate.

Nor a dear little home, with its cost, its cost
   that you have to pay,

earning your living while your life is lost
and dull death comes in a day.

Don't be sucked in by the su-superior,
  don't swallow the culture bait,
  don't drink, don't drink and get beerier and beerier,
  do learn to discriminate.

Do hold yourself together, and fight
  with a hit-hit here and a hit-hit there,
  and a comfortable feeling at night
  that you've let in a little air.

A little fresh air in the money sty,
  knocked a little hole in the holy prison,
  done your little bit, made your own little try
  that the risen Christ should *be* risen.

Wellsian Futures

When men are made in bottles
and emerge as squeaky globules with no bodies to speak of,
and therefore nothing to have feelings with,

they will still squeak intensely about their feelings
and be prepared to kill you if you say they've got none.

Talk

I wish people, when you sit near them
wouldn't think it necessary to make conversation
and send thin draughts of words
blowing down your neck and your ears
and giving you a cold in your inside.

When I Read Shakespeare

When I read Shakespeare I am struck with wonder
that such trivial people should muse and thunder
in such lovely language.

Lear, the old buffer, you wonder his daughters
didn't treat him rougher,
the old chough, the old chuffer!

And Hamlet, how boring, how boring to live with,
so mean and self-conscious, blowing and snoring
his wonderful speeches, full of other folk's whoring!

And Macbeth and his Lady, who should have been choring,
such suburban ambition, so messily goring
old Duncan with daggers!

How boring, how small Shakespeare's people are!
Yet the language so lovely! like the dyes from gas-tar.

1929 *Pansies*

HERBERT FARJEON
Liberty Hall

I've started a school called Liberty Hall
   Upon the latest system;
We take them big, we take them small,
   And try not to mould or twist 'em;
Repression is the great pitfall,
   Of this we live in terror,
So we do our best to do nothing at all
   Lest we should commit some error.

We don't have lessons, we don't have sports,
We don't have rules of any sorts,
And the boys and the girls write their own reports
   In Liberty Hall, the free school;
We don't encourage, we don't suppress,
We don't say No, we don't say Yes,
And when we want, we just undress
   In Liberty Hall, the free school.
We all abhor a dictator,
   And sex is quite unshrouded,
We never, never lock the bathroom door,
   Last night it was simply crowded –
We do just what we think is nice,
The girls play poker, the boys play dice,
Last week I let them cane me twice
   In Liberty Hall, the free school. ...

1936 *Spread It Abroad*

VIRGINIA GRAHAM

A Lullaby in Poor Taste
(To be sung in Westminister)

Hushabye baby, a hush to your crying,
See how the gay little flags are a-flying,

Sleep without fear in your blanket of fleece,
Lullaby Java, rockaway Greece,

Doze in your blue-ribboned nest of inertia,
Pop go the Poles and pat-a-cake Persia.

Run to your dreams where the little lambs play,
Mr Vishinsky has come for the day,

And nothing can harm you O infant most blest,
Ride a cock Palestine, peep-bo Trieste.

Lully my darling, till atom bombs fall,
When up will go baby and mummy and all.

1946   *Consider the Years*

BERTRAND RUSSELL

(God and Bishop Berkeley)

George Berkeley (1685–1753) is important in philosophy through his denial of the existence of matter – a denial which he supported by a number of ingenious arguments. He maintained that material objects only exist through being perceived. To the objection that, in that case, a tree, for instance, would cease to exist if no one was looking at it, he replied that God always perceives everything; if there were no God, what we take to be material objects would have a jerky life, suddenly leaping into being when we look at them; but as it is, owing to God's perceptions, trees and rocks and stones have an existence as continuous as commonsense supposes. This is, in his opinion, a weighty argument for the existence of God.

1946   *A History of Western Philosophy*

HENRY REED
Lessons of the War

I. NAMING OF PARTS

Today we have naming of parts. Yesterday,
We had daily cleaning. And tomorrow morning,
We shall have what to do after firing. But today,
Today we have naming of parts. Japonica
Glistens like coral in all of the neighbouring gardens,
 And today we have naming of parts.

This is the lower sling swivel. And this
Is the upper sling swivel, whose use you will see,
When you are given your slings. And this is the piling swivel,
Which in your case you have not got. The branches
Hold in the gardens their silent, eloquent gestures,
 Which in our case we have not got.

This is the safety catch, which is always released
With an easy flick of the thumb. And please do not let me
See anyone using his finger. You can do it quite easy
If you have any strength in your thumb. The blossoms
Are fragile and motionless, never letting anyone see
 Any of them using their finger.

And this you can see is the bolt. The purpose of this
Is to open the breech, as you see. We can slide it
Rapidly backwards and forwards: we call this
Easing the spring. And rapidly backwards and forwards
The early bees are assaulting and fumbling the flowers:
 They call it easing the Spring.

They call it easing the Spring: it is perfectly easy
If you have any strength in your thumb: like the bolt,
And the breech, and the cocking-piece, and the point of
          balance,
Which in our case we have not got; and the almond-blossom
Silent in all of the gardens and the bees going backwards and
          forwards,
 For today we having naming of parts.

II. JUDGING DISTANCES

Not only how far away, but the way that you say it
Is very important. Perhaps you may never get
The knack of judging a distance, but at least you know
How to report on a landscape: the central sector,
The right of arc and that, which we had last Tuesday,
   And at least you know

That maps are of time, not place, so far as the army
Happens to be concerned – the reason being,
Is one which need not delay us. Again, you know
There are three kinds of tree, three only, the fir and the poplar,
And those which have bushy tops to; and lastly
   That things only seem to be things.

A barn is not called a barn, to put it more plainly,
Or a field in the distance, where sheep may be safely grazing.
You must never be over-sure. You must say, when reporting:
At five o'clock in the central sector is a dozen
Of what appear to be animals; whatever you do,
   Don't call the bleeders *sheep*.

I am sure that's quite clear; and suppose, for the sake of example,
The one at the end, asleep, endeavours to tell us
What he sees over there to the west, and how far away,
After first having come to attention. There to the west,
On the fields of summer the sun and the shadows bestow
   Vestments of purple and gold.

The still white dwellings are like a mirage in the heat,
And under the swaying elms a man and a woman
Lie gently together. Which is, perhaps, only to say
That there is a row of houses to the left of arc,
And that under some poplars a pair

                     of what appear to be humans
   Appear to be loving.

Well that, for an answer, is what we might rightly call
Moderately satisfactory only, the reason being,
Is that two things have been omitted, and those are important.

The human beings, now: in what direction are they,
And how far away, would you say? And do not forget
   There may be dead ground in between.

There may be dead ground in between; and I may not have got
The knack of judging a distance; I will only venture
A guess that perhaps between me and the apparent lovers,
(Who, incidentally, appear by now to have finished,)
At seven o'clock from the houses, is roughly a distance
   Of about one year and a half.

1946   *A Map of Verona*

J. B. PRIESTLEY

(*Chairmanship*)

Quietly malicious chairmanship. There is no sound excuse for
this. It is deeply anti-social, and a sudden excess of it would tear
great holes in our communal life. But a man can be asked once
too often to act as chairman, and to such a man, despairing of
his weakness and feeling a thousand miles from any delight, I
can suggest a few devices. In introducing one or two of the chief
speakers, grossly overpraise them but put no warmth into your
voice, only a metallic flavour of irony. If you know what a
speaker's main point is to be, then make it neatly in presenting
him to the audience. During some tremendous peroration, either
begin whispering and passing notes to other speakers or give the
appearance of falling asleep in spite of much effort to keep
awake. If the funny man takes possession of the meeting and
brings out the old jokes, either look melancholy or raise your
eyebrows as high as they will go. Announce the fellow with the
weak delivery in your loudest and clearest tones. For any timid
speaker, officiously clear a space bang in the middle and offer
him water, paper, pencil, a watch, anything. With noisy cheeky
chaps on their feet, bustle about the platform, and if necessary
give a mysterious little note to some member of the audience.

   If a man insists upon speaking from the floor of the hall, ask
him for his name, pretend to be rather deaf, and then finally
announce his name with a marked air of surprise. After that you
can have some trouble with a cigarette lighter and then take it

to pieces. When they all go on and on, make no further pretence of paying any attention and settle down to drawing outrageous caricatures of the others on the platform, and then at last ask some man you particularly dislike to take over the chair, and stalk out, being careful to leave all your papers behind. And if all this fails to bring you any delight, it should at least help to protect you against further bouts of chairmanship.

1949   *Delight*

CHAPTER 5

The Humour of Situation

A brief section because this kind of humour is no more exclusively English than is Satire. Except by means of the disagreeable vehicle of the funny story, also, it is difficult to illustrate in a brief quotation. The scene from *Evan Harrington* in my first quotation, for instance, depends for its deeply comic effect on our knowledge of the tireless dissimulations of the Countess which precede it.

GEORGE MEREDITH
(*Mr Goren Brings Bad News*)

(*Evan's sister, the Countess, is determined that the fact that their Father was a tailor shall never be revealed.*)

Evan advanced and bowed stiffly.

Mr Goren held out his hand. 'You don't remember me, young man? I cut your first suit for you when you were breeched, though! Yes – ah! Your poor father wouldn't put his hand to it. Goren!'

Embarrassed, and not quite alive to the chapter of facts this name should have opened to him, Evan bowed again.

'Goren!' continued the possessor of the name. He had a cracked voice, that when he spoke a word of two syllables, commenced with a lugubrious crow, and ended in what one might have taken for a curious question.

'It is a bad business brings me, young man. I'm not the best messenger for such tidings. It's a black suit, young man! It's your father!'

The diplomatist and his lady gradually edged back: but Rose remained beside the Countess, who breathed quick, and seemed to have lost her self-command.

Thinking he was apprehended, Mr Goren said: 'I'm going down tonight to take care of the shop. He's to be buried in his

161

old uniform. You had better come with me by the nightcoach, if you would see the last of him, young man.'

Breaking an odd pause that had fallen, the Countess cried aloud, suddenly:

'In his uniform!'

Mr Goren felt his arm seized and his legs hurrying him some paces into isolation. 'Thanks! thanks!' was murmured in his ear. 'Not a word more. Evan cannot bear it. Oh! you are good to have come, and we are grateful. My father! My father!'

She had to tighten her hand and wrist against her bosom to keep herself up. She had to reckon in a glance how much Rose had heard, or divined. She had to mark whether the Count had understood a syllable. She had to whisper to Evan to hasten away with the horrible man. She had to enliven his stunned senses, and calm her own. And with mournful images of her father in her brain, the female Spartan had to turn to Rose, and speculate on the girl's reflective brows, while she said, as over a distant relative, sadly, but without distraction: 'A death in the family!' and preserved herself from weeping her heart out, that none might guess the thing who did not positively know it.

Evan touched the hand of Rose without meeting her eyes. He was soon cast off in Mr Goren's boat. Then the Countess murmured final adieux; twilight under her lids, but yet a smile, stately, affectionate, almost genial. Rose, her sweet Rose, she must kiss. She could have slapped Rose for appearing so reserved and cold. She hugged Rose, as to hug oblivion of the last few minutes into her. The girl leant her cheek, and bore the embrace, looking on her with a kind of wonder.

Only when alone with the Count, in the brewer's carriage awaiting her on shore, did the lady give a natural course to her grief; well knowing that her Silva would attribute it to the darkness of their common exile. She wept: but in the excess of her misery, two words of strangely opposite signification, pronounced by Mr Goren; two words that were at once poison and antidote, sang in her brain; two words that painted her dead father from head to foot, his nature and his fortune: these were the Shop, and the Uniform.

Oh! what would she not have given to have seen and bestowed on her beloved father one last kiss! Oh! how she hoped that her inspired echo of Uniform, on board the Jocasta, had drowned the memory, eclipsed the meaning, of that fatal utterance of Shop!

1861   *Evan Harrington*

ANTHONY TROLLOPE*
(*Agonies of Barchester*)

'Do you like Barchester, on the whole?' asked Bertie.

The bishop, looking dignified, said he did like Barchester.

'You've not been here very long, I believe,' said Bertie.

'No – not long,' said the bishop, and tried again to make his way between the back of the sofa and a heavy rector, who was staring over it at the grimaces of the signora.

'You weren't a bishop, before, were you?'

Dr Proudie explained that this was the first diocese he had held.

'Ah – I thought so,' said Bertie; 'but you are changed about sometimes, a'nt you?'

'Translations are occasionally made,' said Dr Proudie; 'but not so frequently as in former days.'

'They've cut them all down to pretty nearly the same figure, haven't they?' said Bertie.

To this the bishop could not bring himself to make any answer, but again attempted to move the rector.

'But the work, I suppose, is different?' continued Bertie. 'Is there much to do here, at Barchester?' This was said exactly in the tone that a young Admiralty clerk might use in asking the same question of a brother acolyte at the Treasury.

'The work of a Bishop of the Church of England,' said Dr Proudie, with considerable dignity, 'is not easy. The responsibility which he has to bear is very great indeed.'

'Is it?' said Bertie, opening wide his wonderful blue eyes. 'Well, I never was afraid of responsibility. I once had thoughts of being a bishop myself.'

*This admirable passage was the choice of Mr Priestley in his *English Humour*.

'Had thoughts of being a bishop!' said Dr Proudie, much amazed.

'That is, a parson – a parson first, you know, and a bishop afterwards. If I had once begun, I'd have stuck to it. But, on the whole, I like the Church of Rome the best.'

*

The bishop could not discuss the point, so he remained silent.

'Now, there's my father,' continued Bertie; 'he hasn't stuck to it. I fancy he didn't like saying the same thing over so often. By the bye, Bishop, have you seen my father?'

The bishop was more amazed than ever. Had he seen his father? 'No,' he replied; 'he had not yet had the pleasure: he hoped he might'; and, as he said so, he resolved to bear heavy on that fat, immovable rector, if ever he had the power of doing so.

'He's in the room somewhere,' said Bertie, 'and he'll turn up soon. By the bye, do you know much about the Jews?'

At last the bishop saw a way out. 'I beg your pardon,' said he; 'but I'm forced to go round the room.'

'Well, I believe I'll follow in your wake,' said Bertie.

1857   *Barchester Towers*

HAROLD NICOLSON
(*The Right People in the Wrong Places*, 1885)

His appointment to Tehran, which ended in triumphant success, began with difficulties and dismay. He had been warned that it would be madness to take his two babies to Persia during the summer months. He disregarded this advice. Accompanied by an English nurse, they travelled via Constantinople and Trebizond to Batoum. The nurse and children nearly died of sea-sickness. On reaching Batoum Arthur Nicolson and his wife sat upon the beach doing accounts: they came to the conclusion that they were too poor to continue in diplomacy and must exchange at once into the Consular Service. From Batoum they proceeded in the August heat to Tiflis and Baku. They crossed the Caspian: the mountains of Persia were hidden in the steam which rose from the rice-fields. They travelled up from Resht by caravan, moving by night only and resting in muddied caravanserais by day. The women and children were carried in litters slung over the backs of mules – a wooden coffin on each side of the mule in which the traveller lay on cushions. On the third day the English nurse could stand it no longer. Looking over the edge of her litter she had seen, a hundred feet below her, the seething yellow waters of the sefid Rud. She scrambled out of her coffin and asked to be taken home at once to Littlehampton. Nicolson forced her back into the litter with threats of violence. She remained angry for over three years.

1930   *Lord Carnock*

JOHN FOTHERGILL
Wit Antisociable

A witty young man is Jock Weir, son of the engineer peer. He has a spontaneous joy in talking rot that makes it jolly to follow and join in, not that of Reggie Turner, Robbie Ross, and Oscar Wilde, which forbade active collaboration. Oscar Wilde told me that old Sir Somebody was the only man he allowed to talk at his own table. Reggie Turner's wit is so outlandish that one feels desolate after it, much as one does after a pun. When I was 19 and straight from our Lake District fastness, finding myself, shy and tender, in the thick of that witty society at a big dinner-party, Ross's sister, Miss Ethel Jones, took pity on me and talked to me about my home. 'We live at Grasmere,' I told her, and seeing a chance to get in a literary touch, added 'quite near Wordsworth's grave,' but unhappily a silence had just dropped upon the party and Reggie Turner called out from the other end, 'and don't you find it very unhealthy?'

Absinthe and Oscar

At Berneval Oscar Wilde told me – all in his great heavy drawl – of the three stages of Absinthe drinking. 'The first stage is like ordinary drinking, the second when you begin to see munstrous and cruel things, but if you can persevere you will enter in upon the third stage where you see things that you *want* to see, wonderful and curious things. One night I was left sitting, drinking alone, and very late in the Café Royal, and I had just got into this third stage when a waiter came in with a green apron and began to pile the chairs on the tables. "Time to go, sir," he called out to me. Then he brought in a watering-can and began to water the floor. "Time's up, sir. I'm afraid you must go now, sir." – "Waiter, are you watering the flowers?" I asked, but he didn't answer. "What are your favourite flowers, waiter?" I asked again. "Now, sir, I must really ask you to go now, time's up," he said firmly. "I'm sure that tulips are your favourite flowers," I said, and as I got up and passed out into the street I felt – the – heavy – tulip – heads – brushing against my shins.' One day Oscar told us that he had dreamt that he had sat down to dinner with twelve dead men. 'My dear Oscar,' said Robbie Ross, 'I'm sure you were the life and soul of the party.' And when I think of it, with Oscar at the table we were always as good as those dead men ourselves.

*

... When someone asked 'Are there any trains to London on Sunday from this sleepy hole?'

'Yes, indeed,' said Marshall proudly, 'there are two, one at 3 and the other at 3.3.'

*

I had a brindled whippet who had several noises, one of which was a shrill whistle, another was the word 'ham', perfect with no dropping of the aitch. I could generally get from her the kind of noise I wanted. One day two Americans were staying with us, and at breakfast Zoe was at my side. Choosing the moment and the voice, I said to her, 'Zoe, will you have eggs or ham?' 'Ham,' she replied quickly. And so the story of Balaam's ass may be true, though till now I have thought that Balaam, whilst beating the animal, and on a jolting road after a big dish of beans, may have failed precisely to localize the sound, or that some scribe had spelt wrongly the ass that spake.

I came into breakfast another day and, with his back to me at this end of the table, sat Marshall looking down at Zoe. He seemed to be singing. Yes. 'What – er' he sang on C, 'What – er – now go on, Zoe.' 'What-er' he still sang, when Zoe suddenly broke in with her whistle and Marshall, in full-throated

ease, joined in the frightful duet together with 'What-er friend
we have in Jesus' ... He said he was writing a book called, 'Our
dumb friends, how to kill, skin, and stuff them.' ...

1949 (collected edn)   *My Three Inns*

JAMES AGATE
(*The BBC and the Concert Grand*)

Sunday, 15 March. Eckersley told us how after the concert hall at
Broadcasting House was built, there was doubt whether the door
would admit a concert grand. 'Try it,' said somebody. But the
musical director objected on the ground that if his beautiful
Bechstein got stuck it would be damaged. So they instructed the
carpenter to take the measurements and make an exact replica
in ply-wood. This was done, and they then found that they
couldn't get the model out of the carpenter's shop.

1942   *Ego 5*

TOM DRIBERG
(*Margaret Rawlings and the Buchmanites*)

Actress Margaret Rawlings and I were in a minority yesterday.
We were two unhypnotized people at a lunch of two thousand
Buchmanites. Luckily, we sat together, and were able to give
each other moral support. When I say moral I mean moral.

She was the guest of honour. There's an odd story behind that.
Organizers of lunch cast about for a guest of honour; said, in
their simple way, We'll get hold of some actress, she'll be decorative, she'll like the publicity. So they got in touch with an agency.
Miss Rawlings was approached. Would she be guest of honour,
they said, at a Literary Luncheon at which G. B. Shaw was going
to speak? She thought it a great honour, said yes.

Only after she had accepted did she discover what the lunch
was about, did they discover that she was no ordinary actress
but, unfortunately for them, an intelligent woman with strong
views of her own. She said that she would come to the lunch
only if they let her say what she really thought; that if they
wanted her to stay away they must – as her name had been

printed on thousands of cards – announce why she was not there. So they said to come.

Then every sort of pressure was put upon her to induce her either not to speak or to say something which she didn't believe. Buchmanites visited her dressing-room at the theatre, deluged her with cheerful propaganda. She remained un-Changed – or at least regarded attempts to pry into her soul as an impertinence.

Organizers were in great distress before the lunch yesterday. As I was sitting next to Miss Rawlings, they asked me if I couldn't persuade her not to speak her mind. At one moment, they said, the Buchmanites were threatening to walk out on them if she were allowed freedom of speech.

I tried to see it objectively; but it seems to me strange that a religious movement with such high claims should have to resort to such dragooning tactics, should be unable to 'take' criticism.

She made her speech. She was trembling with nervousness before it, puffed quickly at Russian cigarettes. She spoke last but one. There was a lot to sit through first. When Dr Buchman – himself in the chair – was announced, a bugle rang out. Suddenly floodlights were turned on. Up in the balcony long rows of young Buchmanites sang rousing choruses in well-drilled unison. Others held banners aloft.

Then a man downstairs interrogated them, in sharp, parade-ground staccato:

'Who are you?'
'*The youth of the nations!*'
'What do you want?'
'A NEW WORLD!'

And so on. Not a syllable was astray. It was as carefully rehearsed, as brilliantly produced, as a Nazi Party demonstration. I recalled that Buchman had been reported some months ago to have said, 'I thank God for a man like Adolf Hitler.' Unprompted by me, the woman on my left said, 'They make good potential Fascists.'

Then there were individual testimonies – many of them moving, all obviously sincere, many by people picked deliberately for their news value.* An ex-Lord Mayor of Newcastle ... a bishop (from Rangoon) ... A French architect ... a general who trains horses and said that he has 'quiet times' with God and the lads in his stables ... A cowbody (in costume) who sang sort of hill-billy songs with refrains like:

> You got to be willing
> Absolutely willing
> For God to hold the reins His way ...

Two journalists ... a business man who said that Isaiah was an early Grouper.

In this elaborately worked-up atmosphere Margaret Rawlings got up. ('Are you going to start with an apologetic far-be-it-from-me note?' I had asked her. 'No,' she said. 'I'm much too straightforward.') She said: 'I am going to make a plea which to the many hundreds in this room who belong to this movement will seem quite astonishing. I want to make a plea for modesty.' Her childhood had been spent in Japan, she added. One difference between East and West that she had noticed was their different conventions of modesty. In Europe reticence and modesty were reserved for the body. In the East they were unselfconscious about the body – but one important part of man's being was guarded with modesty, reticence, secrecy: his soul.

'To me personally,' she said – there was a whispered buzz of excitement – 'This public exposure of the soul, this psychic exhibitionism, with its natural accompaniment of sensual satisfaction, is *shocking* – shocking in the Victorian sense of the word – as shocking, indecent, and indelicate as it would be if a man took off all his clothes in Piccadilly Circus.'

I was glad that the summing-up speaker who followed praised Miss Rawlings's bravery. But he dragged in that well-known bromide, Sincerity. Sincerity is all that counts. It's a widespread modern heresy. Think again. Bolsheviks are sincere. Fascists are sincere. Lunatics are sincere. People who believe the earth is flat are sincere. They can't all be right. Better make

*There is joy in the presence of the Buchmanites over one celebrity who is captured, more than over ninety-and-nine obscure, undemonstrative Christians.

certain first you've got something to be sincere about, and with.

He also said:

'It doesn't matter if the special [distressed] areas are wiped away in our lifetime or not [he is young] so long as we are doing something about it.'

Tell that to the distressed areas.

He also said:

'Any movement which helps people to get rid of their inhibitions, complexes, and fears *must be good*.'

It sounds fine. Think again. Exactly the same defence could be put up for opium-smoking.

Don't think I am merely carping or sneering at a movement which has done some good to some individuals. I have watched it for years, talked with its leaders, suspended judgement as long as I could. But Buchmanism does not seem to me the best panacea for most people; as a social force it seems potentially dangerous.

1937   *Daily Express*

MARGARET BARTON
(*Garrick's Only Othello*)

Garrick's failure as Othello in March 1745 is generally put down to his humiliation at the laugh that greeted his first entry. To the traditional army officer's scarlet tunic and blackened face, he had the unfortunate idea of adding a high oriental turban with an upstanding plume. He must have hoped that the headdress would add some inches to his height. It was just at this time that Hogarth's series of pictures, *The Harlot's Progress*, were at the height of their popularity, and the scene where the heroine upsets the breakfast table just as a little negro page, in a laced coat and an enormous turban, is bringing in the tea kettle, must have been familiar in reproductions to everyone in the house. Garrick, in his make-up as Othello, bore a fatal resemblance to the boy, and when Quin remarked to his neighbour in an all too audible voice, 'Here's Pompey – but where is the tea kettle?' the laugh that echoed through the theatre destroyed Garrick's confidence in that part for ever.

1948   *Garrick*

OSBERT SITWELL
from Horses on Parade*

It was the leave season, and only two officers were present: one a taciturn, somnolent, mutely disagreeable Scottish cousin of mine, whom I had never hitherto met, the other a spry, pin-headed younger man, with a long, silky moustache and a cavalry lisp. I never discovered if my cousin had a lisp or not, for I never heard him utter sufficient words to make it possible for me to judge: since a routine of port and a fall on his head once a week from horseback kept him in that state of chronic, numb confusion which was then the aim of every cavalry officer.... As neither of my companions spoke, either before the meal or at it, except to say, 'How d'e do?', but ate on in what is best termed a silence of bestial chaos, such as may have preceded the coming of the Word, and since I was of a sociable disposition and hated, too, to see people so plainly frustrated and unhappy, I determined to 'make things go'. I talked on all kinds of interesting subjects and invented a number – on this I must insist – of first-rate jokes for their entertainment. But the surrounding and enveloping silence, an active silence, as it were, and not a mere negation of sound, made it seem gradually as if I were talking to myself in an enormous illuminated cavern, filled with sparkling silver objects. Gowk, my cousin, and Fribble-Sadler said nothing, but slowly drank their claret, and gave each other, from time to time, the sort of glance that the Gorgon Sisters must ever now and then have exchanged among themselves when a stranger was present and as yet unpetrified....

The next morning – it must have been morning, in spite of its night-darkness – the bugles, which seemed only just to have stopped, began to bray again, and set off barking, as invariably they did, the miscellaneous packs of dogs in the Officer's Quarters; a whole rasping chorus of bull-terriers, Irish setters, and half-wit, bandy-legged Sealyhams and Aberdeens. ... Soon Robins was calling me, sidling swiftly about with his quick foot-

*In 1912, 2nd Lieut. F. O. S. Sitwell was attached to a famous regiment of Hussars.

steps and alert movements, and soon we were once more struggling with my boots. Each morning, each day, precisely resembled the last. That year, fog and snow and ice continued for ten weeks, far into the spring, dimming buttons, and tattooing faces with red and blue marks, till they resembled, when you could see them, the masks of the native warriors of Australia or the furthest Pacific isles. Waited on, muzzle and hoof, the horses did not seem to mind the cold. Riding School, the first duty of the day's whole enjoyable round, took place at an hour still lost in the winter darkness – can it have been six o'clock or five? At any rate, so dark was it still that one could only *feel* the snow, not see it. In the centre, under the arc-lamps, shining like moons through their circles of peat-dust that gave them aureoles, stood the riding-master, red-nosed, but silent, large-featured and stiff as an Easter Island figure. Though his chief criticized us little, the sergeant was voluble enough, his language vivid, as he shouted at the rolling, flustered recruits cantering round in a circle without saddles, 'Stop bumping about on your bloody backsides there like a set of Piccadilly 'ores' ... In that high-roofed tin barn I learnt a whole repertory of helpful circus tricks *à la Russe;* such as jumping, without saddle or stirrups, over hurdles with my arms akimbo, or pick-up at the gallop, from under the hoofs of the singularly vicious and oafish horse I had been allotted, a handkerchief which I had been obliged to thrown down in the filthy peat-dust. To be able to perform this last feat, I was assured, would be of inestimable value, both to the country and to myself, in the next war, when it came....

Then came Evensong in the stables, followed, if we were fortunate, by a lecture on *The Care of the Horse Through the Ages*, *The Place of the Horse in the Twentieth Century*, *How the Horse will Replace Mechanical Means of Transport*, or some kindred subject.

In the course of these lectures, we did not hear much of the war that was being prepared for us, except that on occasion a lecturer would give a discourse on *Cavalry Charges in the Coming War*. He would tell us that he hoped it would constitute no breach of trust if he informed us in strictest confidence that the authorities knew a war was drawing near on the Continent, that we should become involved in it, and that it would be a Cavalry War. At last the Horse would, thank God, come into its own.... But we must be prepared, and must not think it was going to be a war after the style of the Peninsular War – that was a mistake we often made. We ought to thank our stars – that was the phrase he used – for the fact that the Boer War had been recently vouchsafed us as a model and dress-rehearsal for this approaching conflict. In many ways, Europe resembled the Great Veldt, and the people of the Veldt, too, resembled those of Europe.

1948   *Great Morning*

CHAPTER 6

Humour of Observation

Observation is the secret of the English Sense of Humour, which depends for its highest effects on the presentation of character by detail clearly and cleanly observed, so that hackneyed traits can be made to seem as fresh and memorable as a snowdrop, and worn-out old cabbage stumps of types, as distasteful as unwanted relatives from over-familiarity, can spring into new life. If we laugh, our pleasure is mixed with the blessed sensation of relief through recognition.

This therefore is the longest chapter; but it is also the most varied. The kind of observation involved can range from the heights of sympathetic comprehension to the jotting-down of tea-time habits in good homey modern comedies. I have chosen by quotations to represent as many different kinds of English observation as possible. The second piece, Chaucer's description of the Pardoner, gives us a glimpse of the power of humour as a positive act of understanding. That the first truly renaissance-minded man should write so indulgently of a despised officer of the then corrupt Catholic Church (the Summoner was too much even for Chaucer's geniality) perfectly shows Chaucer's powers of acceptance. The Smollett represents a type of humour – vigorous and violent – which was once called 'English' but is in fact very far from what we now mean by the 'English sense of humour'. Congreve alone I quote of the Restoration dramatists, because Congreve alone seems to have the necessary humanity for humour. Keats's poem about the cat must stand for the successful humorous descriptions of animals. There are very few of these, though later in the Humorous Age anthropomorphic 'funny' writings about animals were to appear with suffocating frequency. For Dickens I have limited myself to one chestnut passage from Podsnap, which will bear much repetition, and a few passages from 'Mrs Tibb's Boarding House'. This very little known work, which belongs to the Boz period, shows that that awe-inspiring eye is already observing with its exact clarity. The richness of Thomas Hardy in his Melstock Choir vein reminds me how much easier, to my surprise, it is to pick humour out of the tragedies of Hardy than from the comedies of Meredith. In *The Diary of a Nobody*, the art seems to lie in the hard-as-nails presentation of Mr Pooter, a method which, of course, arouses our sympathy and our laughter at the same time. Surely the *Diary* can claim to be the greatest work of humour since Dickens. School stories have been a wonderful mine of humour in this period. I select part of the Eden Phillpotts *Human Boy* cycle, so lucid, so simple, so effective – and, now, neglected. The Aldous Huxley quotation must stand for the Merciless Objectivity school of Post World War One novelists. Miss Nancy Mitford is difficult to represent in a short quotation. The warmer more truly 'humorous' fiction of some more recent writers I recall to the reader with the *Small Back Room* and *Slaves of Solitude*. Patrick Hamilton is always conscious, like John Betjeman, of what might be called the humour of place. The quotations from biographies were chosen to show the humour of the witty selection of the unadorned fact (the Hesketh Pearson method) and contrastingly the fact adorned with the imagination and humorous insight of a writer like Sir Harold Nicolson.

CHAUCER
The Wife of Bath

A worthy *woman* from beside *Bath* city
Was with us, somewhat deaf, which was a pity.

In making cloth she showed so great a bent
She bettered those of Ypres and of Ghent.
In all the parish not a dame dared stir
Towards the altar steps in front of her,
And if indeed they did, so wrath was she
As to be quite put out of charity.
Her kerchiefs were of finely woven ground;
I dared have sworn they weighted a good ten pound,
The ones she wore on Sunday, on her head.
Her hose were of the finest scarlet red
And gartered tight; her shoes were soft and new.
Bold was her face, handsome, and red in hue.
A worthy woman all her life, what's more
She'd had five husbands, all at the church door,
Apart from other company in youth;
No need just now to speak of that, forsooth.
And she had thrice been to Jerusalem,
Seen many strange rivers and passed over them;
She'd been to Rome and also to Boulogne,
St James of Compostella and Cologne,
And she was skilled in wandering by the way.
She had gap-teeth, set widely, truth to say.
Easily on an ambling horse she sat
Well wimpled up, and on her head a hat
As broad as is a buckler or a shield;
She had a flowing mantle that concealed
Large hips, her heels spurred sharply under that.
In company she liked to laugh and chat
And knew the remedies for love's mischances,
An art in which she knew the oldest dances.

The Pardoner

He and a gentle *Pardoner* rode together,
A bird from Charing Cross of the same feather,
Just back from visiting the Court of Rome.
He loudly sang '*Come hither, love, come home!*'
The Summoner sang deep seconds to this song,
No trumpet ever sounded half so strong.

This Pardoner had hair as yellow as wax
Hanging down smoothly like a hank of flax.
In driblets fell his locks behind his head
Down to his shoulders which they overspread;
Thinly they fell, like rat-tails, one by one.
He wore no hood upon his head, for fun;
The hood inside his wallet had been stowed,
He aimed at riding in the latest mode;
But for a little cap his head was bare
And he had bulging eye-balls, like a hare.
He'd sewed a holy relic on his cap;
His wallet lay before him on his lap,
Brimful of pardons come from Rome all hot.
He had the same small voice a goat has got.
His chin no beard had harboured, nor would harbour,
Smoother than ever chin was left by barber.
I judge he was a gelding, or a mare.
As to his trade, from Berwick down to Ware
There was no pardoner of equal grace,
For in his trunk he had a pillow-case
Which he asserted was Our Lady's veil.
He said he had a gobbet of the sail
Saint Peter had the time when he made bold
To walk the waves, till Jesu Christ took hold.
He had a cross of metal set with stones
And, in a glass, a rubble of pigs' bones.
And with these relics, any time he found
Some poor up-country parson to astound,
On one short day, in money down, he drew
More than the parson in a month or two,
And by his flatteries and prevarication
Made monkeys of the priest and congregation.
But first to do him justice first and last
In church he was a noble ecclesiast.
How well he read a lesson or told a story!
But best of all he sang an Offertory,
For well he knew that when that song was sung
He'd have to preach and tune his honey-tongue

And (well he could) win silver from the crowd.
That's why he sang so merrily and loud.

c.1387   *Prologue to the Canterbury Tales*
                          Translated by Nevill Coghill

WILLIAM SHAKESPEARE

(*The Meeting of Beatrice and Benedick*)

BEATRICE: I wonder that you will still be talking, Signior Benedick: nobody marks you.

BENEDICK: What, my dear Lady Disdain! are you yet living?

1599   *Much Ado About Nothing*

(*on Achilles*)

THERSITES: I had rather be a tick in a sheep than such a valiant
   ignorance.   *Troilus and Cressida*
1602

(*on Cressida*)

ULYSSES: Fie, fie upon her!
   There's language in her eye, her cheek, her lip,
   Nay, her foot speaks; her wanton spirits look out
   At every joint and motive of her body.
   O, these encounterers, so glib of tongue,
   That give a coasting welcome ere it comes,
   And wide unclasp the tables of their thoughts
   To every ticklish reader! set them down
   For sluttish spoils of opportunity
   And daughters of the game.

1602   *Troilus and Cressida*

(*When to Plead with Coriolanus*)*

MENENIUS: I'll undertak't:
   I think he'll hear me. Yet, to bite his lip
   And hum at good Cominius, much unhearts me.
   He was not taken well; he had not dined:
   The veins unfill'd, our blood is cold, and then
   We pout upon the morning, are unapt

*Menenius judges Coriolanus's character in terms of his own.

178

To give or to forgive; but when we've stuft
These pipes and these conveyances of our blood
With wine and feeding, we have suppler souls
Than in our priest-like fasts: therefore I'll watch him
Till he be dieted to my request
And then I'll set upon him.

1608   *Coriolanus*

WILLIAM CONGREVE
(*Reasonable Demands of a Wife to Mirabell*)

MRS MILLAMANT: ... I'll never marry, unless I am first made sure of my will and pleasure.

MIRABELL: Would you have 'em both before marriage? or will you be contented with the first now, and stay for the other till after grace?

MRS MILLAMANT: Ah! don't be impertinent. – My dear liberty, shall I leave thee? my faithful solitude, my darling contemplation, must I bid you then adieu? Ay-h adieu – my morning thoughts, agreeable wakings, indolent slumbers, all ye *douceurs, ye sommeils du matin*, adieu? – I can't do't, 'tis more than impossible – positively, Mirabell, I'll lie abed in a morning as long as I please.

MIRABELL: Then I'll get up in a morning as early as I please.

MRS MILLAMANT: Ah! idle creature, get up when you will – and d'ye hear, I won't be called names after I'm married; positively I won't be called names.

MIRABELL: Names!

MRS MILLAMANT: Ay, as wife, spouse, my dear, joy, jewel, love, sweetheart, and the rest of that nauseous cant, in which men and their wives are so fulsomely familiar – I shall never bear that – good Mirabell, don't let us be familiar or fond, nor kiss before folks, like my Lady Fadler and Sir Francis: nor go to Hyde-park together the first Sunday in a new chariot, to provoke eyes and whispers, and then never to be seen there together again; as if we were proud of one another the first week, and ashamed of one another ever after. Let us never visit together, nor go to a play together; but let us be very strange and well-bred: let us be as strange as if we had been married a great while; and as well bred as if we were not married at all.

MIRABELL: Have you any more conditions to offer? Hitherto your demands are pretty reasonable.

MRS MILLAMANT: Trifles! – As liberty to pay and receive visits to and from whom I please; to write and receive letters, without interrogatories or wry faces on your part; to wear what I please; and choose conversation with regard only to my own taste; to have no obligation upon me to converse with wits that I don't like, because they are your acquaintance: or to be intimate with fools, because they may be your relations. Come to dinner when I please; dine in my dressing-room when I'm out of humour, without giving a reason. To have my closet inviolate; to be sole empress of my tea-table, which you must never presume to approach without first asking leave. And lastly, wherever I am, you shall always knock at the door before you come in. These articles subscribed, if I continue to endure you a little longer, I may by degrees dwindle into a wife.

MIRABELL: Your bill of fare is something advanced in this latter account.– Well, have I liberty to offer conditions – that when you are dwindled into a wife, I may not be beyond measures enlarged into a husband?

MRS MILLAMANT: You have free leave; propose your utmost, speak and spare not.

MIRABELL: I thank you.– *Imprimis* then, I covenant, that your acquaintance be general; that you admit no sworn confidant, or intimate of your own sex; no she friend to screen her affairs under your countenance, and tempt you to make trial of a mutual secrecy. No decoy duck to wheedle you a fop – scrambling to the play in a mask – then bring you home in a pretended fright, when you think you shall be found out – and rail at me for missing the play, and disappointing the frolic which you had to pick me up, and prove my constancy.

MRS MILLAMANT: Detestable *imprimis*! I go to the play in a mask!

MIRABELL: *Item*, I article, that you continue to like your own face, as long as I shall: and while it passes current with me, that you endeavour not to new-coin it. To which end, together with all vizards for the day, I prohibit all masks for the night, made of oiled-skins, and I know not what – hogs' bones, hares' gall, pig-water, and the marrow of a roasted cat. In short, I forbid all commerce with the gentlewoman in what d'ye call it court. *Item*, I shut my doors against all bawds with baskets, and pennyworths of muslin, china, fans, atlasses, etc. – *Item*, when you shall be breeding . . .

MRS MILLAMANT: Ah! name it not.

MIRABELL: Which may be presumed with a blessing on our endeavours.

MRS MILLAMANT: Odious endeavours!

MIRABELL: I denounce against all strait lacing, squeezing for a shape, till you mould my boy's head like a sugar-loaf, and instead of a man child, make me father to a crooked billet. Lastly, to the dominion of the tea-table I submit – but with proviso, that you exceed not in your province; but restrain yourself to native and simple tea-table drinks, as tea, chocolate, and coffee: as likewise to genuine and authorized tea-table talk – such as mending of fashions, spoiling reputations, railing at absent friends, and so forth – but that on no account you encroach upon the men's prerogative, and presume to drink healths, or toast fellows; for prevention of which I banish all foreign forces, all auxiliaries to the tea-table, as orange-brandy, all aniseed, cinnamon, citron, and Barbadoes waters, together with ratafia, and the most noble spirit of clary – but for cowslip wine, poppy water, and all dormitives, those I allow.– These provisos admitted in other things I may prove a tractable and complying husband.

MRS MILLAMANT: O horrid provisos! filthy strong-waters! I toast fellows! odious men! I hate your odious provisos.

MIRABELL: Then we are agreed! shall I kiss your hand upon the contract? And here comes one to be a witness to the sealing of the deed.

1700   *The Way of the World*

TOBIAS SMOLLETT

Preparations are made for the Commodore's wedding, which is delayed by an accident that hurried him the Lord knows whither

The fame of this extraordinary conjunction spread all over the county; and on the day appointed for their spousals, the church was surrounded by an inconceivable multitude. The commodore, to give a specimen of his gallantry, by the advice of his friend Hatchway, resolved to appear on horseback on the grand occasion, at the head of all his male attendants, whom he had rigged with the white shirts and black caps formerly belonging to his barge's crew; and he bought a couple of hunters for the accommodation of himself and his lieutenant. With this equipage then he set out from the garrison for the church, after having dispatched a messenger to apprise the bride that he and his company were mounted. She got immediately into the coach, accompanied by her brother and his wife, and drove directly to the place of assignation, where several pews were demolished and divers persons almost pressed to death, by the eagerness of the crowd that broke in to see the ceremony performed. Thus arrived at the altar, and the priest in attendance, they waited a whole half hour for the commodore, at whose slowness they began to be under some apprehension, and accordingly dismissed a servant to quicken his pace. The valet having rode something more than a mile, espied the whole troop disposed in a long field, crossing the road obliquely, and headed by the bridegroom and his friend Hatchway, who, finding himself hindered by a hedge from proceeding farther in the same direction, fired a pistol, and stood over to the other side, making an obtuse angle with the line of his former course; and the rest of the squadron followed his example, keeping always in the rear of each other like a flight of wild geese.

Surprised at this strange method of journeying, the messenger came up, and told the commodore that his lady and her company expected him in the church, where they had tarried a considerable time, and were beginning to be very uneasy at his delay; and therefore desired he would proceed with more expedition. To this message Mr Trunnion replied, – 'Hark ye, brother, don't you see we make all possible speed? go back, and tell those who sent you, that the wind has shifted since we weighed anchor, and that we are obliged to make very short trips in tacking, by reason of the narrowness of the channel: and that as we lie within six points of the wind, they must make some allowance for variation and leeway.' 'Lord, sir!' said the valet, 'what occasion have you to go zig-zag in that manner? do but clap spurs to your horses, and ride straight forward, and I'll engage you shall be at the church-porch in less than a quarter of an hour.' 'What! right in the wind's eye?' answered the commander, 'ahey! brother, where did you learn your navigation? Hawser Trunnion is not to be taught at this time of day how to lie his course, or keep his own reckoning. And as for you, brother, you best know the trim of your own frigate.'

Various were the conjectures of the company on this occasion: some imagined he had mistaken the place of rendezvous, as he had never been at church since he first settled in that parish; others believed he had met with some accident, in consequence of which his attendants had carried him back to his own house; and a third set, in which the bride herself was thought to be comprehended, could not help suspecting that the commodore had changed his mind. But all these suppositions, ingenious as they were, happened to be wide of the true cause that detained him, which was no other than this. – The commodore and his crew had, by dint of turning, almost weathered the parson's house that stood to windward of the church, when the notes of a pack of hounds unluckily reached the ears of the two hunters which Trunnion and the lieutenant bestrode. These fleet animals no sooner heard the enlivening sound, than, eager for the chase, they sprung away all of a sudden, and straining every nerve to partake of the sport, flew across the fields with incredible speed, overleaped hedges and ditches, and everything in their way, without the least regard to their unfortunate riders. The lieutenant, whose steed had got the heels of the other, finding it would be great folly and presumption in him to pretend to keep the saddle with his wooden leg, very wisely took the opportunity of throwing himself off in his passage through a field of rich clover, among which he lay at his ease; and seeing his captain advancing at full gallop, hailed him with the salutation of 'what cheer, ho!' The commodore, who was in infinite distress, eyeing him askance, as he passed, replied with a faltering voice, – 'O damn you! you are safe at anchor; I wish to God I were as fast moored.' Nevertheless, conscious of his disabled heel, he would not venture to try experiment which had succeeded so well with Hatchway, but resolved to stick as close as possible to his horse's back, until Providence should interpose in his behalf. With this view he dropped his whip, and with his right hand laid fast hold on the pummel, contracting every muscle in his body to secure himself in the seat, and grinning most formidably, in consequence of this exertion. In this attitude he was hurried on a considerable way, when all of a sudden his view was comforted by a five-bar gate that appeared before him, as he never doubted that there the career of his hunter must necessarily end. But, alas! he reckoned without his host: Far from halting at this obstruction, the horse sprung over it with amazing agility, to the utter confusion and disorder of his owner, who lost his hat and periwig in the leap, and now began to think in earnest that he was actually mounted on the back of the devil. He recommended himself to God, his reflection forsook him, his eyesight and all his other senses failed, he quitted the reins, and, fastening by instinct on the mane, was in this condition conveyed into the midst of the sportsmen, who were astonished at the sight of such an apparition. Neither was their surprise to be wondered at, if we reflect on the figure that presented itself to their view. The commodore's person was at all times an object of admiration; much more so on this occasion, when every singularity was aggravated by the circumstances of his dress and disaster.

He had put on, in honour of his nuptials, his best coat of blue broad cloth, cut by a tailor of Ramsgate, and trimmed with five dozen of brass buttons, large and small; his breeches were of the same piece, fastened at the knees with large bunches of tape; his waistcoat was of red plush, lapelled with green velvet, and garnished with vellum holes; his boots bore an infinite resemblance, both in colour and shape, to a pair of leather buckets;

his shoulder was graced with a broad buff belt, from whence depended a huge hanger, with a hilt like that of a backsword; and on each side of his pummel appeared a rusty pistol, rammed in a case covered with a bearskin. The loss of his tie, periwig, and laced hat, which were curiosities of the kind, did not at all contribute to the improvement of the picture, but, on the contrary, by exhibiting his bald pate, and the natural extension of his lanthorn jaws, added to the peculiarity and extravagance of the whole.

1751   *The Adventures of Peregrine Pickle*

JAMES BOSWELL
1768   (*Dr Johnson*)

An essay, written by Mr Deane, a Divine of the Church of England, maintaining the future of life of brutes, by an explication of certain parts of the Scriptures, was mentioned, and the doctrine insisted on by a gentleman who seemed fond of curious speculation – Johnson, who did not like to hear anything concerning a future state which was not authorized by the regular canons of orthodoxy, discouraged this talk; and being offended at its continuation, he watched an opportunity to give the gentleman a blow of reprehension. So, when the poor speculatist, with a serious, metaphysical, pensive face, addressed him, 'But, really, Sir, when we see a very sensible dog, we don't know what to think of him.' Johnson, rolling with joy at the thought which beamed in his eye, turned quickly round, and replied, 'True, Sir: and when we see a very foolish *fellow*, we don't know what to think of *him*.' He then rose up, strided to the fire, and stood for some time laughing and exulting.

When I called upon Dr Johnson next morning, I found him highly satisfied with his colloquial prowess the preceding evening. 'Well,' said he, 'we had a good talk.' BOSWELL: 'Yes, Sir, you tossed and gored several persons.'

1769

Talking of a London life, he said: 'The happiness of London is not to be conceived but by those who have been in it. I will venture to say, there is more learning and science within the circumference of ten miles from where we now sit, than in all the rest of the kingdom.' BOSWELL: 'The only disadvantage is the great distance at which people live from one another.' JOHNSON: 'Yes, Sir; but that is occasioned by the largeness of it, which is the cause of all the other advantages.' BOSWELL: 'Sometimes I have been in the humour of wishing to retire to a desert.' JOHNSON: 'Sir, you have desert enough in Scotland.'

1773

The modes of living in different countries, and the various views with which men travel in quest of new sciences, having been talked of, a learned gentleman, who holds a considerable office in the law, expatiated on the happiness of a savage life, and mentioned an instance of an officer who had actually lived for some time in the wilds of America, of whom, when in that state, he quoted this reflection, with an air of admiration, as if it had been deeply philosophical: 'Here am I, free and unrestrained, amidst the rude magnificence of Nature, with this Indian woman by my side, and this gun, with which I can procure food when I want it: what more can be desired for human happiness?' It did not require much sagacity to foresee that such a sentiment would not be permitted to pass without due animadversion. JOHNSON 'Do not allow yourself, Sir, to be imposed upon by such gross absurdity. It is sad stuff; it is brutish. If a bull could speak, he might as well exclaim, – Here am I with this cow and this grass; what being can enjoy greater felicity?'

*

1773

JOHNSON: 'An ancient estate should always go to males. It is mighty foolish to let a stranger have it because he marries your daughter, and takes your name. As for an estate newly acquired by trade, you may give it, if you will, to the dog *Towser*, and let him keep his *own* name.'

Next day I dined with Johnson at Mr Thrale's. He attacked Gray, calling him 'a dull fellow'. BOSWELL: 'I understand he was reserved, and might appear dull in company; but surely he was not dull in poetry.' JOHNSON: 'Sir, he was dull in company, dull in his closet, dull everywhere. He was dull in a new way, and that made many people think him GREAT. He was a mechanical poet.'

1791   *Life of Samuel Johnson, LLD*

OLIVER GOLDSMITH

(*Tony Lumpkin*)

TONY (*Staring at a letter*): A damned cramp piece of penmanship, as ever I saw in my life. I can read your print-hand very well. But here there are such handles, and shanks, and dashes, that one can scarce tell the head from the tail. To *Anthony Lumpkin, Esquire*. It's very odd, I can read the outside of my letters, where my own name is, well enough. But when I come to open it, it's all – buzz. That's hard, very hard; for the inside of the letter is always the cream of the correspondence.

1773   *She Stoops to Conquer*

CREEVEY

(*Mrs Creevey writes of News from Trafalgar*)

Brighton. Wednesday, Nov. 6 1805

I am much flatter'd, dearest Creevey, that you complain when my letters are short ... I went to the Pavillion last night quite well, and moreover am well today and fit for Johnstone's ball, which at last is to be. They were at the Pavilion and she (Miss Johnstone) persecuted both the Prince and Mrs Fitzherbert like a most impudent fool. The former was all complyance and good nature – the latter very civil, but most steady in refusing to go. She said she could not go out, and Miss J. grinned and answer'd – 'Oh! but you *are out* here' – then urged that it had been put off on purpose for Mrs F., who said she was sorry for it, but hoped it wd. be put off no longer. All this Mrs F. told me herself, with further remarks, just before I came away, which I did with Lady Downshire, and left the Johnstones with their affairs in an unsettled state, and with faces of great anxiety and misery. But the attack was renew'd, and the Prince said: 'I shall have great pleasure in looking in upon you, but indeed I cannot let this *good woman* (Mrs F.) come: she is quite unfit for it.' And so we shall see the fun of his looking in or staying all the evening, for poor

Johnstone has been running about the Steyne with a paper in his hand all the morning and invited us all. . . . When I got to the Pavillion last night . . . the Prince sat down by me directly and I told him my headache had made me late, and he was very *affectionate* . . . Harry Grey has just come in with news of a great victory at sea and poor Nelson being kill'd. It has just come by express to the Prince, and it is said 20 sail are taken or destroyed. What will this do? not, I hope, save Pitt; but both parties may now be humble and make peace. . . .

*

Nov. 7, 1805

. . .[The Prince's] sorrow [for Nelson's death] might help to prevent his coming to dinner at the Pavillion or to Johnstone's ball. He did neither, but stayed with Mrs Fitz; and you may imagine the disappointment of the Johnstones. The girl grin'd it off with the captain, but Johnstone had a face of perfect horror all night, and I think he was very near insane. I once lamented Lord Nelson to him, and he said: 'Oh shocking: and to come at such an unlucky time!' . . .

Creevey, ed. John Gore

CHARLES LAMB

on Coleridge to Wordsworth

He is at present under the medical care of a Mr Gillman (Killman?) a Highgate apothecary, where he plays at leaving off laud-m. I think his essentials not touched; he is very bad; but then he wonderfully picks up another day, and his face, when he repeats his verses, hath its ancient glory; an archangel a little damaged.

1816   *Letters*

JOHN KEATS

To Mrs Reynolds's Cat

Cat! who hast pass'd thy grand climacteric
    How many mice and rats hast in thy days
    Destroy'd? – How many tit bits stolen? Gaze
With those bright languid segments green, and prick

Those velvet ears – but pr'ythee do not stick
   Thy latent talons in me – and upraise
   Thy gentle mew – and tell me all thy frays
Of fish and mice, and rats and tender chick.
Nay, look not down, nor lick thy dainty wrists –
   For all the wheezy asthma – and for all
Thy tail's tip is nick'd off – and though the fists
Of many a maid have given thee many a maul,
   Still is that fur as soft as when the lists
   In youth thou enter'dst on glass-bottled wall.

1818

CHARLES DICKENS
from The Boarding-House

Mrs Tibbs was, beyond all dispute, the most tidy, fidgety, thrifty little personage that ever inhaled the smoke of London; and the house of Mrs Tibbs was decidedly the neatest in all Great Coram Street. The area and the area steps, and the street-door and the street-door steps, and the brass handle, and the door-plate, and the knocker, and the fan-light, were all as clean and as bright as indefatigable white-washing, and hearthstoning, and scrubbing and rubbing could make them. The wonder was, that the brass door-plate, with the interesting inscription MRS TIBBS, had never caught fire from constant friction, so perseveringly was it polished. There were meatsafe-looking blinds in the parlour windows, blue and gold curtains in the drawing-room, and spring-roller blinds, as Mrs Tibbs was wont in the pride of her heart to boast, 'all the way up'. The bell-lamp in the passage looked as clear as a soap-bubble; you could see yourself in all the tables, and French-polish yourself on any one of the chairs. The banisters were bees'-waxed, and the very stair-wires made your eyes wink, they were so glittering.

Mrs Tibbs was somewhat short of stature, and Mr Tibbs was by no means a large man. He had, moreover, very short legs, but, by way of indemnification, his face was peculiarly long. He was to his wife what the 0 is in 90 – he was of some importance *with* her – he was nothing without her. Mrs Tibbs was always talking. Mr Tibbs rarely spoke; but if it were at any time possible to put in a word, just when he should have said nothing at all, he did it. Mrs Tibbs detested long stories, and Mr Tibbs had one, the conclusion of which had never been heard by his most intimate friends. It always began, 'I recollect when I was in the volunteer corps, in eighteen hundred and six,'– but as he spoke very slowly and softly and his better half very quickly and loudly, he rarely got beyond the introductory sentence. He was a melancholy specimen of the story-teller. He was the wander-Jew of Joe Millerism.

Mr Tibbs enjoyed a small independence from the pension-list – about 43l. 15s. 10d. a-year. His father, mother, and five interesting scions from the same stock drew a like sum from the revenue of a grateful country, though for what particular service was never distinctly known. But as this said independence was not quite sufficient to furnish two people with all the luxuries of this life, it had occurred to the busy little spouse of Tibbs, that the best thing she could do with a legacy of 700l. would be to take and furnish a tolerable house, somewhere in that partially explored tract of country which lies between the British Museum, and a remote village called Somers Town, for the reception of boarders.

. . .'Are these gals handsome?' inquired Mr Simpson of Mr Septimus Hicks, another of the boarders, as they were amusing themselves in the drawing-room before dinner, by lolling on sofas, and contemplating their pumps.

'Don't know,' replied Mr Septimus Hicks, who was a tallish, white-faced young man, with spectacles, and a black ribbon around his neck instead of a neckerchief – a most interesting person; a poetical walker of the hospitals, and a 'very talented young man'. He was fond of 'lugging' into conversation all sorts of quotations from Don Juan, without fettering himself by the propriety of their application, in which particular he was remarkably independent. The other, Mr Simpson, was one of those young men, who are in society what walking gentlemen are upon the stage, only infinitely worse skilled in his vocation than the most indifferent artist. He was as empty-headed as the great bell of St Paul's; always dressed according to the caricatures published in the monthly fashions, and spelt Character with a K.

'I saw a devilish number of parcels in the passage when I came home,' simpered Simpson.

'Materials for the toilet, no doubt,' rejoined the Don Juan reader.

> ...Much linen, lace and several pair
> Of stockings, slippers, brushes, combs, complete;
> With other articles of ladies' fair,
> To keep them beautiful or leave them neat.

'Is that from Milton?' inquired Mr Simpson.

'No – from Byron,' returned Mr Hicks, with a look of profound contempt. He was quite sure of his author, because he had never read any other – 'Hush!' said the sapient hospital walker, 'Here come the gals,' and they both commenced talking in a loud key.

'Mrs Maplesone and the Miss Maplesones, Mr Hicks. Mr Hicks – Mrs Maplesone and the Miss Maplesones,' said Mrs Tibbs with a very red face, for she had been superintending the cooking operations below stairs, and looked like a wax doll on a sunny day. 'Mr Simpson, I beg your pardon – Mr Simpson – Mrs Maplesone and the Miss Maplesones' – and *vice versa*. The gentlemen immediately began to slide about with much politeness, and to look as if they wished their arms had been legs, so little did they know what to do with them. The ladies smiled, curtsied and glided into chairs, and dived for dropped pocket-handkerchiefs: Mrs Tibbs went through an admirable bit of serious pantomime with a servant who had come up to ask some question about the fish-sauce, and then the two young ladies looked at each other; and everybody else appeared to discover something very attractive in the pattern of the fender.

'Julia my love,' said Mrs Maplesone to her youngest daughter – in a tone just loud enough for the remainder of the company to hear –'Julia'.

'Yes, Ma.'

'Don't stoop.' – This was said for the purpose of directing general attention to Miss Julia's figure, which was undeniable. Everybody looked at her accordingly, and there was another pause.

*

The boarders were seated, a lady and a gentleman alternately like the layers of bread and meat in a plate of sandwiches; and then Mrs Tibbs directed James to take off the covers. Salmon, lobster-sauce, giblet-soup, and the usual accompaniment were *dis*-covered: potatoes like petrifactions, and bits of toasted bread, the shape and size of blank dice.

'Soup for Mrs Maplesone, my dear,' said the bustling Mrs Tibbs. She always called her husband 'my dear' before company. Tibbs who had been eating his bread, and calculating how long it would be before he should get any fish, helped the soup in a hurry, made a small island on the tablecloth, and put his glass upon it, to hide it from his wife.

'Miss Julia, shall I assist you to some fish?'

'If you please – very little – oh! plenty, thank you' (a bit about the size of a walnut put on the plate).

'Julia is a *very* little eater,' said Mrs Maplesone to Mr Calton.

The knocker gave a single rap. He was busy eating the fish with his eyes: so he only ejaculated, 'Ah!'

'My dear,' said Mrs Tibbs, to her spouse after every one else had been helped, 'What do *you* take?' The inquiry was accompanied with a look intimating that he mustn't say fish, because there was not much left. Tibbs thought the frown referred to the island on the tablecloth; he therefore coolly replied, 'Why – I'll take a little – fish, I think.'

'Did you say fish, my dear?' (another frown).

'Yes, dear,' replied the villain, with an expression of acute hunger depicted in his countenance. The tears almost started to Mrs Tibb's eyes, as she helped her 'wretch of a husband', as she inwardly called, him, to the last eatable bit of salmon on the dish.

'James, take this to your master, and take away your master's knife.' This was deliberate revenge, as Tibbs never could eat fish without one. He was, however, constrained to chase small particles of salmon round and round his plate with a piece of bread and a fork, occasionally securing a bit; the number of successful attempts being about one in seventeen.

'Take away, James,' said Mrs Tibbs, just as Tibbs had swallowed the fourth mouthful – and away went the plates like lightning.

'I'll take a bit of bread, James,' said the poor '*master* of the house,' more hungry than ever.

'Never mind your master now, James,' said Mrs Tibbs, 'see about the meat.' – This was conveyed in the tone in which ladies usually give admonitions to servants in company, that is to say, a low one; but which, like a stage whisper, from its peculiar emphasis, is most distinctly heard by everybody present.

A pause ensued before the table was replenished – a sort of parenthesis in which Mr Simpson, Mr Calton, and Mr Hicks produced respectively a bottle of sauterne, cucellas, and sherry, and took wine with everybody – except Tibbs: no one ever thought of him.

Between the fish and an intimated sirloin there was a prolonged interval.

Here was an opportunity for Mr Hicks. He could not resist the singularly appropriate quotation –

> But beef is rare within these oxless isles;
> Goats' flesh there is, no doubt, and kid and mutton,
> And, when a holiday upon them smiles,
> A joint upon their barbarous spits they put on.

'Very ungentlemanly behaviour,' thought little Mrs Tibbs, 'to talk in that way.'

'Ah,' said Mr Calton, filling his glass. 'Tom Moore is my poet.'

'And mine,' said Mrs Maplesone.

'And mine,' said Miss Julia.

'And mine,' added Mr Simpson.

'Look at his compositions,' resumed the knocker.

'To be sure,' said Simpson, with confidence.

'Look at Don Juan,' replied Mr Septimus Hicks.

'Julia's letter,' suggested Miss Matilda.

'Can anything be grander than the Fire Worshippers!' inquired Miss Julia.

'To be sure,' said Simpson.

'Or Paradise and the Peri,' said the old beau.

'Yes; or Paradise and the Peer,' repeated Simpson, who thought he was getting through it capitally.

'It's all very well.' replied Mr Septimus Hicks, who, as we have before hinted, never had read any thing but Don Juan.

'Where will you find any thing finer than the description of the siege, at the commencement of the seventh canto?'

'Talking of a siege,' said Tibbs, with a mouthful of bread – 'when I was in the volunteer corps, in eighteen hundred and six our commanding officer was Sir Charles Rampart; and one day, when we were exercising on the ground on which the London University now stands, he says, says he, "Tibbs (calling me from the ranks) Tibbs –" '

'Tell your master, James,' interrupted Mrs Tibbs, in an awfully distinct tone, 'tell your master if he *won't* carve those fowls, to send them to me.'

*

Mrs Tibbs apologized for being down rather late; the bell was rung; James brought up the urn, and received an unlimited order for dry toast and bacon. Tibbs sat down, at the bottom of the table, and began eating watercresses like a second Nebuchadnezzar. Mr O'Bleary appeared, and Mr Alfred Tomkins. The compliments of the morning were exchanged, and the tea was made.

'God bless me!' exclaimed Tomkins, who had been looking out at the window. 'Here – Wisbottle – pray come here: make haste.'

Mr Wisbottle started from the table, and everyone looked up.

'Do you see,' said the connoisseur, placing Wisbottle in the right position –'a little more this way: there – do you see how splendidly the light falls upon the left side of that broken chimney-pot at No. 48?'

'Dear me! I see,' replied Wisbottle, in a tone of admiration.

'I never saw an object stand out so beautifully against the clear sky in my life,' ejaculated Alfred. Everybody (except John Evenson) echoed the sentiment, for Mr Tomkins had a great character for finding out beauties which no one else could discover – he certainly deserved it.

'I have frequently observed a chimney-pot in College-green, Dublin, which has a much better effect,' said the patriotic O'Bleary who never allowed Ireland to be outdone on any point.

1836   *Sketches by Boz*

GEORGE ELIOT

(The Tullivers are Allowed to See Aunt Pullet's Bonnet)

Uncle Pullet had seen the expected party approaching from the window, and made haste to unbar and unchain the front door, kept always in this fortified condition from fear of tramps, who might be supposed to know of the glass-case of stuffed birds in the hall, and to contemplate rushing in and carrying it away on their heads. Aunt Pullet, too, appeared at the doorway, and as soon as her sister was within hearing said, 'Stop the children, for God's sake, Bessy – don't let 'em come up the door-steps; Sally's bringing the old mat and the duster, to rub their shoes.'

Mrs Pullet's front-door mats were by no means intended to wipe shoes on: the very scraper had a deputy to do its dirty work. Tom rebelled particularly against this shoe-wiping, which he always considered in the light of an indignity to his sex. He felt *it* as the beginning of the disagreeables incident to a visit at aunt Pullet's, where he had once been compelled to sit with towels wrapped round his boots; a fact which may serve to correct the too hasty conclusion that a visit to Garum Firs must have been a great treat to a young gentleman fond of animals – fond, that is, of throwing stones at them.

The next disagreeable was confined to his feminine companions: it was the mounting of the polished oak stairs, which had very handsome carpets rolled up and laid by in a spare bedroom, so that the ascent of these glossy steps might have served, in barbarous times, as a trial by ordeal from which none but the most spotless virtue could have come off with unbroken limbs. Sophy's weakness about these polished stairs was always a subject of bitter remonstrance on Mrs Glegg's part; but Mrs Tulliver ventured on no comment, only thinking to herself it was a mercy when she and the children were safe on the landing.

'Mrs Gray has sent home my new bonnet, Bessy,' said Mrs Pullet, in a pathetic tone, as Mrs Tulliver adjusted her cap.

'Has she, sister?' said Mrs Tulliver, with an air of much interest. 'And how do you like it?'

'It's apt to make a mess with clothes, taking 'em out and

195

putting 'em in again,' said Mrs Pullet, drawing a bunch of keys from her pocket and looking at them earnestly, 'but it 'ud be a pity for you to go away without seeing it. There's no knowing what may happen.'

Mrs Pullet shook her head slowly at this last serious consideration, which determined her to single out a particular key.

'I'm afraid it'll be troublesome to you getting it out, sister,' said Mrs Tulliver, 'but I *should* like to see what sort of a crown she's made you.'

Mrs Pullet rose with a melancholy air and unlocked one wing of a very bright wardrobe, where you may have hastily supposed she would find the new bonnet. Not at all. Such a supposition could only have arisen from a too superficial acquaintance with the habits of the Dodson family. In this wardrobe Mrs Pullet was seeking something small enough to be hidden among layers of linen – it was a door-key.

'You must come with me into the best room,' said Mrs Pullet.

'May the children come too, sister?' inquired Mrs Tulliver, who saw that Maggie and Lucy were looking rather eager.

'Well,' said aunt Pullet, reflectively 'it'll perhaps be safer for 'em to come – they'll be touching something if we leave 'em behind.'

So they went in procession along the bright and slippery corridor, dimly lighted by the semi-lunar top of the window which rose above the closed shutter: it was really quite solemn. Aunt Pullet paused and unlocked a door which opened on something still more solemn than the passage: a darkened room, in which the outer light, entering feebly, showed what looked like the corpses of furniture in white shrouds. Everything that was not shrouded stood with its legs upwards. Lucy laid hold of Maggie's frock, and Maggie's heart beat rapidly.

Aunt Pullet half-opened the shutter and then unlocked the wardrobe, with a melancholy deliberateness which was quite in keeping with the funereal solemnity of the scene. The delicious scent of rose-leaves that issued from the wardrobe made the process of taking out sheet after sheet of silver paper quite pleasant to assist at, though the sight of the bonnet at last was an anticlimax to Maggie, who would have preferred something more strikingly preternatural. But few things could have been more impressive to Mrs Tulliver. She looked all round it in silence for some moments, and then said emphatically, 'Well, sister, I'll never speak against the full crowns again!'

It was a great concession, and Mrs Pullet felt it: she felt something was due to it.

'You like to see it on, sister?' she said sadly. 'I'll open the shutter a bit further.'

'Well, if you don't mind taking off your cap, sister,' said Mrs Tulliver.

Mrs Pullet took off her cap, displaying the brown silk scalp with a jutting promontory of curls which was common to the more mature and judicious women of those times, and, placing the bonnet on her head, turned slowly round, like a draper's lay-figure, that Mrs Tulliver might miss no point of view.

'I've sometimes thought there's a loop too much o'ribbon on this left side, sister; what do you think?' said Mrs Pullet.

Mrs Tulliver looked earnestly at the point indicated, and turned her head on one side. 'Well, I think it's best as it is; if you meddled with it, sister, you might repent.'

'That's true,' said aunt Pullet, taking off the bonnet and looking at it contemplatively.

'How much might she charge you for that bonnet, sister?' said Mrs Tulliver, whose mind was actively engaged on the possibility of getting a humble imitation of this *chef-d'œuvre* made from a piece of silk she had at home.

Mrs Pullet screwed up her mouth and shook her head, and then whispered, 'Pullet pays for it; he said I was to have the best bonnet at Garum Church, let the next best be whose it would.'

She began slowly to adjust the trimmings in preparation for returning it to its place in the wardrobe, and her thoughts seemed to have taken a melancholy turn, for she shook her head.

'Ah,' she said at last, 'I may never wear it twice, sister: who knows?'

'Don't talk o' that, sister,' answered Mrs Tulliver. 'I hope you'll have your health this summer.'

'Ah! but there may come a death in the family, as there did

soon after I had my green satin bonnet. Cousin Abbott may go, and we can't think o' wearing crape less nor half a year for him.'

*

...'He's got a wonderful memory, Pullet has,' she continued, looking pathetically at her sister. 'I should be poorly off if he was to have a stroke, for he always remembers when I've got to take my doctor's stuff – and I'm taking three sorts now.'

'There's the "pills as before" every other night, and the new drops at eleven and four, and the "fervescing mixture when agreeable," ' rehearsed Mr Pullet, with a punctuation determined by a lozenge on his tongue.

'Ah, perhaps it 'ud be better for sister Glegg, if *she'd* go to the doctor sometimes, instead o' chewing Turkey rhubarb whenever there's anything the matter with her,' said Mrs Tulliver, who naturally saw the wide subject of medicine chiefly in relation to Mrs Glegg.

'It's dreadful to think on,' said aunt Pullet, raising her hands and letting them fall again, 'people playing with their own insides in that way! And it's flying i' the face o' Providence; for what are the doctors for, if we aren't to call 'em in? And when folks have got the money to pay for a doctor, it isn't respectable, as I've told Jane many a time. I'm ashamed of acquaintance knowing it.'

'Well, *we've* no call to be ashamed,' said Mr Pullet, 'for Doctor Turnbull hasn't got such another patient as you i' this parish, now old Mrs Sutton's gone.'

'Pullet keeps all my physic-bottles – did you know, Bessy?' said Mrs Pullet. 'He won't have one sold. He says it's nothing but right folks should see 'em when I'm gone. They fill two o' the long store-room shelves a'ready – but,' she added, beginning to cry a little, 'it's well if they ever fill three. I may go before I've made up the dozen o' these last sizes. The pill-boxes are in the closet in my room – you'll remember that, sister – but there's nothing to show for the boluses, if it isn't the bills.'

1860   *The Mill on the Floss*

CHARLES DICKENS
(*Mr Podsnap and the Foreign Gentleman*)

Mr and Mrs Veneering, and Mr and Mrs Veneering's bran-new
bride and bridegroom, were of the dinner company; but the
Podsnap establishment had nothing else in common with the
Veneerings. Mr Podsnap could tolerate taste in a mushroom man
who stood in need of that sort of thing, but was far above it
himself. Hideous solidity was the characteristic of the Podsnap
plate. Everything was made to look as heavy as it could, and to
take up as much room as possible. Everything said boastfully,
'Here you have as much of me in my ugliness as if I were only
lead; but I am so many ounces of precious metal worth so much
an ounce; – wouldn't you like to melt me down?' A corpulent
straggling epergne, blotched all over as if it had broken out in
an eruption rather than been ornamented, delivered this address
from an unsightly silver platform in the centre of the table. Four
silver wine-coolers, each furnished with four staring heads, each
head obtrusively carrying a big silver ring in each of its ears,
conveyed the sentiment up and down the table, and handed it on
to the pot-bellied silver salt-cellars. All the big silver spoons and
forks widened the mouths of the company expressly for the
purpose of thrusting the sentiment down their throats with every
morsel they ate.

The majority of the guests were like the plate, and included
several heavy articles weighing ever so much. But there was a
foreign gentleman among them: whom Mr Podsnap had invited after much debate with himself – believing the whole Euro-
pean continent to be in mortal alliance against the young person
– and there was a droll disposition, not only on the part of Mr
Podsnap, but of everybody else, to treat him as if he were a child
who was hard of hearing.

As a delicate concession to this unfortunately born foreigner,
Mr Podsnap, in receiving him, had presented his wife as 'Madame
Podsnap'; also his daughter as 'Mademoiselle Podsnap', with
some inclination to add 'ma fille', in which bold venture, however, he checked himself. The Veneerings being at that time the

only other arrivals, he had added (in a condescendingly explanatory manner), 'Monsieur Veynairreeng', and had then subsided into English.

'How Do You Like London?' Mr Podsnap now inquired from his station of host, as if he were administering something in the nature of a powder or potion to a deaf child; 'London, Londres, London?'

The foreign gentleman admired it.

'You find it Very Large?' said Mr Podsnap, spaciously.

The foreign gentleman found it very large.

'And Very Rich?'

The foreign gentleman found it, without doubt, énormément riche.

'Enormously Rich, We say,' returned Mr Podsnap, in a condescending manner. 'Our English adverbs do Not terminate in Mong and We Pronounce the "ch" as if there were a "t" before it. We say Ritch.'

'Reetch,' remarked the foreign gentleman.

'And Do You Find, Sir,' pursued Mr Podsnap, with dignity, 'Many Evidences that Strike You, of our British Constitution in the Streets Of The World's Metropolis, London, Londres, London?'

The foreign gentleman begged to be pardoned, but did not altogether understand.

'The Constitution Britannique,' Mr Podsnap explained, as if he were teaching in an infant school. 'We Say British, But You Say Britannique, You Know' (forgivingly, as if that were not not his fault). 'The Constitution, Sir.'

The foreign gentleman said, 'Mais, yees; I know eem.'

A youngish sallowish gentleman in spectacles, with a lumpy forehead, seated in a supplementary chair at a corner of the table, here caused a profound sensation by saying, in a raised voice "ESKER", and then stopping dead.

'Mais oui,' said the foreign gentleman, turning towards him. 'Est-ce que? Quoi donc?'

But the gentleman with the lumpy forehead having for the time delivered himself of all that he found behind his lumps, spake for the time no more.

'I Was Inquiring,' said Mr Podsnap, resuming the thread of his discourse, 'Whether You have Observed in our Streets as We should say, Upon our Pavvy as you would say, any Tokens –'

The foreign gentleman with patient courtesy entreated pardon; 'But what was tokenz?'

'Marks,' said Mr Podsnap; 'Signs, you know, Appearances – Traces.'

'Ah! Of a Orse?' inquired the foreign gentleman.

'We call it Horse,' said Mr Podsnap, with forbearance. 'In England, Angleterre, England, We Aspirate the "H", and We Say "Horse". Only our Lower Classes Say " 'Orse!" '

'Pardon,' said the foreign gentleman; 'I am alwiz wrong!'

'Our Language,' said Mr Podsnap, with a gracious consciousness of being always right, 'is Difficult. Ours is a Copious Language, and Trying to Strangers. I will not Pursue my Question.'

But the lumpy gentleman, unwilling to give it up, again madly said 'ESKER', and again spake no more.

1864   *Our Mutual Friend*

SAMUEL BUTLER
(*The Courting of Christina*)

Papas and mammas sometimes ask young men whether their intentions are honourable towards their daughters. I think young men might occasionally ask papas and mammas whether their intentions are honourable before they accept invitations to houses where there are still unmarried daughters.

*

What a really nice girl might have done with him I cannot tell, but fate had thrown none such in his way except his youngest sister Alethea, whom he might perhaps have liked if she had not been his sister. The result of his experience was that women had never done him any good and he was not accustomed to associate them with any pleasure; if there was a part of Hamlet in connexion with them it had been so completely cut out in the edition of the play in which he was required to act that he had come to disbelieve in its existence. As for kissing, he had never

201

kissed a woman in his life except his sister – and my own sisters when we were all small children together. Over and above these kisses, he had until quite lately been required to imprint a solemn flabby kiss night and morning upon his father's cheek, and this, to the best of my belief, was the extent of Theobald's knowledge in the matter of kissing, at the time of which I am now writing.

*

Over and above the recommendations already enumerated, she had another in the possession of what was supposed to be a very beautiful contralto voice. Her voice was certainly contralto, for she could not reach higher than D in the treble; its only defect was that it did not go correspondingly low in the bass: in those days, however, a contralto voice was understood to include even a soprano if the soprano could not reach soprano notes, and it was not necessary that it should have the quality which we now assign to contralto. What her voice wanted in range and power was made up in the feeling with which she sang. She had transposed 'Angels ever bright and fair' into a lower key, so as to make it suit her voice, thus proving, as her mamma said, that she had a thorough knowledge of the laws of harmony; not only did she do this, but at every pause added an embellishment of arpeggios from one end to the other of the keyboard, on a principle which her governess had taught her; she thus added life and interest to an air which everyone – so she said – must feel to be rather heavy in the form in which Handel left it.

*

'She is heart-whole yet, dear Mr Pontifex,' said Mrs Allaby, one day, 'at last I believe she is. It is not for want of admirers – oh! no – she has had her full share of these, but she is too, too difficult to please. I think, however, she would fall before a *great and good* man.' And she looked hard at Theobald, who blushed; but the days went by and still he did not propose.

Another time Theobald actually took Mrs Cowey into his confidence and the reader may guess what account of Christina he got from her. Mrs Cowey tried the jealousy manoeuvre and hinted at a possible rival. Theobald was, or pretended to be, very much alarmed; a little rudimentary pang of jealousy shot across his bosom and he began to believe with pride that he was not only in love, but desperately in love or he would never feel so jealous. Nevertheless, day after day still went by and he did not propose.

*

Christina was impressionable and could not even hear the name 'Missolonghi' mentioned without bursting into tears. When Theobald accidentally left his sermon case behind him one Sunday, she slept with it in her bosom and was forlorn when she had as it were to disgorge it on the following Sunday; but I do not think Theobald ever took so much as an old toothbrush of Christina's to bed with him.

1872–85   *Way of All Flesh*

GEORGE AND WEEDON GROSSMITH
from The Diary of a Nobody

April 19. Cummings called, bringing with him his friend Merton, who is in the wine trade. Gowing also called. Mr Merton made himself at home at once, and Carrie and I were both struck with him immediately, and thoroughly approved of his sentiments.

He leaned back in his chair and said: 'You must take me as I am;' and I replied: 'Yes – and you must take us as we are. We're homely people, we are not swells.'

He answered: 'No, I can see that,' and Gowing roared with laughter; but Merton in a most gentlemanly manner said to Gowing: 'I don't think you quite understand me. I intended to convey that our charming host and hostess were superior to the follies of fashion, and preferred leading a simple and wholesome life to gadding about to twopenny-halfpenny tea-drinking afternoons, and living above their incomes.'

I was immensely pleased with these sensible remarks of Merton's and concluded that subject by saying: 'No, candidly, Mr Merton, we don't go into Society, because we do not care for it; and what with the expense of cabs here and cabs there, and white gloves and white ties, etc., it doesn't seem worth the money.'

Merton said in reference to *friends:* 'My motto is "Few and

True"; and, by the way, I also apply that to wine, "Little and Good".' Gowing said: 'Yes, and sometimes "cheap and tasty", eh, old man?' Merton, still continuing, said he should treat me as a friend, and put me down for a dozen of his 'Lockanbar' whisky, and as I was an old friend of Gowing, I should have it for 36s., which was considerably under what he paid for it.

He booked his own order, and further said that at any time I wanted any passes for the theatre I was to let him know, as his name stood good for any theatre in London.

April 20. Carrie reminded me that as her old school friend, Annie Fullers (now Mrs James), and her husband had come up from Sutton for a few days, it would look kind to take them to the theatre, and would I drop a line to Mr Merton asking him for passes for four, either for the Italian Opera, Haymarket, Savoy, or Lyceum. I wrote Merton to that effect.

April 21. Got a reply from Merton, saying he was very busy, and just at present couldn't manage passes for the Italian Opera, Haymarket, Savoy or Lyceum, but the best thing going on in London was the *Brown Bushes*, at the Tank Theatre, Islington, and enclosed seats for four; also bill for whisky.

April 23. Mr and Mrs James (Miss Fullers that was) came to meat-tea, and we left directly after for the Tank Theatre. We got a bus that took us to King's Cross, and then changed into one that took us to the 'Angel'. Mr James each time insisted on paying for all, saying that I had paid for the tickets and that was quite enough.

We arrived at the theatre, where, curiously enough, all our bus-load except an old woman with a basket seemed to be going in. I walked ahead and presented the tickets. The man looked at them and called out: 'Mr Willowly! do you know anything about these?' holding up my tickets. The gentleman called to came up and examined my tickets, and said 'Who gave you these?' I said, rather indignantly: 'Mr Merton, of course.' He said: 'Merton? Who's he?' I answered, rather sharply: 'You ought to know, his name's good at any theatre in London.' He replied: 'Oh! is it? Well, it ain't no good here. These tickets, which are *not* dated were issued under Mr Swinstead's management, which has since changed hands.' While I was having some very unpleasant words with the man, James, who had gone upstairs with the ladies, called out: 'Come on!' I went up after them, and a very civil attendant said: 'This way, please, box H.' I said to James: 'Why, how on earth did you manage it?' and to my horror he replied: 'Why, paid for it of course.'

This was humiliating enough, and I could scarcely follow the play, but I was doomed to still further humiliation. I was leaning out of the box, when my tie – a little black bow which fastened onto the stud by means of a new patent – fell into the pit below. A clumsy man not noticing it, had his foot on it and eventually flung it under the next seat in disgust. What with the box incident and the tie, I felt quite miserable. Mr James, of Sutton, was very good. He said: 'Don't worry – no one will notice it with your beard. That is the only advantage of growing one that I can see.' There was no occasion for that remark, for Carrie is very proud of my beard.

April 24. Could scarcely sleep a wink through thinking of having brought up Mr and Mrs James from the country to go to the theatre last night, and his having paid for a private box because our order was not honoured; and such a poor play too. I wrote a very satirical letter to Merton, the wine merchant, who gave us the pass, and said: 'Considering we had to pay for our seats, we did our *best* to appreciate the performance.' I thought this line rather cutting, and I asked Carrie how many p's there were in appreciate, and she said 'One.' After I sent off the letter I looked at the dictionary and found there were two. Awfully vexed at this.

Decided not to worry myself any more about the James's; for, as Carrie wisely said, 'We'll make it all right with them by asking them up from Sutton one evening next week to play at Bezique.'

April 25. In consequence of Brickwell telling me his wife was working wonders with the new Pinkford's enamel paint, I determined to try it. I bought two tins of red on my way home. I hastened through tea, went into the garden and painted some flower-pots. I called out Carrie, who said: 'You've always got some new-fangled craze;' but she was obliged to admit that the flower-pots looked remarkably well. Went upstairs into the servant's bedroom and painted her washstand, towel-horse, and chest of drawers. To my mind it was an extraordinary improvement, but as an example of the ignorance of the lower classes in the matter of taste, our servant, Sarah, on seeing them, evinced no sign of pleasure, but merely said 'she thought they looked very well as they was before.'

April 26. Got some more red enamel paint (red, to my mind, being the best colour), and painted the coal-scuttle, and the backs of our *Shakespeare*, the binding of which had almost worn out.

April 27. Painted the bath red, and was delighted with the result. Sorry to say Carrie was not, in fact we had a few words about it. She said I ought to have consulted her, and she had never heard of such a thing as a bath being painted red. I replied: 'It's merely a matter of taste.'

I PAINTED THE WASHSTAND IN THE SERVANT'S BEDROOM.

Fortunately, further argument on the subject was stopped by a voice saying, 'May I come in?' It was only Cummings, who said, 'Your maid opened the door, and asked me to excuse her showing me in, as she was wringing out some socks.' I was delighted to see him, and suggested we should have a game of whist with a dummy, and by way of merriment said: '*You* can be the dummy.' Cummings (I thought rather ill-naturedly) replied: 'Funny as usual.' He said he couldn't stop, he only called to leave me the *Bicycle News*, as he had done with it.

1894

THOMAS HARDY

Absent-Mindedness in a Parish Choir

'It happened on Sunday after Christmas – the last Sunday ever they played in Longpuddle church gallery, as it turned out though they didn't know it then. As you may know, sir, the players formed a very good band – almost as good as the Mellstock parish players that were led by the Dewys; and that's saying a great deal. There was Nicholas Puddingcome, the leader, with the first fiddle; there was Timothy Thomas, the bass-viol man; John Biles, the tenor fiddler; Dan'l Hornhead, with the serpent; Robert Dowdle, with the clarionet; and Mr Nicks, with the oboe – all sound and powerful musicians, and strong-winded men – they that blowed. For that reason they were very much in demand Christmas week for little reels and dancing parties; for they could turn a jig or a hornpipe out of hand as well as ever they could turn out a psalm, and perhaps better, not to speak irreverent. In short, one half-hour they could be playing a Christmas carol in the squire's hall to the ladies and gentlemen, and drinking tay and coffee with 'em as modest as saints; and the next, at The Tinker's Arms, blazing away like wild horses with the "Dashing White Sergeant" to nine couple of dancers and more and swallowing rum-and-cider hot as flame.

'Well, this Christmas they'd been out to one rattling randy after another every night, and had got next to no sleep at all. Then came the Sunday after Christmas, their fatal day. 'Twas so mortal cold that year that they could hardly sit in the gallery; for though the congregation down in the body of the church had a stove to keep off the frost, the players in the gallery had nothing at all. So Nicholas said at morning service, when 'twas freezing an inch an hour, "Please the Lord I won't stand this numbing weather no longer: this afternoon we'll have something in our insides to make us warm, if it cost a king's ransom."

'So he brought a gallon of hot brandy and beer, ready mixed, to church with him in the afternoon, and by keeping the jar well wrapped up in Timothy Thomas's bass-viol bag it kept drinkably warm till they wanted it, which was just a thimbleful in the Absolution, and another after the Creed, and the remainder at the beginning o' the sermon. When they'd had the last pull they felt quite comfortable and warm, and as the sermon went on – most unfortunately for 'em it was a long one that afternoon – they fell asleep, every man jack of 'em; and there they slept on as sound as rocks.

''Twas a very dark afternoon, and by the end of the sermon all you could see of the inside of the church were the pa'son's two candles alongside of him in the pulpit, and his spaking face behind 'em. The sermon being ended at last, the pa'son gie'd out the Evening Hymn. But no choir set about sounding up the tune, and the people began to turn their heads to learn the reason why, and then Levi Limpet, a boy who sat in the gallery, nudged Timothy and Nicholas, and said, "Begin! begin!"

' "Hey? what?" says Nicholas, starting up; and the church being so dark and his head so muddled he thought he was at the party they had played at all the night before, and away he went, bow and fiddle, at "The Devil among the Tailors", the favourite jog of our neighbourhood at that time. The rest of the band, being in the same state of mind and nothing doubting, followed their leader with all their strength, according to custom. They poured out that there tune till the lower bass notes of "The Devil among the Tailors" made the cobwebs in the roof shiver like ghosts; then Nicholas, seeing nobody moved, shouted out as he scraped (in his usual commanding way at dances when the folk didn't know the figures), "Top couples cross hands! And when I make the fiddle squeak at the end, every man kiss his pardner under the mistletoe!"

'The boy Levi was so frightened that he bolted down the gallery stairs and out homeward like lightning. The pa'son's hair fairly stood on end when he heard the evil tune raging through the church, and thinking the choir had gone crazy he held up his hand and said: "Stop, stop, stop! Stop, stop! What's this?" But they didn't hear'n for the noise of their own playing, and the more he called the louder they played.

'Then the folks came out of their pews, wondering down to the ground, and saying: "What do they mean by such wickedness? We shall be consumed like Sodom and Gomorrah!"

'Then the squire came out of his pew lined wi' green baize, where lots of lords and ladies visiting at the house were worshipping along with him, and went and stood in front of the gallery, and shook his fist in the musicians' faces, saying, "What! In this reverent edifice! What!"

'And at last they heard'n through their playing, and stopped.

' "Never such an insulting, disgraceful thing – never!" says the squire, who couldn't rule his passion.

' "Never!" says the pa'son, who had come down and stood beside him.

' "Not if the Angels of Heaven," says the squire (he was a wickedish man, the squire was, though now for once he happened to be on the Lord's side) – "not if the Angels of Heaven come down," he says, "shall one of you villainous players ever sound a note in this church again; for the insult to me, and my family, and my visitors, and God Almighty, that you've a-perpetrated this afternoon!"

'Then the unfortunate church band came to their senses, and remembered where they were; and 'twas a sight to see Nicholas Puddingcome and Timothy Thomas and John Biles creep down the gallery stairs with their fiddles under their arms, and poor Dan'l Hornhead with his serpent, and Robert Dowdle with his clarionet, all looking as little as ninepins; and out they went. The pa'son might have forfi'ed 'em when he learned the truth o't, but the squire would not. That very week he sent for a barrel-organ that would play two and-twenty new psalm-tunes, so exact and particular that, however sinful inclined you was, you could play nothing but psalm-tunes whatsoever. He had a really respectable man to turn the winch, as I said, and the old players played no more.'

1896   *Life's Little Ironies*

EDEN PHILLPOTTS
from Gideon's Front Tooth*

The great affair of the tooth came on at the beginning of next term; and first I must tell you that next door to Dunston's lived an old man, so frightfully ancient that his skin was all shrivelled over his bones. He didn't like boys much, but he would look over his garden-wall sometimes into our playground and scowl if anybody caught his eye. Various things, of course, went over the wall often, and it was one of the excitements of Dunston's to go into old Grimbal's garden and get them back. Twice only he caught a chap, and both times, despite his awful age and yellowness of skin, he thrashed the chap very fairly hard with a walking-stick; but he never reported anybody to Dunston, and it was generally thought he regarded it as a sort of sport hunting for chaps in his garden. Of course, in fair, open hunting he hadn't a chance, and the two he did catch he got by stealth, hiding behind bushes on a rather dark evening.

Well, the facts would never have been known about this tooth but for Gideon's mean spirit. It happened to be necessary for him to fight me, and though not caring much about it, he couldn't help himself. Besides, though the champion of the Lower School, I was tons smaller than Gideon, and Gideon didn't know till after the fight that I was a champion, the true facts about my greatness being hid from him.

Just before the fight Gideon said, 'Oh! my tooth, by the way. It may be hurt, and it cost my father five guineas.' So, to our great interest he unscrewed one of his two top front teeth and gave it to his second. You couldn't have told it was a sham, so remarkably was it done, and it screwed on to the foundation of the original tooth much like a spike screws into the sole of a cricket-boot. Gideon had fallen downstairs when he was ten and knocked off the tooth, so he told us; but Murray, who is well

*As told by one of the boys in Dr Dunston's Preparatory School.

up in science, said that all Jews' front teeth are rather rocky, because in feudal times they were pulled out with pincers as a form of torture, and to make the Jews give up their secret treasures. Murray said that after many generations of pulling out Nature got sick of it, and that in modern times the front teeth of Jews aren't worth talking about. Murray is full of rum ideas like that, and he hopes to go in for engineering, having already many secret inventions waiting to be patented.

As to Gideon, I licked him rather badly in two rounds and a half. Then he was mopped up and dressed, and screwed in his front tooth again with the greatest ease.

Once it got known about this tooth, and fellows were naturally excited. Steggles said it was on the principle of a tobacco-pipe mouthpiece; and, finding the chaps were keen to see it, Gideon let it be generally known he would freely show it to anybody for threepence a time, and to friends for twopence. But this was a safe reduction to make, because, properly speaking, he hadn't any friends. Seeing there were nearly two hundred boys at Dunston's, and that certainly half, including several fellows from the Sixth, took a pleasure in seeing the tooth, and didn't mind the rather high charge, Gideon did jolly well; and in the case of Nubby Tomkins, he made actually one shilling and threepence, because the tooth had a most peculiar fascination for Nubby, and he saw it no less than five times. After that Gideon made a reduction to him, as well he might. But somehow Slade, the head of the school, was very averse to Gideon's front tooth when he heard about it, and he decided that there must be no more exhibitions of it for money. He told Gideon so himself.

However, a new boy came a week afterwards and heard about the strangeness of the tooth, and offered a shilling, in three instalments, to see it; which was too much temptation for Gideon, and he showed it, contrary to what Slade had said.

Slade, of course, heard, for the new boy happened to be his own cousin, though called Saunders; and then there was a curious scene in the playground, which I fortunately saw. Slade came up to Gideon in the very quiet way he has, and asked him in a perfectly gentlemanly voice for his front tooth. At first Gideon seemed inclined not to give it up, but he saw what an awfully serious thing that would be, and finally unscrewed it, though not willingly.

'Now,' said Slade, 'I'll have no more of this penny peep-show business at Merivale. I told you once, and you have disobeyed me. So there's an end of your beastly tooth. What's this?'

He took something out of his pocket.

'It's a catapult,' said Gideon.

'It is,' said Slade, 'and I'm going to use your tooth instead of a bullet, and fire it into space.'

'It cost five guineas,' said Gideon.

'Don't care if it cost a hundred,' answered Slade, still in a very gentlemanly sort of way. 'We can't have this sort of thing here, you know.'

Slade was just going to fire into space, as he had said, when a robin suddenly settled within thirty yards of us, on the wall between the playground and old Grimbal's. Slade being a wonderful shot with a catapult (having once shot a wood-pigeon), suddenly fired at the robin, and only missed it by about four inches. He said the shape of a front tooth was very unfavourable for shooting. But anyway, the tooth went over into Grimbal's, and we distinctly heard it hit against the side of his house.

Then Slade went away, and we rotted Gideon rather, because not having the tooth looked rum, and made a difference in his voice. He took it very quietly, and said he rather thought his father would be able to summon Slade; and before evening school, having marked down the spot where he fancied his tooth had hit Grimbal's house, he went to look with a box of matches. What happened afterwards he told us frankly; and it was certainly true, because, with all his faults, Gideon never lied to anybody.

'I went quietly over, and began carefully looking along the bottom of the wall, using a match to every foot or so,' he said, 'and I had done about half when I heard a door open. I then hooked it, and ran almost on to old Grimbal. He had not opened the door at all, but was coming up the garden path at the critical moment. Of course, he caught me. He was going to rub it into me with his stick, when I said I should think it very kind if he would hear me first, as I had a perfectly good excuse for being there.

'He said:

' "What excuse can you have for trespassing in my garden, you little oily wretch?"

' "Oily wretch" was what he called me; and I said that my tooth had been fired into his garden that very day, about half past one, by a chap with a catapult; and I lighted a match, and showed him it was missing.

'He said:

' "How the deuce are you going to find a tooth in a garden this size?" And I told him I had marked it down very carefully, and that it had cost five guineas, and that I rather believed my father would be able to summon the chap who had shot it away. He seemed a good deal interested, and said he thought very likely he might, if it was robbery with violence. Then he asked me if I was the boy he had seen beating down the price of a purse at Wilkinson's in Merivale, and I said I was. Then he said "Come in and have a bit of cake, boy;" and I went in and had a bit of cake, and saw on a shelf in his room about fifty or sixty cricket-balls, and various things which he has collared when they went over. He asked me a lot of questions about different things, and I answered them. All he said was about money. He also asked me to be good enough to value the things he had, which came over the wall from time to time; and I did, and he thanked me. They were worth fifteen shillings and ten-pence; and Wright's ball, which everybody thought was stolen by the milkman, wasn't for old Grimbal's got it; and the milk-man should be told and apologized to.

'Well, he knew a lot about money, and told me he had thousands of golden sovereigns, which he makes breed into thousands more.

'He said:

' "You're the only boy I ever met with a grain of sense in his head. Now, if I gave you a cheque on my bankers in Merivale for five pounds today, and wrote to you tomorrow morning to say I had changed my mind, what would you do?"

'I said, "It would be too late, sir, because your cheque would have been sent off to my father that very night, to put out at interest for me." He said, "That's right. Never give back money, or anything." Then he asked me my name, and told me I might come back tomorrow, and look for my tooth by daylight.'

That was Gideon's most peculiar adventure, and, though he never found the tooth or saw old Grimbal again, yet about seven or eight months afterwards, when old Grimbal was discovered all curiously twisted up and dead in bed by the man who took him his breakfast, the result of Gideon's visit to him came out. Old Grimbal had specially put him into his will by some legal method, and Doctor Dunston had Gideon into his study three days after old Grimbal kicked. It then was proved that old Grimbal had left Gideon all the things that came over the wall, and also a legacy of fifty pounds in money, because, according to the bit of the will which the Doctor read to Gideon out of a lawyer's letter, he was the only boy old Grimbal had ever met with who showed any intelligence above that of the anthropoid ape.

Gideon returned all the balls and things to their owners free of charge, but not until the rightful owners proved they were so. And the money he sent to his father; and his father, he told me afterwards, was so jolly pleased about the whole affair that he added nine hundred and fifty pounds to Grimbal's fifty. Therefore, by shooting Gideon's front tooth at a robin, Slade was actually putting the enormous sum of one thousand pounds into Gideon's pocket, which I should think was about the rummest thing that ever happened in the world.

Gideon stopped at Dunston's one term after that. Then he went away, and, I believe, began to help his father to sell diamonds. He was fairly good at French, and very at German; but of other things he knew rather little, except arithmetic, and his was the most beautiful arithmetic which had ever been done at Merivale; for I heard Stokes, who was a seventeenth wrangler in his time, tell the Doctor so.

The Human Boy

HAROLD NICOLSON

(*Tennyson Reads his Poems: 1831*)

... And in this year, 1831, he goes again to No. 67 Wimpole Street, and we find him talking and smoking in Hallam's attic-study under the leads, and their deciding between them that in future they 'will not lose hold of the Real in seeking the Ideal'. We find him, also, reading *Oenone* to Hallam's father. Not the *Oenone* that we know so well, but the first rather hesitating version of the 1832 volume written in the Valley of Cauterets. Nor does this particular recitation appear to have been a quite unqualified success. The old man 'seemed to like Juno's speech, but was called away in the middle of Venus.' The reading was not resumed, nor can Tennyson have relished the part about the old man being called away. But he was to make up for all that later at Farringford and at Aldworth. No chance in those days, no possible chance, of anyone being called away.

(*Tennyson Reads his Poems: 1860*)

How familiar to us has become the description of the life at Farringford! The regularity and the method of it all; the settled habits becoming, as it were, the etiquette of the house, an etiquette, in later years, almost regal in its rigidity. The honoured but apprehensive guest arriving before sunset in a cab from Yarmouth pier; the momentary glimpse of the poet over the hedge mowing the lawn in spectacles and black sombrero, and hiding, as one approached, behind the juniper; the parlour-maid and the very late Gothic of the drawing-room window; the evening sun upon the cedar outside; the mask of Dante glimmering from the dark red walls and the engraving of Sebastiano del Piombo's Lazarus above the mantelpiece; Mrs Tennyson rising, gentle and nervous, towards one from the sofa, in her grey gown; the anxious, expectant pause; the sense of unbearable imminence – and then, slowly framed in the doorway, the dark bulk of the Laureate. In awful silence he would advance into the room, a book held close to his, by then, unspectacled eyes. An evanescent introduction from Mrs Tennyson, and those fierce eyes would be turned upon one in a penetrating myopic scrutiny, and a deep growl of acknowledgement, if not of greeting, would proceed from the mass of tangled mane and beard. Another aching pause, and in a crisis of embarrassment one would pass into the dining-room. It was six-thirty by the clock there; how long could all this be possibly expected to last? There was salt beef and carrots and side dishes on the table. The Laureate would begin to carve. A little fluttering conversation about Yarmouth pier from Mrs Tennyson; a second sudden growl from the Laureate: 'I like my meat in wedges,' and the subject of Yarmouth pier would flutter down to another prolonged and awful silence. And then gradually, in the appropriate and vacant expectancy thus created, the Laureate would embark with grunt and growl upon some broad Lincolnshire story, a story so broad and so North Country that one would wonder tremulously how much one understood, how much, with Mrs Tennyson there, one could rightly be expected to understand; and with the conclusion would come from the Laureate a loud appropriate guffaw, in contrast to which one's own accordant laughter appeared but a slight and timorous cacchination. Gradually under hammer-blows like this the ice would melt, and with the port a certain geniality, heartening but still very insecure, would descend upon the occasion. But there were worse trials to come. At eight one would be taken to the attic room for a pipe; still apprehensive, one would enter, and from a basket the Laureate would choose a pipe and transfer it, already lighted, to one's lips. And then there would be a growl or two about some recent review in an obscure periodical; and more stories; and one would sit there in the smoke, wondering why he was so different from what one had expected – wondering why he called a novel 'a novell', why he pronounced knowledge with a long 'o', why he gave to the word 'too' a thinness of vowel sound which was cockney rather than Lincolnshire; why he spoke of a pageant as a 'paygeant'; why, finally, he sat there, as Mr Gosse has told us in his inimitably vivid way, 'a gaunt, black, touzled man, rough in speech, brooding like an old gipsy over his inch of clay pipe stuffed with shag and sucking in port wine with gusto'.

And then one would descend to the drawing-room, where the curtains had been drawn and the lamps lit; and there was a table in the recessed window, with Mrs Tennyson flickering over the tea-urn and the fruit. And more port. And then the reading would begin.

We have heard a great deal about this reading. It has been described very entertainingly by Mrs Asquith; it has inspired what is perhaps the best of many wonderful passages in Henry James's *Middle Years*. It figures prominently in all the endless references to these palpitating visits. He would sometimes read the *Idylls*; more often he would choose the *Ode to the Duke of Wellington*, lengthening the vowels into:

Bury the greaat Duke with an empire's lamentaation.

Or into:

To the nooise of the moourning of a mighty naaation.

Sometimes, and quite incomprehensibly, he would embark upon *The Northern Farmer*, and at other times he would startle his audience with a very metrical rendering of *The Battle of Brunanburh*. He would never consent to read *In Memoriam*: 'I cannot,' he said, 'it breaks me down so.' But it was *Maud* that was his favourite. 'Come and let me read you *Maud*,' he said to J. T. Fields; 'you'll never forget it.' On occasions, even, he would read German with a strong English accent.

But that he would read one something was a certainty:

           and the poet, little urged,
But with some prelude of disparagement
Read, mouthing out his hollow oes and aes
Deep-chested music.

And thus one would sit there in the red drawing-room, conscious, as Henry James says, 'of the heaviest pressure' one 'had doubtless ever known the romantic situations bring to bear', watching the large brown hand rippling to the movement of the verse, and from time to time clenched with whitening knuckles on the arm of the chair. And through it all the deep bucolic voice would continue, booming and chanting with sudden lifts and with disconcerting hisses and whispers, and, if one's attention wandered for a moment into thoughts of how exactly to phrase the situation in some eventful article or memoir, one would be suddenly pinioned and exposed by a break and a question: 'How exactly do you understand that?'

1923   *Tennyson*

ALDOUS HUXLEY

(*Illidge Joins the Reception Downstairs*)

'But what about clothes,' said Illidge doubtfully. 'I can't come down like this.' He looked down at himself. It had been a cheap suit at the best of times. Age had not improved it.

'Oh, that doesn't matter.' A dog with the smell of rabbits in his nostrils could hardly have shown a more indecent eagerness than Lord Edward at the sound of Pongileoni's flute. He took his assistant's arm and hurried him out of the door, and along the corridor towards the stairs. 'It's just a little party,' he went on. 'I seem to remember my wife having said ... Quite informal. And besides,' he added, inventing new excuses to justify the violence of his musical appetite, 'we can just slip in without ... Nobody will notice.'

Illidge had his doubts. 'I'm afraid it's not a very small party,' he began; he had seen the motors arriving.

'Never mind, never mind,' interrupted Lord Edward, lusting irrepressibly for Bach.

Illidge abandoned himself. He would look like a horrible fool, he reflected, in his shiny blue serge suit. But perhaps, on second thoughts, it was better to appear in shiny blue – straight from the laboratory, after all, and under the protection of the master of the house (himself in a tweed jacket), than in that old and, as he had perceived during previous excursions into Lady Edward's luscious world, deplorably shoddy and ill-made evening suit of his. It was better to be totally different from the rich and smart – a visitor from another intellectual planet – than a fourth-rate and snobbish imitator. Dressed in blue, one might be stared at as an oddity; in badly cut black (like a waiter) one was contemptuously ignored, one was despised for trying without success to be what one obviously wasn't.

Illidge braced himself to play the part of the Martian visitor with firmness, even assertively.

Their entrance was even more embarrassingly conspicuous than Illidge had anticipated. The great staircase at Tantamount House comes down from the first floor in two branches which join, like a pair of equal rivers, to precipitate themselves in a single architectural cataract of Verona marble into the hall. It debouches under the arcades, in the centre of one of the sides of the covered quadrangle, opposite the vestibule and the front door. Coming in from the street, one looks across the hall and sees through the central arch of the opposite arcade the wide stairs and shining balustrades climbing up to a landing on which a Venus by Canova, the pride of the third marquess's collection, stands pedestalled in an alcove, screening with a modest but coquettish gesture of her two hands, or rather failing to screen, her marble charms. It was at the foot of this triumphal slope of marble that Lady Edward had posted the orchestra; her guests were seated in serried rows confronting it. When Illidge and Lord Edward turned the corner in front of Canova's Venus, tip-toeing, as they approached the music and the listening crowd, with steps ever more laboriously conspiratorial, they found themselves suddenly at the focus of a hundred pairs of eyes. A gust of curiosity stirred the assembled guests. The apparition from a world so different from theirs of this huge bent old man, pipe-smoking and tweed-jacketed, seemed strangely portentous. He had a certain air of the skeleton in the cupboard – broken loose; or of one of those monsters which haunt the palaces of only the best and most aristocratic families. The Beastie of Glamis, the Minotaur itself could hardly have aroused more interest than did Lord Edward. Lorgnons were raised, there was a general craning to left and right, as people tried to look round the well-fed obstacles in front of them. Becoming suddenly aware of so many inquisitive glances, Lord Edward took fright. A consciousness of social sin possessed him; he took his pipe out of his mouth and put it away, still smoking, into the pocket of his jacket. He halted irresolutely. Flight or advance? He turned this way and that, pivoting his whole bent body from the hips with a curious swinging motion, like the slow ponderous balancing of a camel's neck. For a moment he wanted to retreat. But love of Bach was stronger than his terrors. He was the bear whom the

219

smell of molasses constrains in spite of all his fears to visit the hunters' camp; the lover who is ready to face an armed and outraged husband and the divorce court for the sake of an hour in his mistress's arms. He went forward, tiptoeing down the stairs more conspiratorially than ever – Guy Fawkes discovered, but yet irrationally hoping that he might escape notice by acting as though the Gunpowder Plot were still unrolling itself according to plan. Illidge followed him. His face had gone very red with the embarrassment of the first moment; but in spite of this embarrassment, or rather because of it, he came downstairs after Lord Edward with a kind of swagger, one hand in his pocket, a smile on his lips. He turned his eyes coolly this way and that over the crowd. The expression on his face was one of contemptuous amusement. Too busy being the Martian to look where he was going, Illidge suddenly missed his footing on this unfamiliarly regal staircase with its inordinate treads and dwarfishly low risers. His foot slipped, he staggered wildly on the brink of a fall, waving his arms, to come to rest, however, still miraculously on his feet, some two or three steps lower down. He resumed his descent with such dignity as he could muster up. He felt exceedingly angry, he hated Lady Edward's guests one and all, without exception.

Point Counter Point
1928

TERENCE RATTIGAN
(*Impressing Diana*)

DIANA *appears at window*, ROGER, THE COMMANDER, *following*.
ROGER: Well, of course, there was only one thing to do. So I gave the order – all hands on deck – (*Stops at sight of* KIT *and* ALAN).
ALAN: And did they come?

French Without Tears
1936

NIGEL BALCHIN
(*The Gun*)

Before I could think of anything to say Jake Gladwin and Mair came in. Gladwin was a big man with a fat white face that was always sweating slightly. He came in and dived into the chair at the head of the table as though he was playing musical chairs and said, 'Well, gentlemen, let's get started,' in his high squeaky voice.

Mair sat down on Gladwin's right, and Waring plumped down next to him. I hesitated about where to sit. I never knew at meetings whether to bag a place near the Old Man at the top, or whether to reckon that we sat in rank order, which brought me pretty near the bottom. Easton and his pal and all the soldiers all went and sat on the opposite side of the table rather pointedly. Luckily, Gladwin's people just went and sat in a heap at the very bottom of the table from sheer force of habit, which made the whole thing look funny.

Gladwin looked down the table and squeaked out, 'Oh, come on, friends, come up higher. Shan't be able to hear you. Won't be able to hear me. Gather round.'

Finally we got sorted out. I sat next to Waring, with the soldiers and Easton opposite and Gladwin's people scattered about.

Gladwin wiped the sweat off his forehead and said 'Gentlemen, I have called this meeting on the Minister's instructions to clear up the position about the Reeves gun. The Minister has his own views about the Reeves. But before making any final decision, he wants to be sure that the various points of view of you gentlemen are fully understood by us. There have been extensive demonstrations and experiments. The question now is, what have those experiments shown and what are we going to do about it?' He gave his forehead a final mop and said in a loud crow, 'That's all I want to say. Now you talk and I'll listen.'

There was a pause. Then Gladwin said, 'I believe Professor Mair has been interested in these experiments. Perhaps he'll give us his conclusions?'

I looked at the Old Man a bit anxiously. The chances were that he would up and do one of his enthusiastic acts, which were always bad salesmanship. But he just went on filling his pipe and said slowly, 'Well, in a few words, Mr Chairman, I should say that the Reeves gun is one of the most promising

221

developments I've seen – from some points of view. But that's only an opinion, and for my part I should prefer to hear other people before being too dogmatic.'

Gladwin nodded. There was silence again. Then the brigadier said, 'Well, frankly, Mr Chairman, we don't like the Reeves.'

'You don't, eh?' said Gladwin. As he must have known they'd been fighting it tooth and nail for weeks, I thought he did pretty well to sound surprised.

'No. It has a lot of snags from the user point of view, and we don't think it has sufficient advantages to offset them.'

'Well, of course that's the question,' squeaked Gladwin. 'What's the balance of advantage and disadvantage? Everything has disadvantages.' He sank back and mopped his forehead as though thinking that up had exhausted him. Nobody seemed to know the next line.

Easton had been sitting staring blankly at the window. He turned and looked through the chairman and said, 'It might possibly be of interest to the meeting, Mr Chairman, to hear the views of the National Scientific Advisory Council, of which I have the honour to be chairman.'

'Please,' said Gladwin in a loud squawk.

'The National Scientific Advisory Council . . .' said Easton.

'Of which he has the honour to be chairman,' Waring muttered in my ear.

'. . . is the body officially deputed by the Cabinet to offer advice on all major scientific issues. The Council appointed a special sub-committee to examine and report on the Reeves gun. Dr Brine, who is with us here today, acted as convener of this sub-committee, which was given the fullest facilities for the examination of this weapon. I suggest that Dr Brine should give the views of his sub-committee.'

'Please,' said Gladwin a bit pathetically, mopping away. I had the feeling that unless somebody really gave some views pretty soon, he would burst into tears.

The blue-chinned man stroked the blue part and said, 'Well, Mr Chairman, my colleagues and I approached this matter purely as scientists.' He said it as though everybody else had approached it as income tax inspectors or jobbing gardeners.

'And our conclusion was that scientifically speaking it was not a sound conception. Not at all a sound conception. In fact, I'll go further and say that no scientist could feel happy about many of the principles involved.' He sat back and looked pointedly at Mair. I glanced at the Old Man. His bottom lip was beginning to stick out – that meant he was bloody angry. The blue-chinned chap was obviously trying to be rude.

I scribbled on a bit of paper, 'Ask if the sub-committee saw the gun fired' and passed it to Mair.

'I'm interested to hear that, Mr Chairman,' said the brigadier, 'Because in our unscientific way that's what we thought.'

'Just what scientific principles did *you* think were unsound?' said Mair quickly.

The Brigadier hesitated and old Holland chipped in. 'We're talking about different sorts of principles,' he said. 'We didn't like it because it had user snags. Dr Brine is talking about principles of – of physics or something like that.'

'Well, then, may we take Dr Brine's statement first?' said Mair, unfolding my note and glancing at it. 'What didn't the sub-committee like?' Before Brine could answer he added, 'Perhaps first he could tell us who were his colleagues?'

Brine said, 'The sub-committee consisted of Professor Char, Dr Goulder, Dr Pease and myself.'

Mair smiled. 'One crystallographer, one vital statistician, one embryologist and one – let's see . . .?' he looked inquiringly at Brine with a charming smile. It couldn't have been more beautifully done if he'd slapped his face.

Easton went very red and said icily, 'If I might answer for Dr Brine, he is, of course, one of the best-known organic chemists in the country.'

'Right,' said Mair. 'Now we've got that straight.' He leant back and added casually, 'By the way – you did see the gun firing, I take it?'

Brine hesitated. Then he said, a bit feebly, 'We were not actually present at the trials.'

'But you've seen the gun *fire*? You didn't just look at it as a piece of furniture?'

'No,' said Brine defiantly. 'We didn't see it firing.'

223

Mair looked at him as though he were astounded. Then he said, 'Oh ... Well, well – never mind. Can we get back to what the committee didn't like?'

It was very pretty. The wretched bloke Brine started off, but it was obvious that no one was going to accept him as evidence after that. What he said was quite all right though not very profound. But he was batting on a ruined wicket. Easton weighed in once or twice, but he was so darned pompous that he only made things worse. So far the Old Man had the meeting cold.

At last old Holland looked up and said, 'Mr Chairman, might we consider this from another aspect? There seems to be some difference of opinion on the scientific side, and I for one am not competent to know who's right or wrong. But our objections to the Reeves aren't particularly scientific. Professor Mair may be quite right in saying that it's a grand idea, scientifically, but what we're interested in is whether it's a good *gun* as it stands.'

This was just the line I wanted to avoid. I glanced at Mair, hoping he'd stall. But by that time he had his tail well up and he went in head first.

'Well now,' he said cheerfully, 'that's surely a matter of fact. We've had experiments and trials. What do they say?'

The brigadier nearly saved him by shaking his head doubtfully and saying, 'Of course trials are one thing, and service in the field is another. Far too many weapons are put out without proper user consultation. That's the trouble.'

This was a grand red herring, because it woke up Gladwin's boys. They recognized the opening notes of one of the eternal rows with the army and started to rally round.

Styles, one of Gladwin's senior people, said, 'One of *our* difficulties, Mr Chairman, is that we can never get at the facts on which these user opinions are based.'

'Hear, hear!' said another of the crowd.

'Our trials may not be very good,' said Styles. 'But at least they're an advance on looking at the thing, firing it twice, and deciding that you don't like the noise it makes.'

The brigadier went rather red and I thought we were safe. They'd quarrel happily now for an hour about whether the army knew what it wanted or not. But old Holland chipped in again and said, 'Mr Chairman, this is an old argument, and it won't get us far. Could we get back to Professor Mair's question – what do the results of the trials show?' He looked across at me and said, 'I'm not a scientist or a statistician. But my reading of the figures I've seen suggests that, in practice, we don't *get* these advantages that have been talked about. I may be wrong.'

'I think Colonel Holland's taking altogether too gloomy a view,' said Mair, still in a high good humour. 'Perhaps, Mr Chairman, you'd allow Mr Rice of my staff to give us the facts. Mr Rice has done all the statistical work on the trials.'

'Please,' squawked Gladwin.

Everybody looked at me. I took the papers out of my bag. I knew the stuff by heart. But it gave me time to think. My hands were shaking slightly. Looking at the figures it suddenly struck me that they probably wouldn't mean anything to the meeting because nobody but some of Gladwin's boys would know the comparative figures for other weapons. I just started to read out the figures rather quickly.

It worked quite well. Gladwin leant back and mopped himself in a bored way, and Brine and the brigadier had that nice vacant look of people who are plodding on through the snow but have lost their way pretty thoroughly. I could see that Gladwin's crowd were a bit doubtful about what to do. They didn't like us, but if they shot at the thing they would be backing the army, which was dead against their principles.

When I finished there was a silence. Then old Holland suddenly said:

'That's fine, Mr Chairman. Now may I ask Mr Rice what it all adds up to?'

I said, 'I hardly think that's for me to say, I was merely giving the results of the trials.'

'And on these results you think that the Reeves is a first rate weapon?'

I hesitated for a moment and then said, 'I think Professor Mair's already given the view of the section.'

'And you share that view?' said Holland quietly.

225

'Oh come!' said Waring. 'That's scarcely a fair question, is it?'

'Why not?' said Holland.

'Well, Mr Chairman,' said Waring. 'I suggest that if Colonel Holland expressed a view, he'd hardly expect us to ask one of his junior officers if he agreed.'

'Quite,' said Gladwin. 'I don't think you can ask Rice to argue with his chief, Holland.'

Old Holland was still looking at me. He sat quiet for a moment and then he started to pat gently on the blotting paper in front of him.

'Mr Chairman,' he said quietly. 'I want to be quite frank. We don't like this gun. We're told that those figures show that we're wrong. Professor Mair suggested that his expert should give us the facts. If Mr Rice, who carried out this work, feels that his facts prove Professor Mair's case, I've no more to say. But surely I'm entitled to ask him what his figures mean?' He gave his blotter a sharp pat. 'After all, this is an important matter. We aren't debating, or defending a point of view. We're trying to get at the facts.' He was still staring at me with his rather pale, washed-out blue eyes. His voice was very quiet. 'If the Reeves gun is accepted, sooner or later men have got to fight with it. If there is anything wrong – if we've been too optimistic or anything has been glossed over ...' He shrugged his shoulder. '*They'll* be the sufferers. We shan't.'

There was a rather uncomfortable silence. This was the first time anybody had said anything as though he really meant it.

'Well, well, Mr Chairman,' said Mair cheerfully. 'Nobody wants to hide anything. If Colonel Holland would like Mr Rice's views, I have no objection at all.' He leaned back and gazed at me inquiringly.

'Well, Mr Rice?' said Holland. He turned the light blue eyes on me again.

I hesitated, and then said slowly, 'I agree with Professor Mair that the idea is excellent ...'

'And the weapon?' said Holland.

'I don't think it's right yet.'

There was a very faint rustle of interest.

'Would you be happy to see it accepted in its present form?' said Holland mercilessly. 'On these figures?'

I could feel Waring's angry eyes on me. My throat was very dry.

I said, 'No. I shouldn't.'

Holland sat back in his chair. 'Thank you,' he said quietly 'That's all I wanted to know.'

Easton said, 'You agree, in fact, with the view of our sub-committee?'

'I don't know how your sub-committee arrived at its view,' I said. 'My opinion is simply based on the figures.'

'I think it's rather important that that should be realized, Mr Chairman,' said Waring. 'Mr Rice is a technician and what he has given is purely a technician's view.'

'Quite,' said Gladwin, mopping his forehead very hard indeed. 'The position's quite understood.'

I looked round the table. It was understood all right.

Gladwin shut the meeting down as soon as he decently could and said something vague about reporting to the Minister.

1943   *The Small Back Room*

BERNARD DARWIN
(*Walter Hagen*)

Much, too much, has been written of Hagen's gifts as a 'show-man' and no doubt he fully understood that his casual manner, with a touch of flamboyant swagger about it, went down well with the crowd. No doubt also he could and did turn it on as some people can turn on, sometimes too palpably, their charm. But the casualness was natural to him and not forced. It helped him to take a strenuous life easily and unexhaustingly. It likewise enabled him to run things fine in point of time and even to be late in a way which might exasperate other people but did not cause Hagen himself to turn a hair. Others might wish to lie in bed or to stay in their baths, but they could not do so because of some malignant sprite whispering in their ears that they might have to hurry to the tee or even be disqualified. Hagen stayed in his bath as long as he pleased and trusted to the

227

chapter of accidents. Possibly he was rather a spoilt child in this matter in that promoters of tournaments knew his value and were always ready to make allowances for what was 'pretty Fanny's way'. There were occasions, notably in a certain match here against Abe Mitchell, when Hagen did considerably ruffle everyone by this inconsiderate lateness. There were not wanting those who said that it was part of a deep-laid scheme to disturb his adversary, much as in older and less scrupulous days men would deliberately fret a nervous adversary by breaking away at the start of a hundred yards race. Personally I think such accusations were utterly unfounded. I do not for a moment believe that he had any such design; this would not have accorded with his code; he was just irretrievably casual and had the bump of punctuality, if there be such a thing, very imperfectly developed.

That Hagen had an overpowering effect on some of his opponents was clear enough. His demeanour towards them, though entirely correct, had yet a certain suppressed truculence; he exhibited so supreme a confidence that they could not get it out of their minds and could not live against it. They felt him to be a killer and could not resist being killed. He had a very shrewd eye for their weaknesses and, strictly within the limits of what was honest and permissible, he would now and then exploit them to his own advantage. I heard a story the other day of Hagen's tactics which seems to me eminently characteristic, and I believe it to be true. He was playing in one of those four consecutive finals of the American P.G.A. tournaments which he won, and with one hole to play the match was all square. Hagen having the honour sliced his drive and the ball sailed away into a wood on the right while his adversary went rigidly down the middle. Hagen carefully examined his ball and emerged from the wood for a minute to have the crowd moved back, as if he were going to make the best of a bad job and play out sideways. He went back into the wood, had another look and then, as if suddenly spying a loop-hole of escape, played a magnificent iron shot through a gap in the trees right on to the green. The flabbergasted enemy put his ball tamely into a bunker and the match was over. Now it would be a poor compliment to

Hagen's intelligence to imagine that he had only just seen this loop-hole. He had seen it at once; he had reckoned that his second shot would be a disappointment to the enemy and that the disappointment would be heightened by the little preliminary drama. That was legitimate whether according to the law or to Hagen's code of ethics. You may approve or disapprove but you cannot but be struck by the cold, clear brain that can thus think things out at such a moment.

(*The 1922 Open*)

There was no fading-away by any of the leading four in the last round. Barnes 73, Whitcombe 75, Hutchison 76 all wrought manfully but Hagen played irresistibly well for his 72, and when he led by a stroke all was apparently over. He himself, and I have a clear vision of him, was smoking a cigar in evident relief and in complete solitude near the first teeing ground. Duncan remained far out in the distance and I resolved, rather against the grain at the end of a tiring day, to go and look for him. Partly a sense of duty urged me on and partly a wild hope. I knew that in Jack White's year both Taylor and Braid had broken 70 on heroic attempts to catch him in the last round and what had happened once might happen again. But the Sandwich of 1922 was a different course from the Sandwich of 1904. Duncan was to be sure incalculable, but the hope was a faint one.

Trudging across the course, cursing my own conscience, I picked up Duncan and his partner by the twelfth green and then I had my reward in six holes of delicious agony. He had but a handful of spectators with him and these were divided between joy and despair. They were full of joy over Duncan's astonishing play up to the flag and of despair because he could not crown these inspired approach shots by holing the putts. As I have said elsewhere, Duncan in a 'crazy' mood does produce those feelings, for the putts look so holeable for those who have not got to hole them. I cannot believe that he had been putting downright badly, but his approaching had given him chances of doing wholly marvellous things and he had not quite clinched them. Still he had good hope and he continued to play superbly and to get no help from Providence on the greens. One shot I seem to remember particularly, a lovely second lashed right up to the fifteenth pin, and a three at that hole would have been worth much fine gold – but the putt never looked in 'off the club'. Still on he went till he had a four for a 68 and a 68 would tie with Hagen. We thought he would do it; the tee shot was perfect and out came his spoon. Clearly he played to let the ball drift in a little from the left, his natural shot with the club. It started away to the left but alas! it never quite came in. In the case of a minor player I should say that here was bad luck, that he hit the ball just too well and truly. That is what most of us would say about a shot of our own, but that will not serve in the case of such a player as Duncan. There is nothing to say but that he did not quite play the shot he intended. His pitch or pitch-and-run was hit hurriedly and ended very short. It was all over; the man who had first set up a mark to be shot at had won again and the spurt had failed. But it remains one of the great spurts of golfing history.

1944   *Golf Between Two Wars*

PATRICK HAMILTON
Dawn over the Boarding House

Dawn, slowly filling Church Street with grey light, disclosed another day of war.

As the weak, winter light grew, however, a charming thing happened: the time of day permitted the withdrawal of black-out curtains, and a few lights shone from the windows of early risers. These remained on for ten minutes or so, and in this period there was a Christmas-card effect, a brief resumption, or rather imitation of the happy and unstrenuous lighting arrangements of the days before the war.

Much the same sort of thing would happen in the evening, when other social benefactors would keep on their lights unscreened until the last moment allowed by the regulations. But these evening lights gave forth, of course, quite a different atmosphere from those of the morning. At the end of the day such lights spoke soothingly of ease, recreation, repose: in the morning they burned intently and dramatically, speaking of renewed tension, of the battle of life, of the arduous endeavour and agitation of the day ahead.

Awareness of what went on outside penetrated hardly at all into the consciousness of those who lay on in bed within the walls of the Rosamund Tea Rooms. To these people, this part of the day in Church Street remained a pallid secret, which was either never disclosed to them at all, or was only disclosed when one of them, for some strange and forceful reason or other, got up to catch the early train to London. Then this adventurer would be delighted and impressed by the freshness, novelty, and quietness of what he saw: would be aware of being let into a secret: but the next day, sleeping on, he would become totally oblivious of its existence once again.

Certain sounds from the street did, indeed, float up into the stuffy, curtained bedrooms – an occasional lorry crashing through, the desultory disturbance of the quiet caused by the milkman and by the street-sweeper, the footsteps of the few people hurrying to the early train, the conversation of girls going to their war-work on bicycles – but the day did not begin at the Rosamund Tea Rooms until Sheila began to bounce about and knock on doors.

Even then the guests did not wake into full life. Instead, there was a dazed period in which each guest, turning in bed, renewed his acquaintanceship with his own problems and the fact that a war was being waged all over the world, and, finally rising and flinging back the curtains, contemplated the awful scene of wreckage caused by his sleep. The feeling of the morning after the night before is not a sensation endured by the dissolute only: every morning, for every human being, is in some sort a morning after the night before: the dissolute merely experience it in a more intense degree. There is an air of debauch about tossed bed-clothes, stale air, cold hot-water bottles, and last night's cast-off clothing, from which even the primmest of maiden ladies cannot hope to escape. Sleep is gross, a form of abandonment, and it is impossible for anyone to awake and observe its sordid consequences save with a faint sense of recent dissipation, of minute personal disquiet and remorse.

This perception, on the part of the guest, of his animal self was made even more dreary by certain impressions which were now wafted towards him of the coarser bedroom selves of his fellow-guests. These impressions were conveyed to him in partially ghostly and mysterious ways – in the uncanny gurgling and throbbing of unlocated water-pipes, which seemed softly and eerily to answer each other all over the house: in the sound of unidentified windows shrieking open or being slammed shut: in sudden furious rushes of water from taps into basins: in the sound of bumps, and of thuds: of tooth-glasses being rattled with tooth-brushes, and of expectorations: of coughs, and stupendous throat-clearings: of noses being blown: even of actual groans. To listen carefully to these noises was to sense a peculiar intensity in the bedroom life of the boarders: it was as if they were taking advantage of their brief privacy to serve too eagerly the physical compulsions of life.

Mrs Payne, pettishly hitting at her gong below, announced the proper commencement of day, and the end of privacy.

1947   *Slaves of Solitude*

JOHN BETJEMAN
Pot-Pourri from a Surrey Garden

Miles of pram in the wind and Pam in the gorse track,
   Coco-nut smell of the broom, and a packet of Weights
Press'd in the sand. The thud of a hoot on a horse-track –
   A horse-riding horse for a horse-track –
   Conifer county of Surrey approached
Through remarkable wrought-iron gates.

Over your boundary now, I wash my face in a bird-bath,
   Then which path shall I take? that over there by the pram?
Down by the pond! or – yes, I will take the slippery third path,
   Trodden away with gym shoes,
   Beautiful fir-dry alley that leads
To the bountiful body of Pam.

Pam, I adore you, Pam, you great big mountainous sports girl,
   Whizzing them over the net, full of the strength of five:
That old Malvernian brother, you zephyr and khaki shorts girl,

Although he's playing for Woking
   Can't stand up
To your wonderful back hand drive.

See the strength of her arm, as firm and hairy as Hendren's;
   See the size of her thighs, the pout of her lips as, cross,
And full of a pent-up strength, she swipes at the rhododendrons,
   Lucky the rhododendrons,
   And flings her arrogant love-lock
Back with a petulant toss.

Over the redolent pinewoods, in at the bathroom casement,
   One fine Saturday, Windlesham bells shall call:
Up the Butterfield aisle rich with Gothic enlacement,
   Licensed now for embracement,
   Pam and I, as the organ
Thunders over you all.

Margate, 1940

From out the Queen's Highcliffe for weeks at a stretch
I watched how the mower evaded the vetch,
So that over the putting-course rashes were seen
Of pink and of yellow among the burnt green.

How restful to putt, when the strains of a band
Announced a *thé dansant* was on at the Grand,
While over the privet, comminglingly clear,
I heard lesser 'Co-Optimists' down by the pier.

How lightly municipal, meltingly tarr'd,
Were the walks through the Lawns by the Queen's Promenade
As soft over Cliftonville languished the light
Down Harold Road, Norfolk Road, into the night.

Oh! then what a pleasure to see the ground floor
With tables for two laid as tables for four,
And bottles of sauce and Kia-Ora and squash
Awaiting their owners who'd gone up to wash –

Who had gone up to wash the ozone from their skins
The sand from their legs and the Rocks from their chins,

To prepare for an evening of dancing and cards
And forget the sea-breeze on the dry promenades.

From third-floor and fourth-floor the children looked down
Upon ribbons of light in the salt-scented town;
And drowning the trams roared the sound of the sea
As it washed in the shingle the scraps of their tea.

* ;

Beside the Queen's Highcliffe now rank grows the vetch,
Now dark is the terrace, a storm-battered stretch;
And I think, as the fairy-lit sights I recall,
It is those we are fighting for, foremost of all.

1948   *Selected Poems*

HUMPHREY HARE

(*Swinburne and Watts-Dunton at The Pines*)

After 1890 the monastic retirement of The Pines became more complete. The visits to the seaside, except for one ultimate expedition to Cromer in 1904, ceased. Visits from friends which up till this time had, though heavily invigilated by Watts, still been reasonably frequent, now came to an end. Indeed, there were no longer many old friends to come ... And where death had been unsuccessful Watts had triumphed. The occasional readings from his own works, which had till now been permitted, Watts decided were too exciting. Private reading from Dickens was substituted, and Watts submitted with a sigh of mingled boredom and relief to listening during these last years to the thrice-repeated Complete Novels. The ordered life at The Pines, too, took on a new, a more exacting symmetry. Every hour of the day was properly employed, suitably organized. It was the only anodyne to what otherwise must have become an excruciating boredom. 'Nothing,' wrote Gosse, 'could be more motionless than the existence of "the little old genius, and his little old acolyte, in their dull little villa".' Their life was 'spent almost as if within a Leyden jar'. Swinburne's daily time-table became set in an unvarying routine, a sort of elaborate, royal etiquette, as if the sovereign *ennui* of Versailles had come to rest, shorn of its grandeur, in a melancholy suburb ... Even his intellectual pleasures, his enthusiasms, remained constant, formed ultimately, as it were, part of the etiquette of The Pines. To the few carefully selected visitors – handpicked by Watts for their talents or their enthusiasms, such as Sir Max Beerbohm, William Rothenstein and T. J. Wise (Swinburne's future bibliographer) – he was shown off by that devoted and possessive presence as if he had been some rare and delicate *bibelot*. His mind lingered in the literary past; he lived in the history of his art. Feuds a century old were more real to him than the events of last week. A reckless guest would be reproved by Watts: 'We don't mention Hazlitt's name here.' Had he not attacked Coleridge? And upstairs in the library the fortunate visitor would be shown the collection of quarto plays and given an enthusiastic discourse on their respective beauties or, perhaps, fired by a chance word, there would be a flow of panegyric, a spate of eulogy, on Shelley, Landor, or Victor Hugo, till Watts anxiously hurried the visitor out. Excitement was another stimulus that must be rationed.

1949   *Swinburne: A Biographical Approach*

ANGUS WILSON
(*A First in English Literature*)

Isobel Sands sat at her walnut escritoire. Three sorts of ink – blue, red and green – were carefully arrayed before her. The examination papers – folios – and her own crib notes – octavo – were each in neat separate piles, weighted down with paper weights. When she had read through a page of examinee's answers she placed it carefully face downwards on a separate pile. After she had read completely the answers of any one candidate, she ticked off his or her name on a printed list at her side. She kept a silver box of cigarettes, a silver match box and a yellow and blue Hausmalerei jug of coffee within reach. She put two small green ticks against A. Rodham's remark that in the last resort Manfred and Childe Harolde must be valued more for their place in the great continental Byron legend than for their intrinsic worth as literature; but against the same candidate's statement that in *Prometheus Unbound* Shelley attacked through God the cruelty of man's impotence before the Natural Order, she wrote in a small, neat hand, 'Does not the key lie more in S.'s own psychology, *e.g.* the father image?'

She was profoundly bored, not so much with the candidates' answers, which usually corresponded to the authorities – any divergence she attributed to imperfect understanding rather than original thought – but with the subject itself. As a professor of English Literature she had no doubt that the whole field lay within her control – not, she regretted, the more exact field of Anglo-Saxon studies which, to her disappointment, she had been foolishly persuaded to leave off after her tripos – but modern literature from Sir Thomas Wyatt, and, in particular, of course, her special study: The Romantic Movement. Though she never quite admitted it even to herself, she had ceased to respond to any work of literature soon after she began her academical career. She had got her First partly through devoted application, partly through an emotional absorption in poetry which had faded with her youth. Her doctorate thesis on 'Natural Images in Lake Poetry' had been completed largely through application alone. She had for many years re-read at intervals the major works of English literature in order to come to them with a fresh eye, but each year of such re-reading had brought less and less fresh ideas to her, and, when her little library was not available during the evacuation of the first years of the War, she had happily relinquished so unrewarding a labour, never to return to it. She read such new works of criticism as appeared and occasionally marked passages for inclusion in her lectures. Otherwise her reading was confined to journalistic works on politics or history that had a 'left' flavour. In her opinion there were two possible approaches to English literature: exact, almost numerical examination of verse structure and images, and the detailing of dates of birth, college entrances or changes of address of authors – this approach she preferred for students unless, as was very rare, they were 'particularly brilliant' – or a philosophical approach, which suggested the underlying meaning of literature by the impressionistic use of a good deal of Hegelian terminology and a lot of figures of speech. Books with this approach she called 'important'. Few 'important' works of criticism appeared nowadays, though she had been very hopeful about Wilson Knight, until she found some concrete statements in his work; these, she felt, were 'rather shallow'. Of her own published works, a critical edition of the text of *Lamia* followed the first approach; 'The Essential Sublimity' and 'Glittering Eye – An Analysis of Narrative Symbol in English poetry', the second. At sixty, she usually said that literature now came second to life with her.

1952   *Hemlock and After*

HESKETH PEARSON
(*Whistler on the Academicians*)

The Royal Academicians were as nervous of him as the critics. He scoffed at them openly and constantly. 'They are the commercial travellers of Art, whose works are their wares, and whose exchange is the Academy,' he wrote. Individually and collectively he had a low opinion of them, though he was able on rare occasions to admire one of their pictures or part of a picture by one of them. Standing before an interior by William Orchardson, he encircled a bit of yellow drapery with his forefinger and said 'It would have been nice to have painted that;' but this may have been because Orchardson had a very high opinion of him. His usual attitude to works in the Academy was summed up when a young dramatist-to-be named Benrimo emerged from Burlington House, saw Whistler, introduced himself, and praised the Master's works effusively. 'Been in there?' asked Whistler, indicating the famous gallery. 'Oh, yes.' 'See anything worth while?' 'Some splendid things, magnificent examples of – ' 'I'm sorry you ever approved of me,' cut in Whistler disdainfully, and turned on his heel. He told Sickert that 'We have only one enemy, and that is funk;' but when someone remarked that R.A.s painted to please the public and so reaped their reward, he did not agree: 'I don't think they do. I think they paint as well as they can.' In other words their paintings were commonplace because they were commonplace. 'It is better to live on bread and cheese and paint beautiful things than to live like Dives and paint potboilers,' he declared, though he knew that poverty, while it necessitated industry, harmed the artist; 'Give a painter money, and see what he'll do. If he does not paint, his work is well lost to the world. If I had had, say, £3,000 a year, what beautiful things I could have done!'

His opinion of the exhibitions at Burlington House was quite honest, but his remarks on individual exhibitors were due to his exclusion from the inner ring, reinforced occasionally by personal animosity and always by an irreverent sense of fun. 'Well, you know, when I first came to England I found I had to put my foot in it, and – well – I have kept it there ever since.' That was the individualist speaking. 'Why do you go for him? He has one foot in the grave,' said someone when Whistler was pitching into an ancient Academician. 'Ah, that's not the foot I want to get hold of!' came the reply, which displayed personal antipathy. But as often as not the situation provoked him to comedy. In speaking of a certain painter as an R.A. he was told that the man was an A.R.A. 'It is a difference without a distinction,' said he. Asked why he was present at an Academy exhibition, he answered, 'Well, you know, one must do something to lend interest to the show – so here I am.' On such occasions it was noticed that he paid scant attention to the exhibits. No doubt he felt that there was nothing new, that each painter had merely repeated himself, and that as he had seen *it* there was no need for him to see *them*. Perhaps his best quip on the subject was delivered when a circular addressed to him at the Royal Academy was endorsed 'Not known at the R.A.' and forwarded to his home. He let the press have it, with a note: 'It is my rare good fortune to be able to send you an unsolicited, official, and final certificate of character.'

His personal contacts with some of the leading Academicians were usually of a droll nature. 'Because Alma-Tadema became an Englishman, the English have to protect all the abominable things he does,' said Whistler; but when the two met at an Arts Club dinner they discussed politics and behaved as if neither of them had ever held a paintbrush. With Poynter he was always on easy terms, sometimes a little too easy. Once they were staying in a country-house and Poynter was painting in the park surrounded by an admiring group. Whistler joined it and asked: 'What are you doing there, Poynter?' 'Oh, I am only touching up a little thing I began here many years ago.' 'That's no excuse, Poynter.' Burne-Jones, much against his will, had given evidence in the Ruskin case, for which Whistler never forgave him; and on the day his large canvas called *The Depths of the Sea*, displaying mermaids in their natural element, was first seen at the Academy, Whistler dashed up to a friend and dragged him off by the arm, saying in his extremely audible voice: 'Come! Come with me! I must show you those unfortunate people in the tank!'

1952   *The Man Whistler*

CHAPTER 7

Self-Portrait

Introspection is a characteristic of English humour, and imparts an English tinge to our letters and autobiographies. Sometimes the effect is spoilt by the sort of apology or self-effacement which is an inverted boast – a fault from which Harriette Wilson, and most of the examples I have given here, are free.

WILLIAM COWPER

... difficult (I say) for me to find opportunities for writing. My morning is engrossed by the garden; and in the afternoon, till I have drunk tea, I am fit for nothing. At five o'clock we walk; and when the walk is over, lassitude recommends rest, and again I become fit for nothing. The current hour therefore which (I need not tell you) is comprised in the interval between four and five, is devoted to your service, as the only one in the twenty-four which is not otherwise engaged.

1781   *Letter to the Rev. William Unwin*

S. T. COLERIDGE

MY DEAR MORGAN – Tomorrow morning, I doubt not, I shall be of clear and collected Spirits; but tonight I feel that I should do nothing to any purpose, but and excepting Thinking, Planning, and Resolving to resolve – and praying to be able to execute.'   *Letter to John H. Morgan*
1814

HARRIETTE WILSON*

(*A Visit from the Duke of Wellington*)

I was getting into debt, as well as my sister Amy, when it so came to pass, as I have since heard say, that the – immortal ! ! ! No; that's common; a very outlandish distinction, fitter for a

*The most celebrated of all Regency ladies of pleasure.

240

lady in a balloon. The terrific ! ! ! that will do better. I have
seen his grace in his cotton nightcap. Well, then, the terrific
Duke of Wellington ! ! the wonder of the world ! ! Having six
feet from the tail to the head, and – but there is a certain techni-
cality in the expressions of the gentleman at Exeter 'Change,
when he has occasion to show off a wild beast, which it would be
vanity in me to presume to imitate; so leaving out his dimensions,
etc., etc. it was even the Duke of Wellington, whose laurels, like
those of the giant in the *Vicar of Wakefield*, had been hardly
earned by the sweat of his little dwarfs' brows, and the loss of
their little legs, arms, and eyes; who, feeling himself amorously
given. – It was in summer. – One sultry evening, ordered his
coachman to set him down at the White Horse Cellar, in Piccadilly, whence he sallied forth, on foot, to No. 2 or 3, in Berkeley
Street, and rapped hastily at the door, which was immediately
opened by the tawdry, well-rouged housekeeper of Mrs Porter,
who, with a significant nod of recognition, led him into her
mistress's boudoir, and then hurried away, simpering, to acquaint
the good Mrs Porter with the arrival of one of her oldest customers. . . .

*

The next morning I received another visit from Mrs Porter,
who informed me that she had just had an interview with my
new lover, and had reported to him all I had desired her to say.

'Since you object to meet a stranger,' continued Mrs Porter,
'His Grace desires me to say, he hopes you can keep a secret,
and to inform you, that it is the Duke of Wellington who so
anxiously desires to make your acquaintance.'

'I have heard of His Grace often,' said I, in a tone of deep
disappointment: for I had been indulging a kind of hope about
the stranger with the great Newfoundland dog, with whose
appearance I had been so unusually struck as to have sought for
him every day, and I thought of him every hour.

'His Grace,' Mrs Porter proceeded, 'only entreats to be
allowed to make your acquaintance. His situation, you know,
prevents the possibility of his getting regularly introduced to
you.'

'It will never do,' said I, shaking my head.

'Be assured,' said Mrs Porter, 'he is a remarkably fine-looking man, and, if you are afraid of my house, promise to receive him in your own, at any hour when he may be certain to find you alone.'

Well, thought I, with a sigh; I suppose he must come. I do not understand economy, and am frightened to death at debts, Argyle is going to Scotland; and I shall want a steady sort of friend, of some kind, in case a bailiff should get hold of me.

'What shall I say to His Grace?' Mrs Porter inquired, growing impatient.

'Well then,' said I, 'since it must be so, tell His Grace that I will receive him tomorrow at three; but mind, only as a common acquaintance!'

Away winged Wellington's Mercury, as an old woman wings it at sixty; and most punctual to my appointment, at three on the following day, Wellington made his appearance. He bowed first, then said –

'How do you do?' then thanked me for having given him permission to call on me; and then wanted to take hold of my hand.

'Really,' said I, withdrawing my hand, 'for such a renowned hero you have very little to say for yourself.'

'Beautiful creature!' uttered Wellington, 'where is Lorne?'

'Good gracious,' said I, out of all patience at his stupidity – 'what come you here for, Duke?'

'Beautiful eyes, yours!' reiterated Wellington.

'Aye, man! they are greater conquerors than ever Wellington shall be; but, to be serious, I understood you came here to try to make yourself agreeable?'

'What, child! do you think that I have nothing better to do than to make speeches to please ladies?' said Wellington.

'*Après avoir dépeuplé la terre, vous devez faire tout pour la repeupler*,' I replied.

'You should see me where I shine,' Wellington observed, laughing.

'Where's that, in God's name?'

'In a field of battle,' answered the hero.

'*Battez-vous, donc, et qu' un autre me fasse le Jour!*' said I.

But love scenes, or even love quarrels, seldom tend to amuse the reader, so, to be brief, what was a mere man, even though it were the handsome Duke of Argyle, to a Wellington ! ! !

Argyle grew jealous of Wellington's frequent visits, and hiding himself in his native woods, wrote me the following very pathetic letter....

*

Wellington was now my constant visitor: a most unentertaining one, Heaven knows! and, in the evenings, when he wore his broad red ribbon, he looked very like a rat-catcher.

'Do you know,' said I to him one day, 'do you know the world talk about hanging you?'

'Eh?' said Wellington.

'They say you will be hanged, in spite of all your brother Wellesley can say in your defence.'

'Ha ! !' said Wellington, very seriously, 'what paper do you read?'

'It is the common talk of the day,' I replied.

'They must not work me in such another campaign,' Wellington said, smiling, 'or my weight will never hang me.'

'Why, you look a little like the apothecary in Romeo already,' I said.

In my walks Brummel often joined me, and I now walked oftener than usual: indeed, whenever I could make anybody walk with me; because I wanted to meet the man with his Newfoundland dog, who was not the sort of man, either, that generally strikes the fancy of a very young female; for he was neither young nor at all gaily dressed. No doubt he was very handsome; but it was that pale expressive beauty, which oftener steals upon us, by degrees, after having become acquainted, than strikes at first sight.

I had, of late, frequently met him, and he always turned his head back, after he had passed me; but whether he admired, or had, indeed, observed me, or whether he only looked back after his large dog, was what puzzled and tormented me. Better to have been merely observed by that fine noble-looking being, than adored by all the men on earth besides, though I, being now at the very tip-top of my heroics.

*

Wellington called on me, the next morning before I had finished my breakfast. I tried him on every subject I could muster. On all, he was most impenetrably taciturn. At last he started an original idea of his own; actual copyright, as Stockdale would call it.

'I wonder you do not get married, Harriette!'

(Bye-the-bye, ignorant people are always wondering.)

'Why so?'

Wellington, however, gives no reason for anything unconnected with fighting, at least since the convention of Cintra; and he, therefore, again became silent. Another burst of attic sentiment blazed forth.

'I was thinking of you last night, after I got into bed,' resumed Wellington.

'How very polite to the Duchess,' I observed. '*Apropos* to marriage, Duke, how do you like it?'

Wellington, who seems to make a point of never answering me, continued, 'I was thinking – I was thinking that you will get into some scrape, when I go to Spain.'

'Nothing so serious as marriage neither, I hope!'

'I must come again tomorrow, to give you a little advice,' continued Wellington.

'O let us have it all out now, and have done with it.'

'I cannot,' said Wellington, putting on his gloves and taking hasty leave of me.

I am glad he is off, thought I, for this is indeed very up-hill work. This is worse than Lord Craven.

As soon as he was gone, I hastened to Curzon Street. The window-shutters of Lord Ponsonby's house were all closed. How disappointed and low-spirited I felt at the idea that His Lordship had left town! Suspense was insufferable; so I ventured to send my servant to inquire when the family were expected in London.

In about a month, was the answer. I must forget this man, thought I, it is far too great a bore: and yet I felt that to forget him was impossible.

1825   *Memoirs*

H. G. WELLS

(Surrender at Keston Fish Ponds)

In those days I had ideas about Aryans extraordinarily like Mr Hitler's. The more I hear of him the more I am convinced that his mind is almost the twin of my thirteen year old mind in 1879; but heard through a megaphone and – implemented. I do not know from what books I caught my first glimpse of the Great Aryan People going to and fro in the middle plains of Europe, spreading east, west, north, and south, varying their consonants according to Grimm's Law as they did so, and driving the inferior breeds into the mountains. But they formed a picturesque background to the duller facts of ancient history. Their ultimate triumphs everywhere squared accounts with the Jews, against which people I had a subconscious dissatisfaction because of their disproportionate share of Holy Writ. I thought Abraham, Isaac, Moses and David loathsome creatures and fit associates for Our Father, but unlike Hitler I had no feelings about the contemporary Jew. Quite a number of the boarders in the Bromley Academy were Jewish and I was not aware of it. My particular pal, Sidney Bowkett, was I think unconsciously Jewish; the point never arose.

I had reveries – I indulged a great deal in reverie until I was fifteen or sixteen, because my active imagination was not sufficiently employed – and I liked especially to dream that I was a great military dictator like Cromwell, a great republican like George Washington or like Napoleon in his earlier phases. I used to fight battles whenever I went for a walk alone. I used to walk about Bromley, a small rather undernourished boy, meanly clad and whistling detestably between his teeth, and no one suspected that a phantom staff pranced about me and phantom orderlies galloped at my commands, to shift the guns and concentrate fire on those houses below, to launch the final attack upon yonder distant ridge. The citizens of Bromley town go out to take the air on Martin's Hill and look towards Shortlands across the fields where once meandered the now dried-up and vanished Ravensbourne, with never a suspicion of the orgies of bloodshed I once conducted there. Martin's Hill indeed is one of the greatest battlegrounds of history. Scores of times the enemy skirmishers have come across those levels, followed by the successive waves of the infantry attack, while I, out-numbered five to one, manoeuvred my guns round, the guns I had refrained so grimly from using too soon in spite of the threat to my centre, to enfilade them suddenly from the curving slopes towards Beckenham. 'Crash,' came the first shell, and then crash and crash. They were mown down by the thousand. They straggled up the steep slopes wavering. And then came the shattering counter-attack, and I and my cavalry swept the broken masses away towards Croydon, pressed them ruthlessly through a night of slaughter on to the pitiful surrender of the remnant at dawn by Keston Fish Ponds.

1934   *Experiment in Autobiography*

ERIC LINKLATER
85831 Pte Linklater, The Black Watch

For the next two or three weeks the war was in a state of singular confusion. We were in the neighbourhood of Ypres again – at Zillebeke and Voormezeele – and wherever we went we were digging trenches and fighting off an enemy who generally appeared from some entirely unexpected quarter. It was the season for low-lying fog, and on one occasion we re-refrained, in the nick of time, from opening fire on a battalion of Cameron Highlanders who, in the most mysterious fashion, came charging towards us out of what we thought was the German line. We were now a composite battalion, made from Cambridgeshires, Cheshires, K.R.Rs, Black Watch, certain Welshmen, and other remnants of the 39th Division; and when, about this time, Haig issued the celebrated order in which he said we were fighting with our backs to the wall, there was laughter from one end of the country to the other; for we had no such illusion of support, and were more likely to be fighting with our backs to the enemy, since the Germans often appeared on both sides of us.

Nothing occurred of any military importance – though a good many lives were lost – but to myself there happened something of startling interest. I nearly became a good soldier. It began with a gumboil and outrageous toothache that swelled my cheek to the likeness of a dumpling, and put me into the vilest temper. When the gumboil subsided, I discovered to my amazement that I had acquired not only confidence, but a new capacity of enjoyment. Rations were plentiful: I ate with good appetite, and swigged my rum with enormous pleasure. I was still afraid, especially of being taken prisoner, and of heavy trench-mortars that shook the earth with the close violence of their explosion; but my fear was under control, and far less tiresome than toothache.

It is true that I never learnt to handle pick and spade very cleverly, and as many of my fellow privates had been miners, my ineptitude was the more apparent by contrast. Once, while we were digging a new line, the Commanding Officer came to inspect our work and stood for a long time behind me. Compared with the deep excavation of my comrades, I had made, I confess, but a shallow hole; and his voice, when at last he spoke, was recognizably unfriendly.

His first question was insulting. 'What are you doing?' he asked.

I turned and stood rigidly at attention: 'Digging a trench, sir.'

'My wife,' he said, 'has a small dog, a Pekinese, that goes out every morning to do its business in the garden. And that little Pekinese dog makes a bigger hole than you do.'

Glumly, amid sycophantic laughter, I waited for the inevitable conclusion. It came. He turned to the N.C.O. beside him and said coldly, 'Take his name, sergeant.'

But I found compensation when, in a rather casual way, I became a sniper. Because of the composite nature of the battalion, organization was a little sketchy, and appointments were made in a somewhat perfunctory fashion. At stand-to one morning the company sergeant-major inquired for marksmen, and though others kept a prudent silence, I stood proudly forward, exclaiming, 'Here, sir!'

'All right,' he said, 'you're a sniper. There's a hole about twenty yards in front of that sap that'll give you a good field of fire. You'd better get into it before the mist rises.'

And then I earned my pay, and in a taut unresting way enjoyed myself. I had found a rifle that was unusually well balanced, and I got the nose of the sear so filed that little more than blood-pressure on the trigger would fire it. It was a good rifle. Twice we were attacked, and the attacks were beaten off; and there were German working-parties within easy range. I earned my rations, and for a few days lived at the full pitch of strenuous excitement.

*

But my little while of active service was nearly over. Early one morning we were driven out of the ruined village of Voormezeele and, in a most unwilling counter-attack, recaptured it an hour or so later. Pressing hard, and vastly outnumbering us, the Germans came back. They turned our flank, and my platoon was left in an unfinished trench that thrust like a tongue into their midst. I was at the extreme end of it, because from there ran a sap I had used for sniping. They were very close. One could see the agitation of their features, and the shape of their helmets appeared more sinister than ever. I had used all my ammunition – I had been shooting badly – and in any case my rifle was too hot to hold. But I had a box of bombs, already detonated, and I threw one that fell short. I was swinging for the second when I heard a wild shout behind me, and looking round saw the trench was empty save for one man, who had come back to warn me that we were retreating. He was an old regular soldier, and had also been a nurse in a lunatic asylum. He was a big good-looking man, but his cheeks had strangely fallen in. He must have lost his false teeth, I thought.

I threw my second bomb, more usefully than the first, and turned to run. I ran so very fast that, although I was the last by a long way to leave the trench, within two hundred yards I had passed several of those who preceded me; including an officer who was looking back with an expression of reluctance that, in the circumstances, appeared strangely ill-timed.

I continued to run till in a mingling of righteous indignation and utter dismay I felt on my head a blow of indescribable force. It was a bullet, and probably a machine-gun bullet; for the rifle-fire of the German infantry was poor.

When I recovered consciousness the surrounding landscape appeared entirely empty. But I could not see very well, and perhaps I was mistaken. A few shots, that were evidently hostile, gave me a rough direction, and with clumsy fingers I took from a pocket in the lining of my tunic a little package of field-dressings. I could not undo it, but stuck it whole on the back of my head, where I judged the wound to be, and kept it in position with my steel helmet, that a chin-strap held tightly on.

Scarcely had I made these arrangements when, my sight growing more foggy, I fell into a water-logged trench. It was deep, and full to the brim, and the sides were so well revetted that I had great difficulty in getting out. I was nearly drowned, indeed, and lost my good rifle there. But the cold water revived me, and now my only feeling of discomfort was extreme weariness. So I threw off my equipment and my tunic and found progress a little easier. Presently, after walking, as I thought, for many miles, someone came to help me, and I saw a cluster of men in kilt and kilt-apron, who looked familiar. I waved my hand to them. It was the very last, the ultimate remnant of the battalion, and already they were forming for the counter-attack. In the after-noon they recaptured Voormezeele.

My wound was dressed and I was given a coat. I lay for some time among dying men, and grew so displeased with such com-pany that I got up and, joining a party of walking wounded, found something to eat. I was ravenously hungry. Then we were put into an ambulance, and the jolting of that was an agony that drove one nearly mad. The ambulance stopped, and we had to get out and walk to a train. Watching us were thirty or forty men of the Chinese Labour Corps. Moon-faced, thickly wadded coolies like those I had been warder among in the long hut at Calais. The same men, perhaps.

They began to laugh at us. We were a ludicrous company, tottering and misshapen, roughly bandaged; but only the dread-ful sanity of China could have seen the joke, I think. Thin of voice, the coolies tittered with laughter; then as their mirth grew, doubled-down and held their sides, or clapped each other on the back. Peal upon peal their laughter rang, and they pointed to the saviours of the western world.

1941   *The Man on My Back*

JAMES AGATE

(On Hardly Using Any French)

Dec. 19 Friday

To judge by the nonsense written about my excessive use of French you would think it amounted to ten per cent or more. Now look at these figures taken from *The Amazing Theatre*. This contains just over 100,000 words. Ten per cent of 100,000 10,000. Actually the book contains 499, say 500 French words, or ·05 per cent. My article on Sunday will have the following:

In Balzac's novel, *La Femme de Trente Ans*, occurs this passage:

La jeune fille n'a qu'une coquetterie, et croit avoir tout dit quand elle a quitté son vêtement; mais la femme en a d'innombrables et se cache sous mille voiles; enfin elle caresse toutes les vanités, et la novice n'en flatte qu'une.

(*Glossary*. Coquetterie – coquetry; Vêtement – vestment; Innombrables – innumerable; Voiles – veils; Vanité – vanity; Novice – novice.)

Ego 5

(Correcting Proofs)

How far should a writer take his readers into his confidence? Shall I 'lose face' if I confess that the *Ego* books are not the careless jottings of idle half-hours? That I think *Ego*, talk *Ego*, dream *Ego*? That I get up in the middle of the night to make a correction? That before the MS of any of my *Ego*'s reaches the publisher it has been through at least a dozen revisions? That it is only when the galley proofs arrive that the real work begins? I suppose that when I had finished with the galleys of *Ego* 7 it would have been difficult to find fifty unaltered sentences. The reason for this is that stuff in print reads differently from the same stuff in typescript. Very well, then. The galleys have been returned to the publishers, and one sits back and awaits the page proofs in the vain belief that there is nothing more to do except see that the galley corrections have been properly carried out. Actually I made over two thousand corrections *on the page proofs of Ego* 7. For the reason that stuff in page reads differently from the same stuff in galley.

C. E. M. JOAD

(*Joad and the Dragon*)

February 18th 1947

A few days ago I read a paper to the Aristotelian Society on the recently published *A History of Western Philosophy*. It wasn't a bad paper; in fact, it was as good as I could make it, for I was told that Russell himself was likely to come to the discussion, and this put me on my mettle.

I am afraid of Russell; at least I used to be. He is so much cleverer than I am that he makes me feel a fool – or used to. But, except on Brains Trusts, where I am so to speak playing on the home ground and feel fairly confident of my ability to take on all comers, I had not crossed swords with Russell for years. Hence, I went to the meeting with mingled trepidation and defiance, telling myself that this time at least I wouldn't be put down, but knowing that I almost certainly should be. I tried to encourage myself by reminding myself that I was no longer a callow youth unversed in controversy but was an old hand with an experienced technique, that I had, indeed, acquired some reputation as a dialectician, and that I had the prestige of Brains Trust success behind me. Moreover, some of the critical points that I had made in my paper seemed to me to be pretty strong.

Nevertheless, I went with trepidation, knowing only too well my weakness. This weakness I attributed to three things. First, there was my old subjection to Russell and the memory of the many occasions on which he had discomfited or nonplussed me in the past; secondly, there was my consciousness of his superior dialectical power, greater reputation, and more vivid personality; thirdly, there was my respect, a respect amounting almost to reverence for one whose mind I held to be so powerfully original as by virtue of its pre-eminence alone to constitute its possessor a great man – not that I don't think him great in other ways; and yet except in respect of the article of moral courage, I don't *know* that he is. This reverential respect which disposes me to listen with humility to what he has to say induces me to think that I am wrong and that he is right, even when this is far from being certainly the case, and puts it wholly out of my power to be pert and contumacious in his presence, or to try to score purely dialectical points.

Knowing all these things it was, I repeat, with trepidation that I went to the meeting. In spite of the awful weather the room was packed with people, some of them my own students. Instead of diminishing, these increased my uneasiness. If my intellectual trousers, as was all too probable, were taken down, it was highly doubtful whether the subsequent exhibition of tutor-spanking would be good for discipline; moreover, I couldn't help remembering how often I had done it to them.

I read my paper in an assertive, rather challenging voice whose vigour, I hoped rather than believed, disguised its underlying nervousness. As I read, I could feel the kick going out of my sentences and the substance oozing from my arguments. Reasonable applause and then the chairman asked Russell to comment! He commented mildly at first, then more trenchantly, charging me now with intellectual error, now with illogicality, now with inconsistency, now with a failure to understand his position, a failure which, he implied, must be due either to a lack of patience and assiduity, or to not having kept myself up to date, or to sheer insufficiency of intellectual equipment.

I interrupted, challenged him, stood up to him as well as I could. It was humiliating how little ice I cut. In part my arguments, when it came to the point, lacked substance. When they had substance, my awe of Russell prevented me from putting them properly. When I tried to put them as well as I knew how, he put me off my stroke by well-timed interruptions, by a shake of the head, by a notable failure to cry *touché* when I thought I had made an undeniable hit. 'Oh,' he would say, with a sort of contemptuous tolerance, 'Oh, you think so? Oh, *do* you?' Then he began trailing red herrings, telling anecdotes and making philosophical jokes.

The audience, quite as as conscious as ever I could be that Russell was a great man, who had come partly to revere and partly to be amused, roared with laughter. Finally, Russell brought the house down with a most diverting account of Leibniz's doctrine of 'Compossibility'. By this time everybody had forgotten me and my paper; they could think only of Russell. All eyes were turned to him; all questions addressed to him. What, they wanted to know, did he think of this? What did he mean by that? (Never did they want to know what I thought of this or meant by that!) Laughing, cracking his dry little jokes, telling his stories, dropping his epigrams, and generally scintillating, Russell had completely stolen the limelight. I looked at my students. All the dialectical tricks I had so often played on them they could now observe being played on me – not surprisingly since had I not, after all, learnt them in the first instance at Russell's dialectical knee?

There was the disabling interrogation, 'Now *what* do you mean by that?'; there was the even more disabling expulsion of breath, the long-drawn out 'Oh' of pitying astonishment, 'Oh, is *that* what you mean?,' when the flustered victim was at last delivered of his halting explanation, followed by 'Oh, it had never occurred to me for a moment that you could have meant *that*,' the implication being that '*that*' was so palpably absurd that nobody in his senses could have meant it or anything like it. 'That' was then subjected to criticism which so riddled and withered it that the victim was left wondering how he could ever have thought anything so manifestly imbecile. Again, there was the non-committal 'Oh! Do you think so?' as if it were a matter of surprise that anybody *could* think so. There was the disarmingly handsome avowal of error. 'There,' said Russell, on some point of manifest unimportance, '*there* I was wrong, completely wrong,' gaining by this unreserved confession everybody's sympathy for fair-minded readiness to admit error, all this, of course, lending increased weight to his vigorous defence of his position on other criticized points of much greater importance. There was the hypocritical confession of a Socratic thick-headedness: 'Now *that* I don't understand! Will you please explain it to me, so that I can grasp what it is that you are saying? . . .' And so on . . .

After this had been going on for some time, I determined on a counter-attack. 'I won't,' I said to myself, 'be put down any

THE SENSE OF HUMOUR

more. I will stand up to him. Yes, in spite of his immense prestige, in spite of his superior dialectical skill, in spite of the enfeebling effects of being put down by him so often in the past and of his remembrance and mine of the fact, in spite of his manifest popularity with the audience, I really will make a stand.'

And, indeed, I might have succeeded if it had not been for Russell's eye. For you can't stand up to a man in discussion unless you can look fairly and squarely at him, unless, in fact, you can meet his eye. And when it came to the point, I found, as I have found before, that I could not meet Russell's eye; not, at least, for more than a moment. I tried it and then had to avert my gaze to hide my embarrassed discomfiture.

Now, I am not shifty-eyed and I can meet most people's eyes with composure. I am interested in the phenomenon of eye-meeting or not-meeting and consider that insufficient attention has been given to it. Is it quite simply that one's realization of superior intellectual, or it may be, moral power or, even, of a more vivid and compelling personality quells and tames one, as the Long-livers in *Back to Methuselah* quell the Short-livers by a look? In Russell's case perhaps it is, but it is certainly not so in every case. There are some people who I know to be my equals; there are even some who I believe to be my inferiors, whose eyes I nevertheless cannot meet.

1948   *A Year More or Less*

J. B. PRIESTLEY
My Tastes

Like you, I am always delighted to declare my tastes, prejudices, preferences. And probably like you too, I hide this delight behind an appearance of awful solemnity. I never look graver and more weighty than at these moments. 'No,' I say, as if sentencing somebody to death, 'I don't care for fried tomatoes.' And I give one of my listeners a searching look, then stare severely at any object in the middle distance, and sit there, mute, heavy, rigid, practically a tablet of stone. Or I hold up a hand that apparently weighs about a hundred and fifty pounds, command silence, and then announce in a massive tone: 'If I'm hot – give

254

me a shower every time.' Sometimes, together with the air of finality that is always there, you will catch a slow sad rhythm, as if a humanitarian prime minister were declaring war: 'No, I can't smoke a Light Virginian flake. It burns my tongue.' And there are times when beneath the grave weighty manner are abysses of bitterness, unfathomable depths of despair, as if all life on this planet had been a blunder: 'Oh, do you?' I cry, seeming to glare at them out of bloody sockets. 'I much prefer the old-fashioned folding ones. Only of course they're so hard to find now.'

1949   *Delight*

CHAPTER 8

The Age of Humour

I think of 1910–40, from the neo-Georgians to the new slang of World War II, as the age most thoroughly tangled with the web of humour, the threads of which permeate not only the essayists and novelists, but the poets and philosophers as well. The comedies of Terence Rattigan, or rather the tone of voice of his dialogue and the featherweight construction – both half lost, unfortunately, in print – embody this spirit. For the beginning of the period, a friend disinterred for me, just in time to be included here, that masterwork of my childhood – embodying the best humorous idea of the decade, 'E.V.L. and G.M.'s' great biographical work illustrated by pictures from Whiteley's catalogue.

I place first, however, a piece which suggests the traps into which humour-for-its-own-sake may fall. Even the delightful wit of Sir John Squire could lose its resilience when humorousness was assumed.

SIR JOHN SQUIRE
(The Godalming Museum)

There was that venerable pile, the Godalming museum. For years I had passed it daily, noting the grave letters MUSEUM above the portal; for years I had resolved to investigate it; and never once had I remembered my firm intention and passionate curiosity when I had had time to go in. 'I will go in now,' I determined, 'even if it means getting a key from the verger's cottage, or whatever it is.' With elated heart I strode on past the butcher's, the baker's, the draper's and the ironmonger's, until I reached the hexagon; and, having tried five sides in vain for a door, found one on the sixth. There, as is everywhere too visual on public institutions, was a board explaining that the Museum could only be seen at certain hours on certain days, none of which this particular day was. Baffled and bitter I muttered to myself: 'It was bad enough, earlier in the year, to go to Cairo without seeing the Sphinx and to Constantinople without seeing the Golden Horn – but at Stamboul there was rain and mist, and in Egypt I did engage to lecture on literature and was kept busy answering questions by brown majors in red fezzes about D. H. Lawrence and James Joyce. But to visit Godalming once more without seeing the Museum – well, it's disgustingly unfair.' I'm quite sure I shall never know what is inside it now. There may be most interesting flint arrow-heads and some of those little serrated things with which early man cut off the ears of his corn. There may be a Cromwellian pike, or some little yellow snakes, going woolly in bottles of spirit; or some dried and tattooed Maori heads, or some Polynesian paddles, or perhaps even the local stocks and ducking-stool, relics of darker days. 'Of course,' my thoughts ran perspicaciously on, 'the place is pretty small, and there couldn't be any really large things here, like those skeletons of whales at South Kensington, for instance.' And then I remembered that even size could sometimes be dealt with by ingenuity.

1937   *The Honeysuckle and the Bee*

E. V. LUCAS AND GEORGE MORROW
(*Experiment in Autobiography*)

Knocking about town as I then did, I naturally got to know many people, especially as I was still unmarried.

For example, Lady Mayfair, the present Queen of Society, I remember as a little toddling child who climbed on my knees.

I knew Monty Wotherspoon, the amateur pyramid champion, intimately.

Monty was one of the old dare-devil crowd. I remember the sensation he caused when, for a wager, he drove a hansom from the Guards' Club to Hurlingham without reins. Poor fellow, his end was very tragic. He was poisoned by his wife. She had rinsed the glass and removed, as she thought, all traces of the poison; but the Law was too much for her.

A. SERVICE PIPE FROM MAIN.
B. INLET TO FILTER.
C. OUTLET OF FILTERED WATER
D. FLUSH TAP
E. ORDINARY WATER TAP.

The autopsy revealed unmistakable signs of the deadly drug.

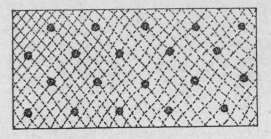

Then there was the Earl of Crewett, who was never seen out of riding breeches : a veritable centaur.

It was Lord Crewett who won the Derby with 'Salad Days'.

1910   *What a Life!*

PROFESSOR WALTER RALEIGH

I am writing a poem* about my death. A very comfortable poem – not sentimental.

> What a nuisance it will be,
> – All that then remains of me!
> Shelves of books I never read,
> Piles of bills undocketed,
> Shaving-brushes, razors, strops,
> Bottles that have lost their tops,
> Boxes full of odds and ends,
> Letters from departed friends,
> Mouldy ties and broken braces,
> Tucked away in secret places,
> Baggy trousers, ragged coats,
> Stacks of ancient lecture-notes,
> And that ghostliest of shows –
> Boots and shoes in horrid rows.
> Cheerful though they are and kind,
> My lovers, whom I leave behind,
> When they find these in my stead
> Will be sorry I am dead.

1918   *Letters*

* A fuller version of this poem appears in *Laughter from a Cloud.*

LOGAN PEARSALL SMITH
(*The Author*)

These pieces of moral prose have been written, dear Reader, by a large Carnivorous Mammal, belonging to that sub-order of the Animal Kingdom which includes also the Orang-outang, the tusked Gorilla, the Baboon with his bright blue and scarlet bottom, and the gentle Chimpanzee.

(*The Shrouded Hours*)

They were talking of people I didn't know. 'How do they spend their time there?' someone asked.

Then I, who had been sitting too long silent, lifted up my voice. 'Ah, that's a mysterious question, when you think of it, how people spend their time. We only see them after all in glimpses; but what, I often wonder, do they do in their hushed and shrouded hours – in all the mysterious interstices of their lives?'

'In the what?'

'In the times, I mean, when no one sees them. In the intervals.'

'But that isn't the word you used?'

'It's the same thing – the interstices –'

Or course there was a deaf lady present. 'What did you say?' she inquired, holding out her ear-trumpet for my answer.

1922   *All Trivia*

HAROLD NICOLSON

On October 3, 1918, the Amir Feisal, accompanied by Colonel T. E. Lawrence, galloped into Damascus at the head of 1,500 Arab cavalry and hoisted the Arab standard. This was an extremely awkward thing to have happened.

1933   *Peacemaking 1919*

TERENCE RATTIGAN
(*Exposition Without Tears*)

ACT ONE

SCENE : *A first-floor flat in Knightsbridge. Large window L., looks on to a quiet street. Door backstage leads into hall, and another R., into bedroom. The room has an air of bachelor distinction, the furniture being considerably better chosen and displayed than the furnishings which are rather drab and ordinary: some good pictures, mainly Dutch landscapes; a bronze head of a girl, not too conspicuously placed.*

The time is about eight o'clock of a summer evening in 1917. The light has begun to fade but, as the curtain rises, we can see the dining-table has been laid in the centre of the room, with two places. The room is empty.

There is the sound of the front door closing and after a moment MARK *enters. He is thirty-two and plainly goes to a tailor in or near Savile Row. He is wearing a dinner jacket, single breasted, and a white waistcoat, and is carrying an object under his arm. This, as he removes the paper, is revealed to be a bottle of champagne, which he unwraps and places on the sideboard. Then he inspects the table, making a couple of meticulous changes. He next looks round the room, paying particular attention to the sofa whose cushions he rearranges. Then, on a sudden impulse, he goes to the window and pulls the heavy curtains, leaving the room in darkness for a moment, until he turns on the lights. These, after a second's consideration, he dims discreetly. Then he rearranges a small vase of flowers on the table. He stands back and examines the effect, but not entirely satisfied sits in one of the chairs at the table. Mouthing soundlessly he makes animated conversation to the other chair, and we see that he has to lean his head to one side to circumvent the flowers. He therefore removes the vase.*

Now, after a final glance round the room, he appears moderately satisfied. He takes a cigarette from a case, lights it, and goes briskly to a telephone.

MARK : (*Into receiver.*) Hullo ... I want Sloane 7939, please. (*As he waits he still glances round the room.*) Cunliffe? ... Yes ... Is her

Ladyship there?... Yes, please,... Hullo, darling... Darling, I'm afraid the most awful thing has just happened. A long dispatch from Mesopotamia has just this second come in, and it looks as it I won't be able to get home till very late ... Oh no, midnight, I should think, at the very earliest. It might be much later than that, even ... Who? Oh, your father. Well, tell him how very sorry I am to miss him, will you?... Oh no, darling, don't bother to do that – I'll have a snack here in the office ... Oh no, that's all right. One has to get used to these things in wartime ... Mesopotamia ... Well, it's the cypher they use, you see, one of the most complicated there is in the world ... Yes. Kiss Denis for me – tell him to be good ... Oh, did he? (*Submissively*) Oh, yes, darling, I quite agree. Very naughty. Yes, darling. I'll talk to him in the morning ... Oh yes, very severe, I promise ... I'm so sorry about tonight ... Goodnight. (*He rings off and jiggles with the telephone for the Exchange.*) Hullo ... Are you there? Yes, I've finished thank you. I want Victoria 8440 ... Hullo, Foreign Office? This is Lord St Neots. Who's in charge of the Middle East department tonight? Well, it's a simple question, I should have thought you could have given me a reasonably simple answer ... Look, dear lady, this is Lord St Neots. I work at the Foreign Office. I have worked at the Foreign Office for the past nine years. I simply want to know ... Now how the dickens can I identify myself on the telephone? I am Viscount St Neots, the son of the Earl of Binfield. I am married. I have one child, a boy, aged five, named Denis, and I live at No.58 Belgrave Square. Now, dear lady, if there is anything else I can tell you about myself I should be only too happy ... (*Furiously*) Well, you can tell Mr Mole from me that he's a blithering idiot. If I were a German spy I wouldn't go dashing about ringing up the Foreign Office asking who's in charge of the Middle East department. I'd jolly well know who was in charge of the Middle East department. Come to think of it, I'd probably *be* in charge of the Middle East department. (*He is rather pleased at this one, and chuckles appreciatively.*) Very well, ring off, if you wish. I have said my say. (*He jiggles the telephone again.*) Hullo, Exchange? Get me Victoria 8440 again would you. I got cut off ... (*In an assumed voice most inexpertly and suspiciously guttural.*) Hullo, Foreign Office.

Please might with the Middle Eastern department to speak? Hullo, Middle East? (*In his normal voice.*) Who's in charge there tonight? Mr Seymour? Good. Put me on to him, would you ... Charley? This is Mark – Do me a little favour, would you? If my home rings up I'm with you, deciphering a long dispatch about Mesopotamia, and can't talk for fear of dropping a stitch ... What ... That's better, isn't it? Gone out for a cup of coffee. You obviously have experience ... No. I have none – honestly I haven't. First time in seven years. Believe it or not, it's true. ... No. Not ashamed of myself, yet. Tomorrow, perhaps. Not now ... Oh by the way, Charley, if my home should ring you'd better have this number, hadn't you. It's Sloane ... Damn, I've forgotten it. I know it so well, too. No, it's not on the receiver ... I tell you what. It's in the book under the name of Oscar Philipson – got that? Oscar Philipson, and the address is 12 Wilbraham Terrace, Knightsbridge ... Yes, that's right. Thank you, Charley, I hope I shall be able to do the same for you one day ... (*As an afterthought.*) Oh, by the way, give my best to your wife.

1950   *Who is Sylvia?*

'GOSH! QUAILS IN ASPIC AGAIN'

Pont

CHAPTER 9

Tragic Humour

There should be a place here for the humour of that highest kind which depends for its pathetic or savage force on its context in tragedy. We think of Hamlet, of the Fool in *Lear*, of Shaw's Saint Joan, or of the splendidly reasonable speeches of Mr Eliot's Knights after the murder of Becket. This passage from Graham Greene's *The Heart of the Matter* depends for its poignancy on context, and the tragic situation of the boy.

GRAHAM GREENE

(Scobie Reads to the Boy)

'Can you read aloud?' Mrs Bowles asked, rising on her toes.

'I suppose so. Yes.'

'You can read to the boy. He's getting bored and boredom's bad for him.'

'Where shall I find a book?'

'There are plenty at the Mission. Shelves of them.'

Anything was better than doing nothing. He walked up to the Mission and found, as Mrs Bowles said, plenty of books. He wasn't much used to books, but even to his eye these hardly seemed a bright collection for reading to a sick boy. Damp-stained and late Victorian, the bindings bore titles like *Twenty Years in the Mission Field*, *Lost and Found*, *The Narrow Way*, *The Missionary's Warning*. Obviously at some time there had been an appeal for books for the Mission library, and here were the scrapings of many pious shelves at home. *The Poems of John Oxenham*, *Fishers of Men*. He took a book at random out of the shelf and returned to the rest-house. Mrs Bowles was in her dispensary mixing medicines.

'Found something?'

'Yes.'

'You are safe with any of those books,' Mrs Bowles said. 'They are censored by the committee before they come out. Sometimes people try to send the most unsuitable books. We are not teaching the children here to read in order that they can read – well, novels.'

'No, I suppose not.'

'Let me see what you've chosen.'

He looked at the title himself for the first time: *A Bishop among the Bantus*.

'That should be interesting,' Mrs Bowles said. He agreed doubtfully.

'You know where to find him. You can read to him for a quarter of an hour – not more.'

*

... The boy watched Scobie come with the bright intelligent gaze of fever.

'My name's Scobie. What's yours?'

'Fisher.'

Scobie said nervously, 'Mrs Bowles asked me to read to you.'

'What are you? A soldier?'

'No, a policeman.'

'Is it a murder story?'

'No. I don't think it is.' He opened the book at random and came on a photograph of the bishop sitting in his robes on a hard drawing-room chair outside a little tin-roofed church: he was surrounded by Bantus, who grinned at the camera.

'I'd like a murder story. Have you ever been in a murder?'

'Not what you'd call a real murder with clues and a chase.'

'What sort of a murder then?'

'Well, people get stabbed sometimes fighting.' He spoke in a low voice so as not to disturb Mrs Rolt. She lay with her fist clenched on the sheet – a fist not much bigger than a tennis ball.

'What's the name of the book you've brought? Perhaps I've read it. I read *Treasure Island* on the boat. I wouldn't mind a pirate story. What's it called?'

Scobie said dubiously, '*A Bishop among the Bantus.*'

'What does that mean?'

Scobie drew a long breath. 'Well, you see, Bishop is the name of the hero.'

'But you said *a* Bishop.'

'Yes. His name was Arthur.'

'It's a soppy name.'

'Yes, but he's a soppy hero.' Suddenly, avoiding the boy's eyes, he noticed that Mrs Rolt was not asleep: she was staring at the wall, listening. He went wildly on. 'The real heroes are the Bantus.'

'What are Bantus?'

'They are a peculiarly ferocious lot of pirates who haunted the West Indies and preyed on all the shipping in that part of the Atlantic.'

'Does Arthur Bishop pursue them?'

'Yes. It's a kind of detective story too because he's a secret agent of the British Government. He dresses up as an ordinary seaman and sails on a merchantman so that he can be captured by the Bantus. You know they always give the ordinary seaman a chance to join them. If he'd been an officer they would have made him walk the plank anyway. Then he discovers all their secret passwords and hiding-places and their plans of raids, of course, so that he can betray them when the time is ripe.'

'He sounds a bit of a swine,' the boy said.

'Yes, and he falls in love with the daughter of the captain of the Bantus and that's when he turns sloppy. But that comes near the end and we won't get as far as that. There are a lot of fights and murders before then.'

'It sounds all right. Let's begin.'

'Well, you see, Mrs Bowles told me I was only to stay a short time today, so I've just told you *about* the book, and we can start it tomorrow.'

'You may not be here tomorrow. There may be a murder or something.'

'But the book will be here. I'll leave it with Mrs Bowles. It's her book. Of course it may sound a bit different when *she* reads it.'

'Just begin it,' the boy pleaded.

'Yes, begin it,' said a low voice from the other bed, so low that he would have discounted it as an illusion if he hadn't looked up and seen her watching him, the eyes large as a child's in the starved face.

Scobie said, 'I'm a very bad reader.'

'Go on,' the boy said impatiently. 'Anyone can read aloud.'

Scobie found his eyes fixed on an opening paragraph which stated, *I shall never forget my first glimpse of the continent where I was to labour for thirty of the best years of my life.* He said slowly, 'From the moment that they left Bermuda the low lean rake-helly craft had followed in their wake. The captain was evidently worried, for he watched the strange ship continually through his spyglass. When night fell it was still on their trail, and at dawn it was the first sight that met their eyes. Can it be, Arthur Bishop wondered, that I am about to meet the object of my quest, Blackbeard, the leader of the Bantus himself, or his bloodthirsty lieutenant . . .' He turned a page and was temporarily put out by a portrait of the bishop in whites with a clerical collar and a topee, standing before a wicket and blocking a ball a Bantu had bowled him.

'Go on,' the boy said.

'. . . Batty Davis, so called because of his insane rages when he would send a whole ship's crew to the plank? It was evident that Captain Buller feared the worst, for he crowded on all canvas and it seemed for a time that he would show the strange ship a clean pair of heels. Suddenly over the water came the boom of a gun, and a cannon-ball struck the water twenty yards ahead of them. Captain Buller had his glass to his eye and called down from the bridge to Arthur Bishop, "The Jolly Roger, by God". He was the only one of the ship's company who knew the secret of Arthur's strange quest.'

Mrs Bowles came briskly in. 'There, that will do. Quite enough for the day. And what's he been reading you, Jimmy?'

'*Bishop among the Bantus.*'

'I hope you enjoyed it.'

'It's wizard.'

'You're a very sensible boy,' Mrs Bowles said approvingly.

1948   *The Heart of the Matter*

CHAPTER 10

The End

BYRON

I would to heaven that I were so much clay,
    As I am blood, bone, marrow, passion, feeling –
Because at least the past were pass'd away
    And for the future – (but I write this reeling,
Having got drunk exceedingly today,
    So that I seem to stand upon the ceiling)
I say – the future is a serious matter –
And so – for God's sake – hock and soda-water!

Don Juan

(Fragment on the back of the Poet's MS. of Canto I.)

Acknowledgements

For permission to use these extracts, I am greatly indebted to the following:

pp. 55–7 Lewis Baumer and Pont illustrations: the proprietors of *Punch*.

p. 65 Ely Culbertson, *The Official Book of Contract Bridge*: the author and Faber & Faber.

p. 67 Ella Wheeler Wilcox, *Answered* (*Poems of Passion*): A. & C. Black.

p. 80 E. S. Turner, *The Shocking History of Advertising*: the author and Michael Joseph.

p. 85 Rupert Hart-Davis, *Hugh Walpole*: the author and the owners of the copyright for the Bennett letters.

p. 89 *The Trial of Arthur Rouse*: the Rt. Hon. Sir Norman Birkett and William Hodge & Co. *Notable British Trials* Series.

p. 93 Baroness Orczy, *Links of the Chain of Life*: Mr. J. Orczy-Barstow and Hutchinson & Co.

p. 94 *Report on Juvenile Deliquency*: The Falcon Press.

p. 97 Ted Kavanagh, *Tommy Handley*: the author and Hodder & Stoughton.

p. 98 'Torquemada', *Crossword Clues*: Mrs Powys Mathers and the *Observer*.

p. 102 Herbert Farjeon, *Nine Sharp*: Mrs Herbert Farjeon.

p. 105 James Agate, *Ego 5*: George G. Harrap & Co.

p. 111 George Bernard Shaw, *Irving in 'Waterloo'*: The Society of Authors.

p. 113 Max Beerbohm, *Around Theatres*: Rupert Hart-Davis.

p. 116 H. G. Wells, *Boon*: Mrs. G. P. Wells.

p. 117 James Agate, *Ego 8*: George G. Harrap & Co.

p. 117 C. A. Lejeune, *Dietrich as an Angel* and *Evening Dress Compulsory*: the author and the *Observer*.

p. 121 Paul Jennings, '*Beatrix Potter Translated*': the author and the *Observer*.

p. 123 John Crow, *The Oxford Dictionary of Quotations*: the author and the *Listener*.

p. 126 Max Beerbohm, *A Christmas Garland*: the author and William Heinemann.

ACKNOWLEDGEMENTS

p. 127 G. K. Chesterton, *Ole King Cole*: the author's executrix and Methuen & Co.

p. 129 J. C. Squire, *Tricks of the Trade*: the author.

p. 130 W. C. Sellar and R. J. Yeatman, *1066 and All That*: R. J. Yeatman and Methuen & Co.

p. 131 J. B. Morton, ('Beachcomber' of the *Daily Express*) '*Little Known Facts Column*: the author and the *Daily Express*.

p. 132 D. B. Wyndham Lewis, *Press Gang*: the author and Hutchinson & Co.

p. 132 Hugh Kingsmill, *Table of Truth*: Jarrolds.

p. 133 Henry Reed, *Thomas Hardy*: the author.

p. 134 Lionel Millard, *Elizabethan Prose*: the author.

p. 134 Stephen Potter, *Script of a BBC Regional Literary Feature*: the author and the British Broadcasting Corporation.

p. 136 Peter Ustinov, *Stage Dialogue We Cannot Do Without*: the author and the editor of *The Author*.

p. 137 Osbert Lancaster, *Drayneflete Revealed*: the author and John Murray.

p. 148 W. R. Sickert, *A Free House*: the author and Macmillan & Co.

p. 152 George Bernard Shaw, *Man and Superman*: The Society of Authors.

p. 153 D. H. Lawrence, *Pansies*: William Heinemann.

p. 155 Herbert Farjeon, *Spread it Abroad*: Mrs Herbert Farjeon.

p. 156 Virginia Graham, *A Lullaby in Poor Taste* from *Consider the Years*: the author and Jonathan Cape.

p. 156 Bertrand Russell, *A History of Western Philosophy*: the author and Allen & Unwin.

p. 157 Henry Reed, *Lessons of the War* from *A Map of Verona*: the author and Jonathan Cape.

p. 159 J. B. Priestley, *Chairmanship* from *Delight*: the author and William Heinemann.

p. 164 Harold Nicolson, *Lord Carnock*: the author and Constable & Co.

p. 165 John Fothergill, *My Three Inns*: the author and Chatto & Windus.

p. 167 James Agate, *Ego 5*: George G. Harrap & Co.

p. 167 Tom Driberg, *Colonnade*: the author and the *Daily Express*.

p. 170 Margaret Barton, *Garrick*: the author and Faber & Faber.

p. 171 Osbert Sitwell, *Great Morning*: the author and Macmillan & Co.

p. 203 George and Weedon Grossmith, *The Diary of a Nobody*: J. M. Dent & Sons.

ACKNOWLEDGEMENTS

p. 207 Thomas Hardy, *Life's Little Ironies*: Macmillan & Co.

p. 210 Eden Phillpotts, *The Human Boy*: the author and Methuen & Co.

p. 215 Harold Nicolson, *Tennyson*: the author and Constable & Co.

p. 218 Aldous Huxley, *Point Counter Point*: the author and Chatto & Windus.

p. 220 Terence Rattigan, *French Without Tears*: the author and Hamish Hamilton.

p. 220 Nigel Balchin, *The Small Back Room*: the author and William Collins, Sons & Co.

p. 227 Bernard Darwin, *Golf Between Two Wars*: the author and Chatto & Windus.

p. 230 Patrick Hamilton, *Slaves of Solitude*: the author and Constable & Co.

p. 232 John Betjeman, *Potpourri from a Surrey Garden* and *Margate 1940* from *Selected Poems*: the author and John Murray.

p. 234 Humphrey Hare, *Swinburne: A Biographical Approach*: the author and H. F. & G. Witherby.

p. 235 Angus Wilson, *Hemlock and After*: Martin Secker & Warburg.

p. 237 Hesketh Pearson, *The Man Whistler*: the author and Methuen & Co.

p. 245 H. G. Wells, *Experiment in Autobiography*: Mrs G. P. Wells and Victor Gollancz.

p. 246 Eric Linklater, *The Man on my Back*: the author and Macmillan & Co.

p. 250 James Agate, *Ego 8*: George G. Harrap & Co.

p. 251 C. E. M. Joad, *A Year More or Less*: the author's executors and Victor Gollancz.

p. 254 J. B. Priestley, *My Tastes* from *Delight*: the author and William Heinemann.

p. 257 E. V. Lucas and George Morrow, *What a Life!*: Methuen & Co.

p. 260 Professor Walter Raleigh, *Letters*: the author and Methuen & Co.

p. 261 Harold Nicolson, *Peacemaking 1919*: the author.

p. 262 Terence Rattigan, *Who is Sylvia?*: the author and Hamish Hamilton.

p. 264 Pont illustrations by kind permission of the proprietors of *Punch*.

p. 265 Graham Greene, *The Heart of the Matter*: the author and William Heinemann.

Index

Index

Some other Penguin books of humour
are described on the
following pages

PENGUIN CARTOON BOOKS

The following new Penguin books of cartoons are being published at the same time as this book:

SEARLE IN THE SIXTIES*
Ronald Searle

L'AMOUR
Raymond Peynet

THE PENGUIN OSBERT LANCASTER*
THE PENGUIN ANDRÉ FRANÇOIS*

A description of the first three will be found on following pages.

Also available:

THE LOVERS
Raymond Peynet

THE PENGUIN MAX**
Giovannetti

THE PENGUIN HOFFNUNG
THE PENGUIN BROCKBANK
THE PENGUIN CHARLES ADDAMS**
THE PENGUIN THELWELL
U.S.A. FOR BEGINNERS *and* THE BIG CITY
Alex Atkinson and Ronald Searle

THE ST TRINIAN'S STORY
Ronald Searle

*NOT FOR SALE IN THE U.S.A.
**NOT FOR SALE IN THE U.S.A. OR CANADA

THE TUNNEL OF LOVE

Peter De Vries

An audacious angle on the battle of the sexes told by a satirist whose aim is dazzling – and devastating.

'Unusually entertaining – his gags are exceedingly funny' – *Sunday Times*

'Mr De Vries could hardly be bettered ... his insights are deadly' – *New Statesman*

Also available

THE MACKEREL PLAZA

NOT FOR SALE IN THE U.S.A. OR CANADA

SEARLE IN THE SIXTIES

Ronald Searle

This Penguin selection of recent Searle cartoons is published in the large 'cartoon-book' format.

The contents are taken from *Punch, Holiday, Life, Look, Sports Illustrated, Réalités, Le Canard enchaîné*, and other magazines and sources. They include a series of tours round Paris, Las Vegas, Dublin, Berlin, Alaska, and the U.S.A., in which Searle 'gets' the national characteristics to perfection. There are also a few caricatures of political leaders, and the series of fantasy portraits of authors and others ('as the imagination sees them . . .'), featuring C. P. Snow, Muriel Spark, Iris Murdoch, Lawrence Durrell, Robert Graves, and several others.

A number of other typical Searles, rich in feathers, scrolls, hat-pins, and general fru-fru, completes an entertaining collection.

NOT FOR SALE IN THE U.S.A.

THE PENGUIN OSBERT LANCASTER

From John o'Groats time-honoured Lancaster
    Extends his realm to Littlehampton's strand,
Where waspish Maudie and her stalwart Earl
    Stand guard upon the Channel, gin in hand.

This royal throne of kings, this sceptered isle,
    This earth of majesty, this seat of Mars . . .
Ah, Osbert shows it all, and daily proves
    The fault, dear reader, lies not in our stars.

His mini-cartoon nips across the years
    From war to peace and back to war on ice:
Ay, me . . . this dear, dear land. Still, laughs like these
    Might still be reckoned cheap at twice the price.

A selection of the inimitable Osbert Lancaster's cartoons,
from the *Daily Express* and elsewhere.

NOT FOR SALE IN THE U.S.A.

L'AMOUR

Raymond Peynet

Love's more than gratitude,
Certitude, aptitude:
Love has a magnitude –
    Love is immense.

Love in all latitudes,
Love in all attitudes
(Ooh – la – la . . . think of it),
Love without platitudes
    Peynet presents.

This is his book of it –
Pictures he took of it:
You like the look of it . . .?
    Then part with your pence.

SCHOLARSHIP AT STAKE

Jane Hope

Scholarship at Stake contains two of Jane Hope's front-line dispatches from the class-room, *The Scholarship Stakes* and *Standing Room Only*. In the first she conjures up the perils of higher education as she dissects the Scholarship Entrance Examination with a satiric wit and sardonic humour which are only matched by her devastating drawings. In the second, down at a lower level of learning, she is wickedly funny on the nutty problem of unwieldy classes in cramped spaces. If these are the nation's schools, we can only Hope.

NOT FOR SALE IN THE U.S.A OR CANADA

THE WORLD OF
A. J. WENTWORTH B.A.

H. F. Ellis

If, in *Punch* or out, you have never had the pleasure of meeting A. J. Wentworth B.A., you are in need of an introduction. But you'll have to shout. If he hears you above the din of the class-room, as he sits awash, like King Canute, in the rising waves of indiscipline, he will probably take you for a parent or a visiting inspector. You can be sure of a courteous welcome and a string of reminiscences about life at Burgrove Preparatory School (Gravel Soil. Boys prepared for Common Entrance and the Royal Navy). Encourage him and he will tell you how he carried his bat, for solemn ineptitude, throughout a long and undistinguished career – at school, in the army, and in rural retirement. But don't laugh: the dignity of A. J. Wentworth B.A. is very easily injured.

'In our present shortage of schoolmasters here is one not to be missed' – *The Times Literary Supplement*

This volume contains *The Papers of A. J. Wentworth B.A.* and *A. J. Wentworth B.A. (Retd).*

NOT FOR SALE IN THE U.S.A.

STEPHEN POTTER

'It is astonishing that Stephen Potter should have been able to sustain this joke so long. ... What is so good in these books of Potter's is the brevity and compactness of the presentation. As in any practical manual, the principles are stated and concisely illustrated. Nothing goes on too long' – Edmund Wilson in the *Nation*

'A man less witty than Mr Potter might have worked his devices to death; it is far otherwise with the Master of Station Road, Yeovil. On he goes, continually scintillating and rarely probing into his victim without a preliminary anaesthetic of good humour' – C. E. Vulliamy in the *Spectator*

The following titles are available in Penguins:

GAMESMANSHIP
'The Art of Winning Games Without Actually Cheating'

LIFEMANSHIP
The sequel to *Gamesmanship* which covers the whole art of life.

ONE-UPMANSHIP
'Being some Account of the Activities and Teaching of the Lifemanship Correspondence College of One-Upness and Gameslifemastery'

SUPERMANSHIP
'How to continue to stay top without actually falling apart'

NOT FOR SALE IN THE U.S.A.

For a complete list of books available please write to Penguin Books whose address can be found on the back of the title page